Life's Work

T0366863

Life's Work

Geographies of Social Reproduction

Edited by

**Katharyne Mitchell, Sallie A. Marston and
Cindi Katz**

Blackwell
Publishing

Contents

Notes on Contributors

Robert Andolina is an assistant professor of political science at Bates College in Maine, USA. Previously he was a postdoctoral research associate in geography at Cambridge and Newcastle Universities in the UK. He works on indigenous social movement and development politics in Ecuador and Bolivia, and has publications on indigenous movement ideology and political discourse, including "The Sovereign and Its Shadow: Constituent Assembly and Indigenous Movement in Ecuador" in *Journal of Latin American Studies* (forthcoming) and "El Proyecto Político de la CONAIE como Lucha Anticolonial," in *En Defensa del Pluralismo y la Igualdad: Los Derechos de los Pueblos Indígenas y el Estado* (edited by Ileana Almeida and Nidia Arrobo, Abya Yala, Quito, 1998).

Altha J Cravey is an associate professor of geography and the director of undergraduate studies at the University of North Carolina in Chapel Hill. As a former construction electrician and member of the International Brotherhood of Electrical Workers, she became interested in geographies of work, gender, and globalization. Author of *Women and Work in Mexico's Maquiladoras* (Rowman and Littlefield Inc, 1998), she is currently involved in field projects in Mexico and the US South that explore the mutual influence of racialized, gendered labor markets and government policies.

Maria Fannin is a PhD student in the Department of Geography at the University of Washington. Her research interests include the production of space and identity, cultural studies of medicine and the body, and reproductive politics. Her PhD research focuses on the politics of midwifery in Quebec, Canada.

Melissa Hyams is currently a visiting assistant professor in the Department of Geography at Northern Illinois University. Her research interests lie in identity, embodiment and processes of social and spatial inclusion/exclusion. Through qualitative analysis of young Latina teenagers' group narratives, her recent doctoral research considered the ways in which day-to-day social relations of gender, sexuality, race and age are shaped by and give shape to local spaces and bodies and "global" US-Mexico border and body spaces.

Cindi Katz is a professor of geography in the departments of Environmental Psychology and Women's Studies at the Graduate Center of the City University of New York. Her work concerns social reproduction and the production of space, place, and nature, children and the environment, and the consequences of global economic restructuring for everyday life. She has published widely on these themes as well as on social theory and the politics of knowledge, in edited collections and in journals such as *Society and Space, Social Text, Signs, Feminist Studies, Annals of the Association of American Geographers, Social Justice,* and *Antipode*. She is the coeditor with Janice Monk of *Full Circles: Geographies of Gender over the Life Course* (Routledge, 1993), and she recently completed *Disintegrating Developments: Global Economic Restructuring and Children's Everyday Lives*, forthcoming in 2004 (University of Minnesota Press). She is currently working on a project called "Retheorizing Childhood" and another on the social wage.

Nina Laurie is a senior lecturer in the Department of Geography at Newcastle University, UK. She has worked on issues of social development in Latin America for more than fifteen years, with specific interests in gender and development, indigenous issues and social exclusion in the Andes. She works collaboratively with colleagues at CESU, San Simón University, Bolivia and in the Postgraduate Centre in San Marcos University, Peru through DFID/British Council Higher Education Links. She is coauthor of *Geographies of New Femininity* (Longman, 1999).

Jean Lave is an anthropologist, a professor of social and cultural studies in education and an affiliate professor of geography at the University of California, Berkeley. She is currently working on a book on social practice theory, learning, and everyday life. She has carried out ethnographic research in Brazil, Liberia, the US, and, most recently, Portugal. Her previous books include *Cognition in Practice* (1988), *Situated Learning* (with E Wenger, Cambridge University Press, 1991), *Understanding Practice* (edited with Seth Chaiklin, Cambridge University Press, 1993) and *History in Person: Enduring Struggles, Contentious Practice, Intimate Identities* (edited with Dorothy Holland, School of American Research Press, 2001).

Rosemary Marangoly George is an associate professor in the Department of Literature and the director of the Critical Gender Studies Program at the University of California, San Diego. She is the author of *The Politics of Home: Postcolonial Relocations and Twentieth Century Fiction* (Cambridge University Press, 1996; University of California Press, 1999) and edited *Burning Down the House: Recycling Domesticity*

(Westview/Perseus, 1998). Her scholarship on postcolonial feminist issues has been published in *Diaspora, Differences, Cultural Critique, Feminist Studies* and other academic venues. She is currently working on a book entitled *Texts Slip Their Moorings: Literature Outside the National Framework.*

Sallie Marston is a professor of geography at the University of Arizona in Tucson. Her work focuses on space, difference, and politics. She is the author of numerous articles on urban space and political questions of gender, ethnicity, race, and sexuality published in, among other journals, *Transactions of the Institute of British Geographers, Annals of the Association of American Geographers, Progress in Human Geography, Society and Space, Political Geography, Urban Geography*. She is on the editorial board of several journals and the author of two textbooks, *Places and Regions in Global Context: Human Geography* and *World Regions in Global Context: Peoples, Places, and Environments*. She is the coeditor with Susan Aiken, Ann Brigham, and Penny Waterstone of *Making Worlds: Gender, Metaphor, Materiality*. She is currently working on a monograph that explores identity politics and new state practices around the spaces of discourse and representation, entitled *Acting Out in Public: The St. Patrick's Day Parade and Struggles over the Production of Meaning and Identity in the Streets of New York*.

Katharyne Mitchell is an associate professor in the Department of Geography at the University of Washington. She is coeditor of *The Companion Guide to Political Geography* and has published in the areas of immigration, urban geography, and transnational studies in journals such as *Transactions of the Institute of British Geographers, Society and Space, Antipode, Political Geography, Urban Geography*, and *Economic Geography*. She is currently completing a monograph entitled *Transnationalism and the Politics of Space*. Her latest research focuses on the impact of transnational migration on conceptions of education, with a particular emphasis on how children are educated to become citizens of a particular nation-state. This ongoing research has been funded by the Simpson Center of the University of Washington, the Spencer Foundation, and the John D and Catherine T MacArthur Foundation.

John Morgan is a lecturer in geography education at the University of Bristol, England. Before this, he worked as a schoolteacher and is now involved in initial teacher education. His research interests focus on the theory and practice of geography education.

Alison Mountz is a doctoral candidate in geography at the University of British Columbia. Her work examines the social geography of transnational migration and its governance through bureaucracy. After conducting transnational research with Central American migrants and refugees, she embarked on an institutional ethnography of the response of Citizenship and Immigration Canada to human smuggling.

Geraldine Pratt teaches in the Geography Department at the University of British Columbia and is editor of *Environment and Planning D: Society and Space*. She is co-author (with Susan Hanson) of *Gender, Space and Work* (Routledge, 1995). Her recent work engages the theme of migration to Canada, especially the migration of Filipino women through the Live-in Caregiver Program.

Sarah Radcliffe is at the Department of Geography, University of Cambridge. Her research interests include spatial and sociopolitical transformations in the Andes, gender and feminist theory, and debates around development. Her books include *Remaking the Nation: Place, Politics and Identity in Latin America* (1996) and *Viva! Women and Popular Protest in Latin America* (1993).

Life's Work:
An Introduction, Review
and Critique

Katharyne Mitchell, Sallie A Marston and Cindi Katz

Introduction

This special issue of *Antipode* addresses the ways in which people produce value in all domains of their lives. We are particularly interested in the relationship between the production of value "at work" and the social reproduction of labor-power along with the conditions that enable its deployment. Consider these three vignettes of contemporary life:

A man strolls quickly through the airport. He is dressed in a business suit and carries a computer and a cup of coffee. He wears a headset. As he walks, he discusses plans involving the future direction of his company. At the baggage claim, the baggage cart reads: "I am your idea. Push me." Above him on the wall is the image of a corporate man, dressed much as he is. The advertisement reads: "You are the office."[1]

A woman is talking on the phone. While she talks she is moving through the kitchen, cooking dinner, setting the table, and washing her children's hands. She is speaking about the sexual activities she would like to perform for the person on the other end of the line. When she hangs up she has just made $20.00.[2]

A woman is sewing clothes at her home. Her children are doing their homework at the kitchen table. The phone rings; it is her husband calling from the Dominican Republic. He asks about the weather in New York and the children's schoolwork. She asks about their home and their crops, which have just been harvested. They discuss their plans to meet. She completes another three shirtsleeves during this phone conversation.[3]

At the most fundamental level, social reproduction is about how we live. One of the main problematics energizing generations of Marxists is the relationship between how we live at work and how we live outside of it. This preoccupation is based on the assumption that social formations arise from the dominant mode of production and necessarily reflect and reproduce that mode in order to continue it through time. The thinking goes that, in a capitalist system, the reproduction of both the means of production and the forces of production (labor-power) must be ensured; otherwise, the circuit(s) will be broken, production will cease, and capitalism will ultimately founder. The constitution and maintenance of "labor-power"—how people survive, what they do and buy that sustains them and brings them pleasure—are thus subjects of great interest to many political-economists and others working in this tradition.

Outside of the research of a number of Marxist feminists whose ideas we discuss below, however, the primary fascination with "how we live outside of work" has been largely a matter of understanding the constitution of labor-power in relation to production. If most feminist work on labor inside and outside the home has maintained the *categorical* binary of production and reproduction, the *substantive* distinctions between the two have been consistently and productively blurred (cf Dalla Costa 1972; Folbre 1994; Mies 1982). Likewise, while some socialist-feminist theorists have focused on the relative weight given to the structuring forces of capitalism and patriarchy, many—particularly those in critical development studies—have been at the forefront of challenging and even imploding that binary (cf eg Beneria 1985; Deere 1977; Mackintosh 1979; Sargent 1981; *SIGNS* 1981).

We would like to do three things in this introductory chapter. The first is to critically explore the conceptual separation of production and reproduction that still underpins much of the thinking about how individuals and social groups participate in life's work. From Marx through Althusser to Leacock and Dalla Costa, the theoretical imperative has been to elucidate the correspondences and contradictions among structures and between them and particular social relations, to understand the form, logic, and practices through which capitalism as a socioeconomic system is able to sustain its dynamic via the capacity to reproduce itself on an expanded scale. While drawing greatly on this tradition of scholarship, we also point to the limits of abstract theorizing, advocating not just the long view—as in the work of Braudel—but also the topographical and embodied view.[4] This incorporates—quite literally—an understanding of the constitution of subjects through time and in space, one that shows the continuities and discontinuities within and between structures and social relations and demonstrates how abstract theories often reify problematic categorical distinctions between the spheres of production and reproduction.

Our second aim is to examine the ways in which this analytical separation, always problematic, is particularly unwieldy in the contemporary period of capitalist transformation. As our three vignettes indicate, the everyday practices of widely disparate subjects manifest a growing obfuscation of the boundaries between "work" and "nonwork."

This interpretation is deeper than that suggested by those who speak of the penetration of the lifeworld by the market, and of a different order than earlier feminist writings that made the work of "nonwork" clear. What we are signaling is the interpellation of subjects as *life workers*—the rendering of permanently mobilized bodies in new kinds of technologies of power. The new flexible subjects of late capitalism "are the office"; their spheres of domesticity "are the factory"; their attitudes are those of *"formation permanente,"* as Donzelot (1991:273) has written.[5] This widespread and profound shift in both the material spaces and cognitive understandings of life's work is galvanized by and facilitates the complete breakdown of the barriers between worlds, such that the domain of work and the domains of home and leisure are indistinguishable from each other—and for many *this now forms the contemporary "habitus."*[6]

The third project is to investigate the changing relationship of social reproduction and individuals involved in life's work to the contemporary state. In Althusserian logic, it is in the superstructures that society reproduces the relations of production outside production, for production. These superstructures include both the "repressive" institutions of the state, such as the army, the prisons, and the courts, and those "ideological state apparatuses," such as schools, the family, and religion. But we need to rethink this creaky logic, especially as it applies to the specifics of social reproduction. Drawing on the work of political theorists, anthropologists, geographers, and others, we probe the production of state institutions and practices across domains, challenging the logic of separation itself as well as Althusser's famous privileging of "the economic" "in the last instance." The inseparability of production and reproduction should make clear the undialectical artifice of distinguishing base from superstructure. Neither capitalism nor life's work is so neat.

One of the areas that command our attention in particular is the formation of the "neoliberal subject" in relation to the current regime of accumulation and in relation to the state. In order to understand how and why life's work is changing in the contemporary era, we must know more about the ways in which individuals make and understand themselves as workers, consumers, students, parents, migrants, and lovers, and how these subject positions are constituted and entrenched spatially through the discourses and material social practices of public and private, inside and outside, alien and citizen, home and away, natural and unnatural, imaginary and real, and work and leisure, among others. The devolution of more and more "choice" to a seemingly ever more autonomous individual who must rationally calculate the benefits and costs of all aspects of life—from health care (which diagnostics or treatment?) to children (how many?) to production (how to improve it?/how to succeed at it?/whether to conform to it?/how to derive pleasure from it?)—is part of a much broader set of practices that tend to increase productivity and profits for the employer while reducing the responsibility of both the employer and the state in managing and sustaining the reproduction of labor-power. These shifts not only call into question what kind of "autonomy" is on offer, but also demonstrate its distinctly economistic flavor. In the contemporary "security" state, the particularity of that "autonomy" rubs uncomfortably against growing state management of surplus labor and a loss of autonomy in other realms that is often overwhelming. But the economic devolution associated with neoliberalism is the perfect expression of contemporary capitalist ideology, which brings the logic of the rational market to all aspects of life and in so doing redefines the nexus of the economic and the social (cf Martin 2002).

What is important to remember here, however, is that this devolution is not imposed; rather, it becomes the accepted norm through time as it infiltrates and articulates with other commonsense understandings in society. In this volume, we want to foreground the ways in which these ideologies about the proper role of the individual at home and work *become* commonsense understandings as they are entrenched in various kinds of spatial practices and symbols through time. The production of commonsense understandings entails a lot of work and is an important part of the work of social reproduction. Each piece in this collection focuses on an aspect of this work. The intensity and breadth of these efforts point to the many instances in which these hegemonic articulations fail and individuals contest and disrupt the normativizing understandings of work, schooling, home, and leisure under contemporary capitalism. In the course of life's work, social actors encounter, absorb, rework, and disrupt these efforts, and there is a distinct spatiality or historical geography to these material social practices and their outcomes. Thus, all of the contributions to this special issue highlight the following idea: that how we live *in space*—in and between schools, homes, neighborhoods, workplaces, and institutions of civil society and the state, as mobile subjects both inside and outside the intertwined projects of domesticity, schooling, and nation, among others—constitutes us as contemporary subjects in life's work.

Theorizing the Relations between Production and Reproduction

In his later work, Marx became less preoccupied with identifying and analyzing the emergence of capitalism as an economic system and more with how that particular system was maintained through time. In his quest to understand the necessary conditions for the reproduction of capitalism, he began to elaborate on the various structures and social practices that aided its perpetuation, especially vis-à-vis their capacity to contain the contradictions he perceived to be inherent to capitalism. In the second volume of *Capital*, he focused on circulation and reproduction—how "the social phenomena of capitalist society return to themselves" (Caffentzis 1999:158). For Marx, the innumerable exchanges inherent within any capitalist economy were part of a vast, multistranded network of individual circuits, all of which together formed the aggregate social capital. These individual or microcircuits were functional as single coherent entities, yet they never operated in isolation (see Marx 1967:351–358).

Marx spent considerable time elucidating the properties of these individual circuits, demonstrating the intricate interconnections among them as well as the vast potential for expansion of the system, as each circuit could operate to galvanize another. As a mature socioeconomic system, capitalism seemed capable of sustaining its dynamic through its capacity to reproduce itself on an ever-expanding scale. This reproduction was made possible through the dynamic articulation of countless individual circuits of capital, each operative in different stages of the exchange process. Caffentzis (1999:159) illustrates this scenario well:

> We can imagine capitalist A (i) selling the produced commodity to another capitalist B who uses it as means of production, (ii) taking part of the money so realized and buying some luxury goods from capitalist C, (iii) buying labor power from worker D and new means of production from capitalist E who, in turn energizes, new circuits of other individual capitals.

What Marx quickly noted, however, was the fatal flaw in this seemingly unstoppable revolution of the circuits of exchange. The failings were the same as those that existed within the bourgeois labor process itself, for example: "[T]he antithesis, use-value, and exchange value; the contradictions that private labor is bound to manifest itself as direct social labor, that a particularized concrete kind of labor has to pass for abstract human labor; the contradiction between the personification of objects and the representation of persons by things" (Marx 1906:113–114). These antitheses of capitalist production, Marx argued, are resynthesized in at least two ways. The first has occurred economically, in the course of concrete labor becoming value becoming abstract labor, and the whole circuit of economic value production that has been the predominant focus of most Marxists. But the second way in which the antitheses of capitalism have been remade is socially. Thus, Marx (1906:578) wrote, "Capitalist production produces not only commodities, not only surplus-value, but it also produces and reproduces the capitalist relation; on the one side the capitalist, on the other the wage-laborer." Class struggle—the inherently antagonistic relations between the capitalist and the laborer—would not diminish during the process of exchange.

In fact, with the multiple, interlinked, circulating, and reproductive functions of exchange, the possibilities for the replication of this antagonistic dynamic and its associated contradictions were greatly increased. For example, if too long an interval in time occurs between "complementary phases" of the metamorphosis of a commodity—such as between its production, sale, and purchase—"the intimate connexion between them, their oneness, asserts itself by producing a crisis" (Marx 1906:113–114). All kinds of slow-downs and stoppages could lead to this "extended" interval time, including those associated with factors of social reproduction or "material life" occurring outside of the production-consumption nexus. Further, it may not necessarily be the "same" contradiction developed and reproduced at the same time within different economic, political, cultural, or ideological spheres that leads to this type of break in the circuit, but rather because different contradictions have condensed and fused at a particular moment, thus producing a major overall rupture or crisis.[7] The reproduction of these multiple contradictions inherent within all spheres of capitalist organization thus allowed Marx to see the possibilities of systemic crisis within the system and to forecast the end of capitalism itself.

What is useful here is to examine how Marx's ideas about reproduction relate specifically to the social relations between capitalists and laborers at the point of production. Two interlinked assumptions are made that are pertinent for our discussion. First, as Caffentzis, Dalla Costa, and many others have pointed out, Marx's analysis of the reproduction/crisis nexus was based on the assumption of workers as "waged" workers. Marxist theory generally elides the great numbers of unwaged workers, including homemakers and people on public assistance, subsistence farmers, students, and the vast numbers involved in underground economies all around the world. Explanations of the reproduction of the social relations of production often neglect the many forms of labor that are not contracted or paid for in a monetary exchange. As feminists, antiracists, and others have noted, much of this work is done by women, racialized minorities, and those whose legal status is precarious (cf eg Ehrenreich and Hochschild 2003; Folbre 2002; Parrenas 2001).

This point ties in with the second assumption that concerns the constitution of the individual as a "free" laborer. Marx's discussion on this point is best described in the first part of the second volume of *Capital* (1967), in which he talks about the circuit of money-capital. Here, he wants to be clear that in order for money-capital to be transformed into productive capital, the capitalist must begin by buying the means of production, such as buildings and machinery, and then must purchase labor-power. In order for the capitalist to be able to purchase labor-power effectively (ie quickly and assuredly), however, the laborer must already have been separated from his/her own means of production and must have no effective means of survival other than through the sale of his labor-power. "Money can be expended in this form only because labour-power finds itself in a state of separation from its means of production" (Marx 1967:30). The timing of this process is what interests Marx, for if the labor-power is purchased too soon (prior to the purchase of the means of production), the capital invested in this labor-power remains idle; similarly, if the means of production are purchased too soon (before labor-power can be purchased) the capital invested there lies idle. Thus, before the entire production process can be undertaken, it is necessary for a class of individuals to have been formed *as workers*, so that when the time arrives for the capitalist to purchase labor-power as a commodity, there is already a willing and immediate supply.

> In order that the sale of one's own labour-power (in the form of the sale of one's own labour or in the form of wages) may constitute not an isolated phenomenon but a socially decisive premise for the production of commodities, in order that money-capital may therefore perform, on a social scale, the above-discussed function $M\text{-}C\!\!\left\langle{}^{L}_{MP}\right.$ historical processes are assumed by which the original connection of the means of production with labour-power was dissolved—processes in consequence of which the mass of the people, the labourers, have, as non-owners, come face to face with the non-labourers as the owners of these means of production (Marx 1967:30–31

Thus, for Marx, the class relation between the capitalist and the laborer is formed through "historical processes" prior to the moment when they come together as buyer and seller of labor-power. It was these processes, such as the enclosure movement in England, that constituted the individual as a waged worker through his/her separation from the means of production, and which formed the class of "free" labor necessary for the capitalist production process to occur.

The assumption here that carries through much of Marxian analysis —and that we believe obscures the contemporary picture in particular —is the idea that an individual is constituted as a laborer (within a class of laborers) in a capitalist system solely through the coercion to work in order to survive (and "reproduce" him or herself). This assumption ties in with the previous one about labor as "waged" labor. Even within primarily capitalist social formations, there are pockets of economic activity existing outside of or in relation to capitalism that are not based entirely on the type of capitalist social relations outlined by Marx.[8] These forms of economic activity can be waged or non-waged, but might operate along quite different lines than a "pure" or homogenous capitalist system. For example, the "ethnic enclaves" existing in many cities, the "informal sectors" of others, and the hybrid economies of countries as different as China and the UK are composed of a mix of capitalist and noncapitalist activities existing in relation to each other.[9] In many of these paracapitalist activities, the relations between employers and workers operate within a dense social network of obligations and ties. Within these sectors and societies, individuals are constituted as laborers through numerous intersecting and often colliding processes. The "coercion" to work may come from an ethnic group, a husband, a "coyote" (people smuggler), or a parent, and may involve historical processes other than or in excess of those associated with the separation of the individual from the means of production. Similarly, the individual might operate in both waged and unwaged economic activities over the course of a lifetime, or even within the course of a single day. The constitution of the individual as a "laborer," engaged in waged or unwaged work or both, is thus a product of the heterogeneous spaces and uneven practices of capitalist development, but also the many other partial and uneven structuring processes associated with material life.

Another theorist of the production/social-reproduction linkage whom we would like to emphasize is Fernand Braudel, whose three-volume series on civilization and capitalism weaves together the forces of production and reproduction in a nearly seamless manner. Unlike Marx, Braudel conceives of the economy—both past and present—as a plural, shifting, and highly contextual set of processes that are partly capitalistic and partly not, depending on time and place. For him, the story of capitalism is not a story of necessary advancement along a linear path, a story of "gradual progress towards the rational world of the market, the firm, and capitalist investment" (Braudel 1981:23; see also Braudel 1982:461). Rather, it is a story of mixture and hybridity, of acceleration and deceleration, and of different spheres of economic activity, each with its own logic and set of practices. As a result of this methodological starting point, he examines social reproduction with a slightly different lens than those of most Marxists, one that conceives of "material life" as something widespread, varied, and central to all forms of economic development, including early and advanced capitalism. He sees material life and economic life as distinct from each other, yet joined through so many points of exchange that they are fundamentally part of one piece of machinery. Thus, while Braudel's image of a vast number of intersecting circuits and exchanges circulating and reproducing each other on an ever-expanding scale is reminiscent of Marx's depiction of capitalist circulation in the second volume of *Capital*, the profound distinction exists in his view that these exchanges incorporate "nonmarket" economic activity or the "infra"economy of material life in an absolutely essential and inextricable embrace.

Braudel, like Marx, is interested in how history—the events of the past—remains with the living. Part of his explicit method is to give a long-term view of historical processes and to present a dialectic of past/present. But he is careful not to posit a strong break with the traditions of the economic and material life of the past. Instead, he sees historical and contemporary economic processes as interrelated, as necessary for each other. In his view, capitalism does not devour and destroy other economic systems; it needs them in order to reproduce itself. Under certain conditions, many of the elements of material life may block the progress of capitalism, but in other circumstances, they act to subsidize capitalism's "upper tier"—which, in Braudel's conception, is constituted by the "real" capitalists, those who control the instruments of credit, exchange rates, and international trade. These upper-sphere capitalists of the past were the "transnational" economic actors of the 15th–18th centuries. Today they are comprised primarily of supranational agents and institutions such as the World Trade Organization (WTO), the International Monetary Fund, and the World Bank. They exist in every era, and they survive and reproduce themselves because of the ongoing work of the "other" tiers of economic activity, including the market, the household, and the practices associated with material life broadly understood, which subsidize them.

In terms of thinking about social reproduction, a second strong point of Braudel's work is his emphasis on the differing motivational forces that have affected people and caused them to engage in various kinds of work. For example, in his discussion of luxury in the first volume of his series, he notes how desire—for example, the desire to have certain kinds of luxury commodities—is intrinsically connected with social hierarchy and has been a strong driving force throughout history. Desire is not just individual: it is also class-based and even constitutive of civilizational accelerations and conflicts (cf Bourdieu 1984). Throughout his work, Braudel illuminates the historical processes that constitute individuals as workers and workers as classes, demonstrating that these are multiple, rather than being based solely on separation from the means of production.

Braudel's interest in these types of motivating forces—distinct from, yet always interlinked with capitalist processes—was part of a burgeoning intellectual interest in ideology in the late 1960s and 1970s in which a number of scholars attempted to theorize the relationship between production and reproduction through differing frameworks of correspondence, discourse, hegemony, and homology (among others). This vast, and very interesting literature is too broad for a detailed discussion here, but we want to point to a few differing theories of articulation, and also to discuss some of the limits common to these various frameworks.

With the exception of Marx's own analysis, one of the most well-known Marxist analyses of social reproduction is that of Althusser. He (1971:127, 135) asks, "What, then, is the *reproduction of the conditions of production*?" and then focuses primarily on the ongoing reproduction of wage labor, or the "reproduction of the relations of production." Althusser (1971:143; emphasis in original) is interested in the manifold ways in which individuals are interpellated as working subjects through institutions such as the family, the legal system, religion, and education. His work on the linkages between production and social reproduction draws on the writings of Gramsci, but loses all the sense of social practice and life that make Gramsci so vital, emphasizing instead the processes through which the fundamental structures and relations of society continually re-create the existing mode of production—a mode in which the structures of dominance of one group over another are maintained. Rather than a direct *reflection* between economic base and the political, cultural, and social superstructure, however, both Gramsci and Althusser foreground the ways in which the so-called superstructural elements of society create and sustain the *conditions* in which capitalist production can flourish. As Hall (1981:21–22) puts it, this mode of theorizing "regards the superstructures as having the role, above all, of drawing society into 'conformity' with the long-term requirements and conditions of a capitalist economic system." Or, as Althusser (1971:132) succinctly writes, "I shall say that the reproduction of labour power requires not only a reproduction of its skills, but also, at the same time, a reproduction of its submission to the rules of the established order."

There are innumerable variations on this theme of the coupling or articulation of production and social reproduction (or base and superstructure) within Marxist theory.[10] What distinguishes theories of reproduction from those associated with the more functionalist notion of "correspondence" is in the emphasis on practice, on the relative autonomy of different spheres of everyday life, and on the interest in questions of ideology or hegemony and the contest over these. Theories of social reproduction attend not only to how subjects are haled in multiple ways through the institutions of society—institutions structured and maintained within relations of dominance that simultaneously contain their own internal logics and trajectories—but also to how these institutions and the uneven social relations that uphold them are the sedimented outcome of material social practice. Their very basis and continued existence are secured—or not—in the dialectic of production and reproduction, in large measure through the compass of practices and social relations that we are calling "life's work." Here is where Althusser's work falls flat, foreclosing the liveliness and possibility of taking practice seriously. If he opens up a number of new ways of thinking about the structures or "apparatuses" through which ideology functions in society, his work reifies in problematic ways the binary distinctions between production and reproduction, positioning the former as the base or infrastructure and the latter as the superstructure. Furthermore, while the institutions and processes constituting the superstructure are conceived as relatively autonomous, it is the economic that, nevertheless, remained determining of social relations in the last instance.

The primary critique we wish to make, however, concerns less the overly structuralist nature of Althusser's and others' formulations of reproduction than the theoretical abstractions that allow this work to miss certain fundamental aspects of society. For example, Althusser lists institutions as part of the ideological state apparatus randomly— or, as he puts it, with "no particular significance" (1971: 143). These include, among other things, the religious, the educational, the family, the legal, and the political. For Althusser, the differences among these institutions are not analytically relevant, and as a whole they are given equal theoretical weight. Yet if the constituent elements of social reproduction are looked at—what one of us (Katz 2001b:711) has referred to as the "messy, fleshy" components of material life: shopping, cooking and cleaning, daily paperwork, social networking, minding the family store during or after hours, participating in religious or civic organizations, caring for children and the elderly (which often includes mediation with educational, medical, and religious institutions)—it becomes clear that these activities have historically fallen primarily to a few specific groups to accomplish, mostly women, but also other, largely disenfranchised members of society. Most of social reproduction throughout recorded history—that is, the work considered "outside" of production, either unwaged or paid so poorly it cannot serve to reproduce the laborer himself or herself—has been conducted by slaves and their descendants, colonial and postcolonial subjects, children, and women. Thus, in order to really understand how labor-power is constituted as a class and capitalism is reproduced as an economic system and a set of social relations, we must understand how these particular groups are constituted as workers—waged and unwaged—within this system. Further, we must problematize the very categories of production and social reproduction, which determine the nature and value of "work" in far too limited ways.

What Althusser misses, as a result of his abstraction of institutions away from the nitty-gritty of the everyday practices of laboring subjects, is this understanding of difference: the difference *between* subjects, which infects and affects the entire production/reproduction nexus; the difference *between* institutions and their relative degrees of importance in the overall reproductive cycle; and the ways in which these differences are brought to bear in producing a differentiated labor force daily and over the long term. Marx made the same fundamental error of transforming all questions of difference—for example, when discussing the subordination of women—to general philosophical critiques of human history. As Mitchell (1971:78) trenchantly observes,

> [Marx] retained the abstraction of Fourier's conception of the position of women as an index of general social advance. This in effect makes it merely a symbol—it accords the problem a universal importance at the cost of depriving it of its specific substance. Symbols are allusions to or derivations from something else. In Marx's early writings, "woman" becomes an anthropological entity, an ontological category, of a highly abstract kind.

Similarly, in his discussion of the family, Engels (1972), although observant of "difference" and mindful of the work of making workers, locates the subordination of women in their inability to engage in "socially productive work"—that is, work that is outside the home and waged. In his analysis, it is owing to the depredations caused by private property that women are caught in subordinate positions in society. The privatization of property and the development of commodity production initiated the formation of the individual family as an economic unit (as distinct from kinship units). The subsequent separation of "productive" waged work (men's) and "reproductive" family work (women's) created the schisms leading to the oppression of women. Engel's answer vis-à-vis women's liberation thus rests on women's ability to engage in waged labor in "public industry." Despite the advances in this mode of thinking with respect to the question of the differences among laborers and in the valuation of labor, the theoretical underpinnings of the work still rests on economic abstractions that ignore the history of patriarchy and many of the other hegemonic and coercive structures affecting women's engagement in social reproduction. As Mitchell (1971:79) writes, "Engels effectively reduces the problem of woman to her capacity to work." Like Marx, Engels reveals an economistic and highly abstract conceptualization of the actual disciplining forces through which reproductive labor-power is constituted.

Since the 1970s, a number of feminists have tackled the issue of social reproduction, querying the very notion of value and paying significantly greater attention to alternative structuring forces such as patriarchy and racism. Dalla Costa and James (1972), for example, were among the first to question the separation of waged labor as productive labor versus the assumption of family labor as "nonproductive." They argued that the family is a center for the production of value, not merely the space of reproductive functions such as consumption and childrearing. In this sense, they reconceptualized the Marxian understanding of value by locating it as something created through the work needed to produce and reproduce labor-power, not simply through the production of commodities. Their work, as

Leacock (1986:257) has noted, "became central in the intense debates of that era over the relation between women's domestic labor and the production of surplus value and the corollary relation between patriarchal family structure and the capitalist system." Other feminists criticized this position, arguing that women marginalized within a family unit were not productive of value, but rather served as the perfect "reserve army" of labor, effective in depressing working-class wages and also in mystifying—for both sexes—the structure of capitalist exploitation (eg Leacock 1986; Saffioti 1978).

Dalla Costa and James (1972), Fortunati (1989), Federici (1995), and many other Marxist-feminist theorists brought the question of unwaged reproductive work to the foreground and thus launched an effective critique of Marxist theory, which until that time had omitted the question of the productivity of housework. Marx himself measured value creation only in the process of commodity production, and never recognized the ways in which unwaged labor was consumed in the production of labor-power. Of course, social reproduction is not reducible to the reproduction of labor-power. "[T]he complex circuits of exchanges that Marx described in *Capital II* remain crucial for an explanation of social reproduction" (Caffentzis 1999:176). But bringing in the question of labor-power's reproduction—primarily by women—significantly augments and transforms Marx's formulations.

The early work by feminists and postcolonial theorists showed, both theoretically and practically, how the laboring classes were divided through differences of gender, race and colonial status and how the effects of these differences were not just epiphenomenal to the reproduction of the capitalist system, but absolutely central to it. The underlying power relations among differing groups in society were part of historical processes other than the separation of the laborer from the means of production, but they were also often greatly exacerbated by this separation. More recent work has continued to probe these types of connections and articulations among capitalism, patriarchy, and racism (and other structures of dominance) in theorizing life's work, but there often remains a separation between the theory and the actual spaces of material reproduction. Poststructuralist or psychoanalytical explanations, for example, are frequently abstracted away from the experiences and social relations of individuals in quotidian life. As we saw with earlier theories relying on abstract, ontological assumptions, this move affects the operational value of the theory itself.

For example, in many societies, the impulse to work—and to work in specific kinds of ways—is felt on a deep, psychological level and is tied in with feelings of individual productivity and personal value. Elucidating how people come to have these driving emotions requires a nuanced understanding of the multiple disciplining processes that influence the formation of individual and group subjectivities in the contemporary era. If, as Foucault observed, modern power operates through numerous microcircuits and technologies of control and is primarily productive rather than repressive, we need to investigate the ways in which individual and societal understandings of the creation of value, from the scale of the individual body to the corporate body and beyond, are produced. We need to examine the multiple inter-linked forces within which the body of the laborer is constituted and hegemonic norms develop. "Today political and economic demands are coming to be made more on behalf of the wage-earner's body than of the wage-earning class" (Foucault 1980:58).

But more than this, these are bodies and knowledges that are firmly invested in and strategically monitored through space. The spatiality of everyday life is an absolutely crucial formulation. Foucault (1980:149) wrote:

> A whole history remains to be written of *spaces*—which would at the same time be the history of *powers* (both these terms in the plural)—from the great strategies of geo-politics to the little tactics of the habitat, institutional architecture from the classroom to the design of hospitals, passing via economic and political installations. It is surprising how long the problem of space took to emerge as a historico-political problem. (emphasis in original)

What, then, are the contemporary spaces of life's work within which individuals are coming to have a sense of value? Pred (1990), Lefebvre (1991), and Hayden (1997), among others, have examined this question at a range of scales, making clear the potent spatiality of social reproduction. What are the new technologies of power and knowledge that are being brought to bear on laboring bodies? "What," asks Martin (1997:244), "might be the next step in the historical development of the body and kinds of powers regulating it that would come into existence along with a dramatic shift in political economic organization, such as that being brought about by flexible accumulation? What changes in our bodies might be necessary for such a shift to occur?"

If we are arguing that many arenas of work—life's work—are neglected as "nonwork" in the literature because they are outside traditionally recognized domains of production, we are also signaling a blurring of work and nonwork in an entirely different register. In this instance, it seems, the contemporary blurring of work and nonwork is accepted and understood as normal or even positive in some cases, largely because of the seductive influences of new technologies and spaces within current regimes of flexible accumulation. For many contemporary subjects, work—even nonstop work—is what makes you a person; it is what gives you value as a modern, rational agent. Even for those laboring under superexploitative conditions in the global South, or in "emerging" economies such as China's, this hegemonic refrain of work as conferring individual value, existing in juxtaposition with the ubiquitous images and narratives of modernity, has become commonplace.[11] Similarly, migrants negotiate the prospect of nonstop work even as they negotiate the prospect of nonstop movement between the spaces of work. And the managerial-professional class is wired to work in cars, on flights, at children's soccer games, and at the dinner table—but, to compensate for any lingering resentment this might cause, their "play" can now be accommodated at work, as work ostensibly metamorphoses into play. Throughout this volume, we show how diverse institutions and policies—such as those pertaining to education, childhood, migration, and housing, among many others—are facilitating new forms of awareness and new imaginations and practices concerning the "spaces" of work.

Conceptualizing the State and Social Reproduction

One of the most persistent debates in contemporary theorizing about globalization relevant to our discussion of social reproduction is whether the (territorially bounded) nation-state is becoming less or more central to capitalism through the "denationalization" of economies and the rise of suprastate organizations such as the WTO (Ohmae 1990, 1996; Sassen 1996). "Hyperglobalists" believe that the impact of globalization on the capitalist political economy has been so profound that it is leading to the diminution of the powers of the modern state, if not its ultimate disappearance. They contend that because the modern state is organized around a bounded territory, and because globalization is creating a new transnational economic space, the nation-state is increasingly unable to respond to the needs of the new global economy. Our position is that contemporary capitalism is very much dependent upon individual nation-states to support, protect, and extend its global reach. The changing sociospatial contexts of subjects involved in life's work are shaped and constrained by the state in contemporary capitalist society, perhaps even more than ever before. Indeed, the state is not disappearing; instead, it is dramatically restructuring, such that its juridical-legislative systems, bureaucratic apparatuses, economic entities, modes of governmentality, and war-making capacities continue to define, discipline, control, and regulate the residents of its territorial orbit (and those who wish to enter it) in most of the old ways as well as in startlingly new ones (Ong 1999). Indeed, it is in the dynamic articulation of countless new circuits of capital, manifested in the flow of people and things—circuits that are complex, overlapping, and often contradictory—that the role of the state becomes ever more important in managing, shaping, regulating, and supporting them.

In fact, as Castells (1996) has made clear, what the increasing importance of transnational flows and connections—from flows of capital to flows of migrants—indicates is that the nation-state is less a container of political or economic power than a complex site of flows and connections. The rise of supranational organizations, then, is not evidence of the decline of the nation-state, but rather a new arena for their operation. We see the massive increase in flows of trade, foreign direct investment, financial commodities, tourism, migration, crime, drugs, cultural products, and ideas as evidence of the need for different state forms (global and regional) whose roles are to manage and regulate these flows in the interests of global capital formation (Hardt and Negri 2000; Held et al 2000; Hirst and Thompson 1999). The result is that globalization has increasingly drawn the modern state into a complex of supranational, regional, and multilateral systems of governance. As the nation-state has been drawn into these new activities, it has abandoned, reduced, or reconfigured many of its previous responsibilities for social reproduction, especially with respect to social welfare provision (Katz 2001a), though it continues to exert great power through various disciplining strategies—witness US welfare reform policies that encourage marriage, advocate abstinence, and coerce work in exchange for public assistance.

Yet the increasing retreat of modern Western states from social welfare provision is a fairly recent phenomenon. The very emergence of the welfare state in parts of the world such as Europe and Anglo North America is a product of the late 19th and early 20th century, as the idea of social citizenship began to gain credence (Marshall 1950). "Social citizenship implies a relationship between states and individuals in which the former provides welfare benefits in cash or in kind for the latter on a formal basis and by legal right" (Painter 1995:77). The result is the social welfare state, the precise form of which varies from place to place. In the US, the social welfare state emerged first as a local phenomenon, largely through the efforts of women in the progressive movement, who worked to reconfigure the local state from a laissez-faire, tax-collecting entity to a complex bureaucracy responsible for imposing standards, issuing licenses, collecting garbage, providing utilities, maintaining and protecting the water supply, institutionalizing fire and police services, developing schools, and the like (Marston forthcoming). By the mid-20th century, individually based social welfare provision had become the responsibility of the national state enacted through public health insurance, support for dependent women and children, unemployment insurance, and old-age pensions.

In the US—as contrasted with the UK, for example—the impulse to create a welfare state was a direct response to rapidly increasing industrialization, immigration, and the movement of freed slaves into northern and midwestern cities. The cultural diversity these processes created caused "old stock" Americans a great deal of anxiety, as existing norms were challenged by new ideas and practices. In many ways, the welfare state was called upon to incorporate these new groups into the US polity through the institutionalization of middle-class norms deployed through public policies and programs directed at the poor, the indigent, and new immigrants. As Gordon (1994) has argued, although the welfare state's stated purpose was to equilibrate access to key social resources among all its citizens, social welfare policies need also to be seen as forms of social reform and control.

Yet by the onset of the world economic crisis in the 1970s, modern welfare states throughout Europe and Anglo North America and in Japan began to experience dramatic fiscal crises, as demands upon their resources were not matched by revenues. In response, states began a slow but determined process of abandoning social programs that supported the social reproduction of labor and shifting resources to more directly facilitate capital investment and growth, both domestically and abroad. The result is that in the 21st century, social reproduction has been dramatically privatized, as the state has abandoned its century-old role as the purveyor of public goods and services that enable the social reproduction of labor, the conditions of production, and production itself.

Perhaps what is most distressing about contemporary nation-state restructuring in Anglo North America and other regions where federal forms of government prevail is the massive devolution of nation-state support for social reproduction to lower territorial levels of government, private charities, and nongovernmental organizations, the resource bases of which are typically far less rich than those of any nation-state and the governance of which is often less publicly accountable. Thus, in addition to the nation-state's retreat from social reproduction, there is dramatically declining support for social reproduction at the local level with respect to education, the environment, health care, and other traditional "collective consumption" public goods, from public transportation to garbage collection. As Harvey (2000:87) and others have written, the contemporary nation-state's relationship to labor is about cutting back on the social wage, fine-tuning immigration so that only certain types of workers can be admitted, usually only for limited periods of time, and turning education over to the private sector or supporting "faith-based" education through vouchers. At the same time, it encourages corporate advertising and product distribution as a way of subsidizing the declining resource base of the local state.

One result of the nation-state's new relationship to labor is that it has had to develop new borders as it seeks to assign identity in ever more restricted ways. With respect to immigration policy, Kearney (1991:59), for instance, writes:

Capitalism in general effects the alienation of labor from its owner, but immigration policy can be seen as a means to achieve a form of this alienation that increases greatly in the age of transnationalism, namely the spatial separation of the site of the purchase and expenditure of labor from the sites of its reproduction, such that the locus of production and [social] reproduction lie in two different national spaces.

And yet, while discussions of globalization have begun to recognize the impacts of political and economic restructuring on social reproduction, they tend to underappreciate how state practices with respect to social reproduction are produced and deployed by the social agents that make up state bureaucracies (Gupta 1995; Heyman 1995). Our aim is to expose these practices to the light of day at the level at which they are viscerally experienced and reproduced in practice. Thus, at the same time that we assert that the state is not disappearing, we want also to make abundantly clear that we find mainstream constructions of the state inadequate to understanding how it operates upon and influences the particularities of life's work. Our commitment as feminist, Marxist, and poststructural theorists is to conceptualize the state, not as a disembodied or reified object that somehow sits above the fray of everyday life, but as a relationship that is enacted through the practices of social agents at work, at home, and in other quotidian spaces (Hyndman 2001; Painter 1995). As historians, geographers, sociologists, anthropologists, cultural-studies scholars, and feminist theorists have been arguing for over a decade, state and society are mutually constitutive, such that the state needs to be confronted less as an abstraction with autonomy from the rest of society than as a manifestation of the materialized social practices of human agents enacting life's work in complex ways. In short, the state is the restless outcome of human agency that is produced and negotiated through the social and cultural meanings of the multiply manifested normative environment of contemporary capitalism. The point is that the state is able to perform its power through the materialized daily practices of agents who are part of the state apparatus—through its bureaucracies and agencies—or who interact with the state as clients, claimants, or inmates. Such an approach to the state places human practice and cultural logics at the center of discussions about the state and recognizes social reproduction as inseparable from those practices and logics.

Writing almost a decade ago, Corrigan (1994) argued that the key question for theorists interested in state formation was not *who* rules, but *how* rule is accomplished and how patriarchy, racism, nationalism, homophobia, and classism become visible as constitutive features of rule. Such an approach requires us to rethink how we understand the state theoretically and methodologically in our attempts to examine its role in social reproduction. And, as geographers, we need to locate our questions within the context of the changing spaces of rule and ruling, asking not only how those spaces are made, remade, or altered by the very subjects whose everyday practices constitute them, but how hegemony is secured—or might be frayed—in the overlapping spaces where home and work, the public and the private, state and society converge. If, as in our conceptualization, the state is the contested product of the formal and informal practices of multiply situated subjects and social reproduction is about how we as subjects live at and outside of work, then the categorical binaries of state and society, work and home, production and social reproduction cannot be maintained. Our conceptualizations also require us to return once again to the critique advanced by feminists in the 1970s: that theory and practice cannot be separated either, and that everyday life is both politically and practically important as a site of research and progressive social change.

Contributions to This Volume

Each of the pieces in this collection pulls apart and examines the multiple social relations, spaces, practices, and possibilities of life's work. If it is through these practices that capitalism and other relations of domination and exploitation, together with their mobile subjects, are produced, maintained, and remade, then they hold the possibility for altering, undermining, and undoing these relations—for making new subjects. Glimmers of these possibilities spark through the minutia and magnificence of life's work and are sometimes recognized by life's workers. But to be transformative—to confound reproduction and maybe make something else—requires not only conscious appropriation of these sparks of recognition, but new modes of practice that build and rework the connections among the many spaces, actors, and material social practices of life's work. The power of life's work and the possibilities of its transformation are brought to the fore in the contributions to this volume, which address the broad arenas of education, migration and citizenship, and domesticity and the making of transnational modernity.

In the section on "Education and the Making of the Modern (Trans)national Subject," John Morgan, Jean Lave, and Nina Laurie, Robert Andolina and Sarah Radcliffe look at the cultural forms and material practices of educational and other institutions that contribute to the maintenance and consolidation of national and other forms of identity. Each addresses the everyday practices and ordinary spaces of social reproduction in general and identity formation in particular. Morgan's piece examines the "imagined geographies" of Britain portrayed in postwar school geography textbooks to consider how the mundane practices of schooling contribute to the production of a particular national subject. Focusing on the reception of these texts—which, Morgan argues, work as maps that at once naturalize social constructions of geography and identify and authorize particular modes of knowing—the piece shows how particular narratives about Britain and its relation to the world are constructed at the nexus between books, teachers, and students. In an insightful reading of a number of school geographies, Morgan reveals how they have handled and purveyed a shifting environmental consciousness, redefinitions of national space, and reappraisals of Britain's place in the world, but at the same time remained anchored in conservative representations of the nation and "citizenship education."

In their piece on indigenous professionalization in Bolivia, Laurie, Andolina and Radcliffe examine how these courses trade on and propel the mobile politics of "culturally appropriate development" in a transnational and local terrain. Working across scales, the authors reveal the sorts of "social reproduction involved in 'becoming indigenous' in the Andes" and how uneven access to political space among all the actors involved in "development" is contingent upon particular representations of social roles, including those associated with ethnicity. Drawing on extensive field research in Bolivia and Ecuador, they make a compelling argument that the role of transnational development institutions in promoting indigenous professional education weakens relationships between the national state and indigenous movements. Their piece is carefully attentive to the spaces wherein these practices are carried out and negotiated, revealing the ways in which the social reproductive practices of indigenous professionalization under neoliberalism simultaneously empower and circumscribe social actors operating at multiple scales.

Lave's piece examines how particular futures and identities are produced among the residents of the British enclave of Porto in Portugal. In her lively ethnographic account of British port merchants and their community, Lave reveals the means through which the old merchant groups continue to exert power over the enclave and its imagined future, even as they lose ground to an ascendant group of multinational corporate managers. As in the Bolivian case, social actors at the local scale secure their reproduction as particular kinds of subjects through producing and maintaining more forceful connections at the transnational scale than the local. Making clear the tight weave between cultural practices and political economy, and attentive to the local spatiality of social reproduction—in particular, the struggle around a pair of schools, but also those around the church and the cricket club—and its global inflections, Lave provides a nuanced sense of the work involved in "getting to be British" in a transnational context. In so doing, she demonstrates what is at stake in all forms of identification, and the work and daily compromises involved in securing them.

In the section on "Domesticity and Other Homely Spaces of Modernity," Maria Fannin, Melissa Hyams, and Rosemary Marangoly

George look at the relationship of the "home" to the emergence and consolidation of bourgeois, diasporic, and gendered subjectivities in capitalist transnational societies. Their pieces engage the means through which "home" is constructed in mutual and productive tension with other sites, such as the body, the hospital, the street, and the world. Looking at the spatiality of particular practices of social reproduction, these authors render visceral the strategic contingencies through which public and private or self and other get framed as distinct.

In her piece on birthing, Fannin traces the shifts from home to hospital to "homelike" hospital in US birthing practices over the course of the 20th century. She reveals the entangled historical geographies of embodiment, domesticity, privacy, agency, and security that lie at the heart of these changes as she carefully unpacks their relationships to the politics of social reproduction and the economics of health care in the US. In a detailed discussion of birth settings and practices since mid-century, Fannin makes clear that birth is a spatial as much as a social practice, arguing that its configuration speaks volumes about maternal subjectivity, the institutional settings of social reproduction, and the political economics of childbearing in particular and health care more generally.

Hyams also tracks the themes of embodiment and subjectivity, in her piece on "adolescent Latina bodyspaces." In a vivid ethnography, Hyams traces the means through which a group of teenage girls in Los Angeles become gendered, racialized, and classed subjects. Her account demonstrates how the global processes of capital restructuring are worked out on and through these young women's bodies and the ways they imagine themselves in the world. In a nuanced discussion of the spaces of social reproduction—wherein she troubles the obvious distinctions between public and private, using the language of inside/ outside to rework the meaning and sensibility of everyday places such as the bedroom, the home, the street, the neighborhood, and shops or malls—Hyams fleshes out contemporary ideas of "entangled power" In so doing, she engages what resistance might be under the conditions in which these girls were coming of age.

George reflects on cultural productions of home to reimagine the social reproduction of "Indian" national and diasporic subjects in a transnational sphere. Looking at three "fictional cities" created by two Indian writers and a painter, she explores the workings of these social texts to see how reproduction "unfolds within the cultural realm." Her piece engages the circulation and reception of these cultural forms to make sense of how they produce particular kinds of subjects, identifications, and affiliations. The essay provocatively considers how these productions rub against those coming from other institutional spaces in the differentiated reproduction of diasporic "Indian" subjects. In teasing out hegemonic ideas of home and nation in the paintings and fiction that are her focus, George provides a glimpse of how national identities and social relations might be made differently.

The section on "Modern Migrants/Flexible Citizens: Cultural Constructions of Belonging and Alienation" continues many of these themes in a different register. Geraldine Pratt, Altha Cravey, and Alison Mountz address the issue of immigration and social reproduction from a variety of angles. Their pieces examine how contemporary home spaces are being reworked by transnational exchanges of people, money, and emotions. Each piece offers insights into how social actors with limited access to citizenship rights—political, social, and economic —are frustrated or defeated by the awesome power of the state to restrict or prohibit their capacity to belong to the imagined community of the nation, and/or how they endeavor to construct alternative sources of support as the state increasingly withdraws from its previous social welfare responsibilities.

Pratt's essay takes a sobering look at the consistent devaluation of childcare by middle-class households and the Canadian state through an examination of childcare practices and practitioners—some of whom have arrived through special immigration programs—in suburban Vancouver. Observing the trend on the part of the national government towards abandoning responsibilities for the social welfare of women and children, as well as the everyday practices of middle-class Canadian households that render childcare as gendered and low-skilled work, she draws on survey and interview data to point to a national crisis in childcare in Canada. She argues quite convincingly that redressing this crisis requires rethinking standard conceptualizations of the economy beyond the usual male-oriented categories of production ("cars, trucks, and steel"), giving questions of domestic work and social reproduction —such as childcare—equal value with more traditional economic production in our analyses.

Cravey's inventive piece on mostly male Mexican migrants in central North Carolina provides important insights into gendered variations on immigration and the ways in which they create "home" places out of public spaces in an attempt to recover some of the emotional losses that their singular (nonfamilial) migration necessarily incurs. Through highly textured ethnography, she shows the numerous ways in which transnational labor migrants inadvertently work to offset the costs of social reproduction for capital and national states and the ingenious ways new forms of domestic practices take hold in transnational immigrant households. She also sees in these transnational migrant biographies creative potential to confront globalization in new ways, as novel identities are called forth under altered conditions and new spaces for political, social, and cultural interaction are constructed.

In her piece on human smuggling in Canada, Mountz argues that the state is not only constitutive of but constituted by spheres of social reproduction. Using the case of Fujian Chinese migrants who were smuggled into Canada in 1999 and later denied refugee status and deported, she shows how identity construction is a manifestation of social reproduction. Through a complex ethnography of the federal department of Citizenship and Immigration Canada, Mountz constructs an "everyday epistemology" of the state such that identities of belonging and exclusion are seen to be the result of bureaucratic actors determining the central elements of the social production and reproduction of the polity based on binary categories such as good or bad, deserving or undeserving, legitimate or illegitimate immigrants. Mountz, Cravey, and Pratt each take on some of the complex implications of the new flows of transnational migrants and explore the ways in which their presence in the economies of Anglo North America complicate our current understandings of social reproduction in theory and in practice.

In their attention to the various ways in which life is made outside of work, the contributors to this volume reveal how differentiated subjects of transnational capitalism are produced in the course of everyday practices. As we hope these pieces make clear, analysis of the enormity and variation of "life's work" can reveal not only the many means through which value is produced outside of the workplace, but also the importance of retheorizing the problematic divide between production and social reproduction. This project is essential if we are to understand—and have the hope of changing—the constitution of subjects through time and in space, the social relations of production and reproduction that make them sensible in a broader sphere, and the continuities and discontinuities within and between the social relations and structures wherein life's work is put into play.

Acknowledgments

Thanks to Lucy Jarosz and Matt Sparke for their insightful and critical readings of an earlier draft of this manuscript, and a huge thank you to Ros Whitehead who not only makes all things possible, but does it with great style and enormous patience. We could not have completed this volume without her assistance.

Endnotes

[1] The phrase "I am your idea, push me" is part of a global advertising campaign by the company Accenture.

[2] A scenario similar to this one is portrayed in the 1993 film *Shortcuts*.

[3] Empirical case studies of this kind of cross-border living are common in contemporary transnational migration research. See for example, the work of Luis Eduardo Guarnizo (1994) and Nina Glick Schiller (2001).

[4] See Katz (2001a) for a greater discussion of the idea of spatial topographies.

[5] *Formation permanente* is the state of being in continual retraining or constant mobilization in the domain of work. According to Donzelot (1991), this way of being in the

world is becoming normalized within the regime of flexible capitalism and represents a profound shift vis-à-vis the relation between the position of the subject and society. [6] Bourdieu's notion of the *habitus* rests on the material practices of everyday life. These practices become so routine and normalized that they take on the character of the self-evident—that which is "natural" to a given order and way of being in the world. See Bourdieu (1984). [7] The idea of "condensation" is expressed by Althusser as "overdetermination". See the essay, "Contradiction and over-determination", in *For Marx* (1969). See also Stuart Hall (1981). [8] For a discussion of the idea of capitalism as multiply constituted in different contexts around the world, see Mitchell (1995) and Thrift and Olds (1996). For a more radical poststructuralist critique of the theoretical privileging of capitalism over other forms of economic activity, see Gibson-Graham (1996). [9] See, for example, Blim (1996), Light and Karageorgis (1994), Portes (1994), and Phizacklea (1990). [10] For an enlightening discussion of these variations, see Hall's (1981) review of the literature on schooling, state, and society, especially pages 15–29. [11] See, for example, Yan's (2002) wonderful dissertation, which outlines the struggles of rural migrant women in China. Through their efforts to find employment as domestic workers in Beijing and Shanghai, these women seek to become modern subjects; in their minds, it is only through their capacity to labor in the "big" city that they are able to become fully *ren* (human).

References

Accenture (2003) http://www.accenture.com (last accessed 17 March 2003)

Althusser L (1969) *For Marx.* Translated by B Brewster. London: Allen Lane

Althusser L (1971) *Lenin and Philosophy and other Essays.* Translated by B Brewster. New York: Monthly Review Press

Beneria L (1985) (ed) *Women and Development: The Sexual Division of Labour in Rural Societies.* New York: Praeger

Blim M (1996) Cultures and the problems of capitalisms. *Critique of Anthropology* 16:79–93

Bourdieu P (1984) *Distinction: A Social Critique of the Judgement of Taste.* Translated by R Nice. Cambridge, MA: Harvard University Press

Braudel F (1981) *The Structures of Everyday Life: The Limits of the Possible.* Translated by S Reynolds. New York: Harper and Row

Braudel F (1982) *The Wheels of Commerce.* Translated by S Reynolds. New York: Harper and Row

Caffentzis C G (1999) On the notion of a crisis of social reproduction: A theoretical review. In M Dalla Costa and G Dalla Costa (eds) *Women, Development and Labor of Reproduction: Struggles and Movements* (pp 153–187). Trenton: Africa World Press

Castells M (1996) *The Information Age: Economy, Society, and Culture.* Vol. 1, *The Rise of Network Society.* Oxford: Blackwell

Corrigan P (1994) State formation. In GM Joseph and D Nugent (eds) *Everyday Forms of State Formation: Revolution and the Negotiation of Rule in Modern Mexico* (pp xvii–xix). Durham, NC: Duke University Press

Dalla Costa M (1972) Women and the subversion of the community. In M Dalla Costa and S James (eds) *The Power of Women and the Subversion of the Community* (pp 19–54). Bristol: Falling Wall Press

Dalla Costa M and James S (eds) (1972) *The Power of Women and the Subversion of the Community.* Bristol: Falling Wall Press

Deere C D (1977) Changing social relations of production and Peruvian peasant women's work. *Latin American Perspectives* 4(1–2):48–69

Donzelot J (1991) Pleasure in work. In G Burchell, C Gordon and P Miller (eds) *The Foucault Effect: Studies in Governmentality* (pp 251–280). Chicago: University of Chicago Press

Ehrenreich B and Hochschild A R (2003) *Global Woman: Nannies, Maids, and Sex Workers in the New Economy*. New York: Metropolitan Books

Engels F (1972) *The Origin of the Family, Private Property, and the State*. New York: Pathfinder Press

Federici S (1995) Wages against Housework. In E Malos (ed) *The Politics of Housework* (pp 187–194). Cheltenham: New Clarion Press

Folbre N (1994) *Who Pays for the Kids? Gender and the Structures of Constraint (Economics as Social Theory)*. New York: Routledge

Folbre N (2002) *The Invisible Heart: Economics and Family Values*. New York: New Press

Fortunati L (1989) *The Arcane of Reproduction: Housework, Prostitution, Labor, and Capital*. New York: Autonomedia

Foucault M (1980) *Power/Knowledge: Selected Interviews and Other Writings, 1972–1977*. Edited by C Gordon, L Marshall, J Mepham, and K Soper. New York: Pantheon

Gibson-Graham J K (1996) *The End of Capitalism (As We Knew It)*. Oxford: Blackwell

Gordon L (1994) *Pitied but Not Entitled: Single Mothers and the History of Welfare, 1880–1935*. New York: The Free Press

Guarnizo L (1994) Los Dominicanyorks: The Making of a Binational Society. *Annals of the Academy of Political and Social Science* 533: 70–86

Gupta A (1995) Blurred boundaries: The discourse of corruption, the culture of politics, and the imagined state. *American Ethnologist* 22(2):375–402

Hall S (1981) Schooling, state, and society. In R Dale, G Esland, R Fergusson, and M MacDonald (eds) *Education and the State: Schooling and the National Interest* (pp 3–30). Sussex: Falmer Press

Hardt M and Negri A (2000) *Empire*. Cambridge, MA: Harvard University Press

Harvey D (2000) Reinventing geography. *New Left Review* 4(July/August):75–97

Hayden D (1997) *The Power of Place: Urban Landscape as Public History*. Cambridge, MA: MIT Press

Held D, McGrew A, Goldblatt D and Perraton J (2000) *Global Transformations: Politics, Economics, and Culture*. Cambridge, UK: Polity Press

Heyman J M (1995) Putting power in the anthropology of bureaucracy: The Naturalization Service at the Mexico-United States border. *Current Anthropology* 36(2): 261–287

Hirst P and Thompson G (1999) *Globalization in Question: The International Economy and the Possibilities of Governance*. 2nd ed. Cambridge, MA: Polity Press

Hyndman J (2001) Mind the gap: a conversation between feminist and political geography. Manuscript, Department of Geography, Simon Fraser University

James S (1975a) *Sex, Race, and Class*. Bristol: Falling Water Press

James S (1975b) Wageless of the world. In W Edmonds and S Fleming (eds) *All Work and No Pay* (pp 62–86). Bristol: Falling Water Press

Katz C (2001a) On the grounds of globalization: A topography for feminist political engagement. *Signs: Journal of Women in Culture and Society* 26(4):1213–1234

Katz C (2001b) Vagabond capitalism and the necessity of social reproduction. *Antipode* 33(4):709–728

Kearney M (1991) Borders and boundaries of state and self at the end of empire. *Journal of Historical Sociology* 1(4):52–74

Leacock E (1986) Postscript: Implications for organizations. In E Leacock and H Safa (eds) *Women's Work: Development and the Division of Labor by Gender* (pp 253–267). Boston: Bergin and Garvey

Lefebvre H (1991) *The Production of Space.* Translated by D Nicholson-Smith. Oxford: Blackwell

Light I and Karageorgis S (1994) The ethnic economy. In N Smelser and R Swedberg (eds) *The Handbook of Economic Sociology* (pp 647–671). Princeton, NJ: Princeton University Press

Mackintosh M (1979) Domestic labour and the household. In S Burman (ed) *Fit Work for Women* (pp 173–191). London: Croom Helm

Marshall T H (1950) *Citizenship and Social Class.* Cambridge, UK: Cambridge University Press

Marston SA (forthcoming) A long way from home: Domesticating the social production of scale. In R McMaster and E Sheppard (eds) *Scale and Geographic Inquiry: Nature, Society, Method.* Minneapolis: University of Minnesota Press

Martin E (1997) Managing Americans: Policy and changes in the meanings of work and the self. In C Shore and S Wright (eds) *Anthropology of Policy: Critical Perspectives on Governance and Power* (pp 239–257). New York: Routledge

Martin R (2002) *Financialization of Daily Life.* Philadelphia: Temple University Press

Marx K (1906) *Capital.* Vol 1. New York: Bennett A Cerf

Marx K (1967) *Capital.* Vol 2. New York: International Publishers

Mies M (1982) *The Lacemakers of Naraspur: Indian Housewives Produce for the World Market.* London: Zed Books

Mitchell J (1971) *Woman's Estate.* New York: Pantheon Books

Mitchell K (1995) Flexible circulation in the Pacific Rim: Capitalisms in cultural context. *Economic Geography* 71(4):364–382

Ohmae K (1990) *The Borderless World: Power and Strategy in the Interlinked Economy.* New York: Harper Collins

Ohmae K (1996) *The End of the Nation-State: The Rise of Regional Economies.* New York: Free Press

Ong A (1999) *Flexible Citizenship: The Cultural Logic of Transnationality.* Durham, NC: Duke University Press

Painter J (1995) *Politics, Geography, and "Political Geography."* New York: Arnold

Parrenas R S (2001) *Servants of Globalization: Women, Migration, and Domestic Work.* Stanford, CA: Stanford University Press

Phizacklea A (1990) *Unpacking the Fashion Industry.* New York: Routledge

Portes A (1994) The informal economy and its paradoxes. In N Smelser and R Swedberg (eds) *The Handbook of Economic Sociology* (pp 426–449). Princeton, NJ: Princeton University Press

Pred A (1990) In other wor(l)ds: Fragmented and integrated observations on gendered languages, gendered spaces, and local transformation. *Antipode* 22(1):33–52

Saffioti H I B (1978) *Women in Class Society.* New York: Monthly Review Press

Sargent L (1981) (ed) *Women and Revolution: A Discussion of the Unhappy Marriage of Marxism and Feminism.* Boston: South End Press

Sassen S (1996) *Losing Control: Sovereignty in an Age of Globalization.* New York: Columbia University Press

Schiller N and Fouron G (2001) Georges Woke Up Laughing: Long-distance Nationalism and the Search for Home. Durham: Duke University Press

Shortcuts (1993) Motion picture. Directed by Robert Altman

SIGNS: Journal of Women in Culture and Society (1981) Special Issue on development and the sexual division of labor. 7(2)

Thrift N and Olds K (1996) Refiguring the economic in economic geography. *Progress in Human Geography* 20(3):311–337

Yan H (2002) "Development, Contradiction, and the Specter of Disposability: Rural Migrant Women in Search of Self-Development in Post-Mao China." PhD dissertation, Department of Anthropology, University of Washington

Part 1

Education and the Making of the Modern (Trans)national Subject

Chapter 1
Imagined Country:
National Environmental Ideologies
in School Geography Textbooks

John Morgan

Introduction

Within educational literature, it is widely accepted that schooling plays an important role in social reproduction (Apple 1979; Bourdieu and Passeron 1977; Bowles and Gintis 1976). However, less has been written about the role that specific school subjects play in such processes. Accordingly, this essay is about the role that school geography plays in social reproduction. It is a contribution to a small but growing body of geographical literature that asks questions about the purposes of geography teaching. Huckle (1985) suggests that geography teaching fulfils both a general and a more specific role in social reproduction. The general role is to sustain a "hidden curriculum," whilst the more specific role is

> related to the overt curriculum and theoretical ideology. The reality, rather than the rhetoric, of school geography suggests that the majority of lessons cultivate a voluntary submission to existing social, spatial and environmental relations. The subject is generally presented as a body of unproblematic facts, many of them dull, boring, or redundant. Pupils are given a dehumanized and depoliticized view of the world and their success or failure depends largely on their ability to reproduce ideas, skills and attitudes which sustain the status quo. (Huckle 1985:293)

Huckle's assessment of the role of geography teaching in social reproduction was written in the mid-1980s. Since then, the practices of geography teaching in Britain have been subject to the process of curriculum centralisation (Coulby 2000), with a common national curriculum in operation since 1991 (Rawling 2001). This has led a number of commentators to argue that geography teaching is being linked to attempts to make it serve the needs of the nation-state. For example, Ball (1994:36) argues that the original Working Group, set up to advise on the content of the National Curriculum, produced a report that sought to reposition the UK in "some mythical golden age of empire." Similarly, Hall (1990:314) draws a direct link between the knowledge to be taught in schools and national ideology:

> Why should California feature so strongly, without any requirement to undertake a serious study of China? The naming of the Falkland Islands could be seen as one instance of highlighting detail for its own sake and the re-establishment of Capes and Bays which had taken 50 years of hard campaigning to disestablish in the late sixties; alternatively, its inclusion might be seen as a political statement which reifies our Imperial Tradition, which is symbolically out of keeping with our economic future within a European Community. Is Colonel Blimp to haunt us forever, either through the specification of factual knowledge as an end in itself, or of particular places which are tombstones of the past?

These accounts go beyond the idea that the content of school geography is neutral and disinterested, and stress the importance of geographical knowledge in processes of social reproduction. Political geographers make similar arguments. For instance, Radcliffe (1999) discusses the processes by which state power is used to consolidate national identities. By means of power relations, the nation-state attempts to provide closure and boundedness to its own project. Geographical practices, resting on the territorial and sociospatial inventories of bounded nations, are central to the state's techniques of power. The "imagined geographies" upon which a social sense of identity rests can be manufactured and circulated by the state through its institutions, orders and discourses.

Radcliffe (1999) explains how geographical professionalism and skills have often provided the knowledge/power with which to promote these imaginative geographies. The state reinforces the "obviousness" of the national territory through the creation of the palimpsest of the national map, which is "logoized" into an immediately recognisable symbol. Citizens are "corralled" into certain identities through the creation of discursive power effects around the lines on the map. These structures of feeling are shaped by spaces and practices such as state schooling and a national educational curriculum, as well as by imageries diffused by the media to the general population. The overall effect is to build up a national imaginative geography, an imagined space in which other practices in the name of the state are justified and legitimated. Radcliffe's (1999) work is important for the argument in this essay because it makes clear that school geography is implicated in the processes of "nation-building." However, rather than seeing this as somehow a process of top-down imposition, she stresses the contribution of "everyday" practices, such as those that take place in "ordinary" spaces such as geography classrooms.

Similarly, Sharp (2000a) points out that geopolitics, or the spatialising of international politics, is inherent to any representation of political processes, whether at the global, regional, national or local scale. Sharp (2000a:333) argues that whilst the majority of critical geopolitics focuses at the state level, where policy is enacted, dominant images of the world and its workings emerge, not from a single source, "but from the complex—and fragile—workings of hegemony." It is through institutions such as the media and education that people are drawn into the political process as subjects of various political discourses: "The media and education explain the linkages between their audiences and what is being explained in order to provide a context of interpretation. People are told what various changes and occurrences both at home and around the globe mean to them personally" (Sharp 2000a:333).

Sharp (2000a:334) goes on to argue that the scripting of global politics in popular culture is also significant, in that it is "within the sphere of popular culture that national cultures are formed and reinforced": "A national culture represents a common source of narratives and understandings which attempt to produce a sense of belonging. These narratives and beliefs are drawn upon to define and explain new situations and their importance to individuals in the community." Sharp (2000a:335) suggests that the wider context of interpretation is important because geopolitical descriptions and arguments often rely upon accepted models, metaphors and images: "These are naturalised —made into 'common-sense' statements—through reproduction in *education* and popular culture. Through these institutions, people learn about different places, whether this is a list of 'factual' data or a more metaphorical narrative" (emphasis added).

This introductory section has sought to show that "school geography matters." The content of school geography lessons serves to provide students with ideas, skills and attitudes that support existing social and economic arrangements. The next section expands on how these processes take place though common educational practices in school geography.

School Geography's Role in Cultural Production

Ross (2000:154) summarises the role that geography plays in the school curriculum: "The subject of geography necessarily defines social space and territory, given its concern with boundaries (national and physical), zones of activity and notions of regionality: these are inevitably part of the process of identifying people with places, in terms of the identity and nature of a nation." Ross (2000) is suggesting that, rather than *describing* the world "out there," geography lessons are *constitutive* of that "real world." For example, in 1998, it was announced that the Fujitsu Microelectronics Plant in Newton Aycliffe in northeast England would shut down. Is the closure of a microelectronics factory in northeast England a local, regional, national or international event? One answer is that it depends on the scale at which we choose to study it. Following Smith's (1993) argument the closure of the Fujitsu factory has a very different meaning as a global event than it has as a local event: the two are clearly coincident, though not identical.

The question of the scale at which this example should be studied in geography classrooms is not immediately clear. On the one hand, it could be used as an example of local employment changes and the impact of such changes on a locality. It could also be seen as part of a study of regional and national changes, specifically ideas about a "North-South" divide in the UK or about regional policies. Alternatively, it could be interpreted as an example of the difficulties firms face in operating in a European Community in which exchange-rate variations exist and thus raise the question of national sovereignty. Then again, it might be studied as an example of the shifting patterns of global employment change and the inability of national governments to control events within their own economic space (this was the interpretation offered by the British government when Prime Minister Tony Blair visited the workers who faced redundancy). The point is that this example or event looks different and needs to be treated differently depending on which scale the geography teacher decides to adopt as an interpretative frame. There is nothing "natural" about the selection of scale.

This leads to the idea that the outcomes of these "framings" have tangible and material consequences in terms of how students understand particular aspects of their lives. For instance, the decision to teach at the global scale means that a particular slant is put on the event. In school geography, this might be about the inevitability of global shifts in economic production, given the footloose nature of transnational corporations. The message for geography students, then, might be that governments can do little to challenge the logic of global capital. Gibson-Graham (1999) has usefully discussed the pedagogical implications of this. Reflecting on her experience with teaching economic geography, she (1999:81) notes:

[I]n those exciting early days, I had yet to take seriously the "performativity" of social representations—in other words, the ways in which they are implicated in the worlds they ostensibly represent. I was still trying to capture "what was happening out there" ... Students were drawn to the certainty and urgency of tracing the "emergence of

global capitalism" in particular industrial sectors and regions, and
the classroom became a site where the new world order was critically
"pinned down." At that point I was not thinking about the social
representation my students and I were creating as constitutive of
the world in which we would have to live. Yet the image of global
capitalism that we were producing was actively participating in con-
solidating a new phase of capitalist hegemony. Through my pedagogy
... I was representing an entity called the "global capitalist economy,"
and that representation was becoming common sense to a generation
of students.

This example suggests that it is through stories or representations
such as this that we develop understandings of the world and how to
live in it. The contest between rival stories produces our notions of
reality, and hence our beliefs about what we can and cannot do. The
stories through which we make sense of the world are everywhere. In
the media, they are not just in the articles and programmes labelled
"fiction" and "drama," but in those on current affairs, sport, party
politics, science, religion and the arts, and in those specified as education and for children. The argument is that geography teaching
in schools is a form of "cultural production." Just as societies need to
produce materially in order to continue, so they must also produce
culturally. They need *knowledges* to keep production going, and
geography is just one part of this set of knowledges. While geography
may provide some people with technical skills, its more general
function is concerned with providing people with an understanding of
their location in the world. Cultural production provides concepts,
systems and—apparently—"natural" understandings to explain who
"we" are collectively and individually, who "others" are and how the
world works (Sinfield 1997).

Geography Textbooks
This argument clearly has its roots in the idea that school curricula
perform the role of cultural transmission associated with writers
such as Apple, Bourdieu and Passeron, and Bowles and Gintis. The
rest of this essay focuses on geography textbooks, which are seen
as one mechanism whereby this cultural transmission occurs. Apple
(1988:85) is clear about the importance of textbooks in this
process:

> How is the "legitimate" knowledge made available in schools? By
> and large it is made available through something to which we have
> paid far too little attention—the textbook. Whether we like it or not,
> the curriculum in most American schools is not defined by courses
> of study or suggested programs, but by one particular artefact, the
> standardized, grade-level specific text in mathematics, reading,

social studies ... The impact of this on the social relations of the classroom is also immense. It is estimated, for example, that 75 percent of the time elementary and secondary students are in classrooms and 90 percent of their time on homework is spent on text materials.

Blaut (1998:46) has reiterated this statement about the importance of the textbook as a means of transmitting "legitimate" forms of knowledge:

A school textbook is truly a key social document, a kind of modern stele. In the typical case, a book becomes accepted as a high school (or lower-level) textbook only after it has been reviewed very carefully by the publisher, school boards and administrators, all of whom are intensely sensitive to the need to print acceptable doctrine. They are concerned to make it certain that children will only read those facts in their textbook which are considered to be acceptable as facts by the opinion-forming elite of the culture. The resulting textbook is, therefore, less an ordinary authored book than a vetted social statement of what is considered valid and acceptable for entry into the mind of the child. For this reason, research on textbooks is, in fact, ethnographic research.

These statements suggest that an examination of the textbooks used in school geography can shed some light on the construction of students' "geographical imaginations." There exist a number of important statements about the role of school geography textbooks in constructing readers' ideas about the world. Whilst the earliest studies sought to identify and excise ideological biases in contemporary textbooks and teaching materials, more recent approaches have focused on qualitative analysis of geographical textbooks. Within geography education, notable examples include Gilbert's (1984) *The Impotent Image* and Henley's (1989) discussion of the forms of language used in school geography textbooks. Ahier's (1988:123) analysis of school history and geography textbooks suggests how the texts serve to reinforce social differentiation (between social groups) and social integration (at the level of the nation): "[I]f most history books located the child at the end of a long process of national development, *then most geography books address their child-readers as very specifically located in space around which all other space is measured, placed and compared*" (emphasis added).

In such "ideology critiques," there is a tendency to assume that texts have a deep, hidden meaning that is capable of being revealed by the informed reader. Gilbert (1989) noted that the structures and metanarratives of ideology critique are too singular and complete. There is too much emphasis on making "heroic," oppositional readings at the expense of investigating the social processes involved in the realisation of textual meaning. Another way of putting this is to suggest that the focus has been on what the texts say, rather than what teachers and students get from them (Lee 1996). More recent work in human geography, influenced by the so-called cultural turn, is more willing to defer the moment at which the meaning of the text is "fixed." Such approaches have sought to stress the importance of the context in which they were read (Maddrell 1996; Ploszajska 2000). Marsden (2001) has written a history of the school textbook in the United States and Britain. In Britain, he detects an "antitextbook ethos" amongst educators, where "ideology critique" has been used to judge textbooks. Though this essay follows in this "critical" tradition, I would argue that, far from invalidating such texts, such critical awareness of their content and approach can be useful in providing meaningful learning for students. Indeed, my own initial interest in these texts came from my experience of using them in classrooms.

Recent studies of school geography textbooks might be seen as an addition to the growing number of studies on geographic representations in books, paintings, music, festivals, maps and—more latterly—textbooks. Following Short (2001a), it is possible to see geography textbooks as a type of map. Phillips (1997:14) argues that maps "*may* be spatial, visual, graphic representations, but the information they represent *must* be spatial." Accordingly, the cartographic map is a special kind of map, one in which space is used to represent space, but it is not the only form of map. Harley (1992) conceptualised the relationship between maps and other forms of representation by showing how both can be read as cultural texts. Cartography, he argued, is geographical discourse. Given this broad definition of maps, the geography textbook, replete with vivid geographical imagery, is as much a map as any formal cartographic image.

Geographic textbooks share with other maps—particularly cartographic maps—a measure of authority, a power to naturalise constructions of geography and identity. As maps, geography textbooks possess the "aura of knowledge." They are commonly regarded as scientific, objective and mechanical. It seems that they depict the world as it really is.

National Environmental Ideologies in School Geography Textbooks

The second part of this essay considers some of the specific content found in geography textbooks that deal with one national space—Britain. In his book, *Imagined Country*, Short (1991:xvi) uses the term "national environmental ideology" to refer to myths mobilised in the course of state formation and nation-building: "Societies occupy space as well as time, an occupancy which provides a rich source for the production of national legends and social metaphors. Ideologies, as used here, refer to myths of wilderness, countryside and city which are used in the creation of a national identity. National environmental ideologies are myths which reference particular territories and specific societies." This section of the essay focuses on specific aspects of national environmental ideologies found in school textbooks on the geography of Britain in the postwar period. The texts span an important era in the recent historical geography of Britain, a time when there were important social, economic, cultural and environmental changes. In line with the discussion in the first part of the essay, the argument here is that these textbooks, rather than offering readers a transparent "window on the world," play their part in constructing particular narratives about Britain and its place in the world. School geography textbooks are taken as an example of Sharp's (2000b) argument that geographers need to get away from a "naïve realist" position that reads fictional and factual texts as reliable guides to landscape. Sharp suggests the need for a critical reading of such texts. The following sections are based on a reading of 18 school geography textbooks published in the postwar period that deal with the geography of Britain. In reading them, I have attempted to assess their content and identify some of the ideological messages in the ways in which they treat their subject matter. I have tried to comment on their inclusions and omissions, and to place them in their wider context.

Environmental Crises

The first "national environmental ideology" or "myth" considered here is the relationship between people and the physical environment. In *An Environmental History of Great Britain: From 10,000 Years Ago to the Present*, Simmons (2001:238) discusses the period from 1950 to the present and notes that "In environmental terms, no age has perhaps been more conscious of 'the environment,' yet no other has brought about such a strong impact. This may have helped to produce some of the unease which has been a feature of life in the last 40–50 years, though not of course the only basis." Textbooks on the geography of Britain during this period have reflected this evolving environmental consciousness. Early texts tended to stress the "fortunate" position of Britain at the centre of the modern world. Britain's climate was thought to be the most obvious and natural reason for the success of its people, being neither too hot nor too cold and having great seasonal variety. This theme was common in texts influenced by the geographical determinism associated with regional approaches. Later books reflect a clear shift from a description of the abundance of natural resources through recognition of the need for conservation to a sense of environmental "crisis."

Taking energy as an example, Marsden's (1978) *The Changing Geography of Britain* captures the shifting perception of Britain's energy needs at a time when it was recognised that coal was no longer king. Throughout the chapter on energy there is a progressive broadening of focus, from the location of specific mines on specific coalfields towards a discussion of the role that coal plays in Britain's industrial development. The prominence of the coal industry over other energy sources reflects the importance of the resource. Subsequent sections focus on North Sea oil and gas, pointing out that the first oil from the North Sea was landed at the Isle of Grain in June 1975 and that by 1982, Britain was self-sufficient in oil and natural gas. The chapter stresses the relationship between energy resources and Britain's economic development. There is an unmistakable narrative of progress running through the account, which is explained by technological advance. The employment benefits of these changes are stressed, and the text displays little evidence of concern about environmental issues. Even in relation to nuclear power stations, the original fears about safety are played down: "At first, all the stations built were placed in fairly isolated parts of Britain. After many years of safe operation, it is now thought that new stations might be built near urban areas without risk. Hence two of a later generation of nuclear power stations, at Hartlepool and Heysham, are in urban areas" (Marsden 1978:90).

By 1990, this optimistic picture of inexorable progress driven by the discovery of new sources of energy and technological advance was looking less convincing. In *A Contemporary Geography of Britain*, in describing the way in which the daily lifestyles of "Mr and Mrs Average" made demands on limited energy resources, Walford (1990:170) observed: "[F]or some time oil was a cheap energy source, but recent international decisions to cut back on production have pushed up its price again; gas has also been relatively cheap in Britain (largely because of the introduction of natural North Sea gas, to replace manufactured town gas) but the price has been rising recently."

There are some important differences between the accounts offered in these textbooks. For a start, the 1984–1985 miners' strike left its mark, so that discussions about the rate at which coal reserves were declining or becoming "uneconomic" had to be weighed against the political costs and social costs of pit closures: "[I]t is not easy to uproot families and whole neighbourhoods and move them on, just because the good coal seams have run out" (Walford 1990:172). The discussions of the various energy sources are marked by a concern with how fast they are likely to be used up, reflecting a general awareness of the need for energy conservation. In addition, Walford's textbook is much more concerned with environmental issues and the recognition that large-scale schemes to harness energy can have repercussions. This is particularly true in the case of the nuclear industry, where reference is made to the recent events at Chernobyl. In this text, there is a tendency to place Britain's energy needs and issues in a more international context, and there is a much more explicit recognition of the role that governments play in the decision to exploit energy sources.

In general, the textbooks display some important shifts in the "stories" they tell about the relationship between people and environment. The older story about man's (sic) increasing domination of the environment and about Britain's favourable location gives way to a bleaker assessment of people's impact on the environment. There are some important points to make about this shift, however. First, many of these textbooks tend to see environmental issues as managerial ones that can be solved by rational planning and resource management. The textbooks are inclined to adopt a "technocentric" view of environmental issues, and, although they become increasingly uncertain about the prospects for unlimited resource use, they are confident about the ability of people and governments to effectively manage resources and solve resource issues. Second, in general the textbooks treat environmental issues as essentially "local" issues unrelated to wider structural forces in the world economy. Evidence of a "global imaginary" is not strongly developed in these texts.

Divisions of National Space

Following Anderson's (1991) argument, the "nation" is an example of an "imagined community." School geography textbooks might be seen as one example of a technology with which this imagined community is maintained and reproduced over time. All textbook authors face the question of how to depict the obvious diversity and fragmentation of geographical space while making it clear to readers that there *is* such thing as a "British" nation. However, they do not handle this decision in the same way. Some of the texts make no attempt to "theorize" the regions they use: the regions are simply there, to be described. The national space is a container into which the various regions somehow fit. The traditional geographical question of how to draw boundaries around places is generally not asked; if it is, a rational, "scientific" justification is offered. The most common approach is to base such divisions on structural aspects of the geography of Britain. The approach in a number of these textbooks is the detailed inventory of the contents of the geographical regions. The effect of this is to provide a textual unity to the fragmented geographical diversity.

However, over the period considered here, other ways of representing the national space are introduced, which reflect, in part, changing approaches to the study of geography. In general, the shifting approaches to the division of Britain move from a physical (or structural) division to human, mainly economic division. Thus, Kirby and Robinson's (1981) *Geography of Britain: Perspectives and Problems* uses the idea of the metropolitan core areas (Southeast, East Midlands, West Midlands and East Anglia), the peripheral regions (Wales, Scotland, Northern Ireland and the Southwest) and the intermediate regions. Each of these has its own set of geographical issues. Nonetheless, the tenor of the text is optimistic: these diverse regions are all part of the same Keynesian welfare state, and government economic policies are suggested as the way to ensure that the problems of these regions are solved: "Perhaps the greatest economic and social problem facing the governments of the developed world at the present time is how to correct these regional imbalances, and to regenerate decaying and decayed areas which have lost their economic vigour, are suffering out-migration and have become depressed socially and psychologically" (Kirby and Robinson 1981:219).

Other divisions of the national space are possible, such as the organisation of the text along lines of urban and rural environments—a division that is, of course, deeply rooted in the national consciousness. The choice of places to be studied is important in considering the ways in which these textbooks construct their view of Britain. Thus—and perhaps not surprisingly—many of the books make great play of London and the Southeast as the dominant region. The texts go out of their way to stress the "modernity" of the Southeast. By contrast, there is some evidence that the older industrial regions are represented as belonging to an earlier time. This is an example of the sort of "place-myth" that Shields (1991) describes. Notably, there is little attempt to reflect the existence of "Celtic geographies," despite the growing importance of the internal divisions associated with demands for political devolution from the mid-1970s onwards (Harvey et al 2002).

The overall picture that one gets from a reading of textbooks of this period is one of growing confusion about how to divide up the national space. A number of solutions to the problem exist, yet—in the 1980s in particular—there are no clear answers. Of course, these must in some way be related to the changing shape of Britain's geography, which became increasingly divided and contested during this time. Thus, textbook sections that ask about the existence of the "North-South divide" reflect economic and social division. In the 1970s, textbook writers are able to write with confidence about the role of the government in managing resources rationally in order to solve spatial problems. By the 1980s, there is less ebullience and optimism, to the extent that textbooks resemble the "cartographies of distress" described by Mohan (1999:2), which map the social conflict and division that characterised life in Britain in that period. An example of this tendency is seen in Beddis's (1985) *A New Geography of Britain*. Despite its attempts to offer a framework that could include a wide number of social groups that had been affected by social, political and economic change, this textbook ultimately leaves the reader with a stronger sense of what divided Britain in the 1980s than of what held it together. The key words here are "contrast" and "difference" and a surprisingly fine-grained differentiation of the nation according to different types of places.

Britain in the World

Despite the problems associated with the representation of geographical and social diversity within Britain, all these textbooks take it for granted that there is such a place as "Britain," and that it can be treated as a single, homogenous unit for analysis. This is most obvious when it comes to making comparisons with the "rest of the world." The following statement from Tolson and Johnstone's (1970:7–8) *A Geography of Britain* is typical: "At the end of the Ice Age, water from the melting ice swamped the land. The seas rose and flooded the coasts, making Britain an island separating her from the continent of Europe." Thus, in one statement Britain's physical and political separation are effectively conflated (an example of the way in which geographical discourse can serve to culturalise the natural and naturalise the cultural). Stephenson's (1984:5) *Geography of the British Isles* contains the following statement, which chimed well with Britain's adventures in the South Atlantic in the previous year:

> The position of Britain has helped her to become a major world power. The surrounding seas made it necessary for Britain to become a seafaring nation in order to trade with other lands ... The growth of commerce and shipping enabled Britain to trade with most parts of the world, to become a major sea power and to expand her territories overseas. Today, the British Empire has virtually ceased to exist, but the English language is spoken in most parts of the world and is an important link in the British Commonwealth of Nations. The position of the British Isles also makes it an important centre of international air routes.

This story of national greatness is maintained in the face of its increasingly tenuous hold on reality.

Whilst these might be considered to be examples of the types of "Anglocentrism" left over from a bygone age, it is sobering to consider Knapp's textbook *Britain in Today's World*. The book was published in 1988, and thus avoids the explicit racism that pervaded earlier texts. Its approach was to take a number of geographical themes and provide comparisons, contrasts and links between Britain and the developing world. Despite the honest attempt to represent the complexity of the world, however, the result is the representation of the world around a crude economically-developed/economically-developing dualism. The message is that Britain is more "advanced" than other nations.

A Changing Geography

Many of the textbooks examined attempt to represent the changing geography of Britain. Indeed, some have the words "new" and "changing" in their titles. How do they represent these changes? It is important to point out that despite their focus on the "new" and on "change," none of these textbooks offers readers an explanation of how or why Britain's geography is changing.

This is not to suggest that the authors do not have their own ideas about this. In their academic text, *The Transformation of Britain*, Ball, Gray and McDowell (1989) suggest that in the 1980s, there were four "stylised generalisations" of Britain and its relationship with the past. The *radical break thesis* held that the 1980s constitute a radical break with earlier postwar decades. Whilst this thesis is clearly linked with the political impact of Thatcherism, there are also broader understandings, such as the idea that fundamental economic change has been taking place in Britain and elsewhere—for instance, the idea that in the economic sphere, manufacturing has shifted from Fordist mass production to post-Fordist flexible specialisation. *Golden Age ideologies* suggest that at some time in the past, "they got it right." *Inexorable progress* is presented as an idea that structures most people's views of modern society. Progress is seen in the increased material wealth available to all, in contrast to the situation 20, 40 or 100 years ago. Development may exert a price, and awareness of the environmental cost is growing, but the benefits are generally regarded as outweighing the costs. Finally, *social-conflict models* are based on the idea that societies are divided along lines of class and that older models of social pluralism no longer serve. This is obviously quite a complex idea for school geography textbooks to get across. However, some of the textbooks examined—such as the 1989 book *British Issues in Geography* (Flint and Flint 1989)—do adopt an approach that stresses the existence of social conflict.

It would be surprising if these textbooks involved simple adherence to one of these narratives. In reality, the representation of Britain each book offers tends to draw upon a number of these approaches. By far the most common is that of technological progress and advancement. Most of the textbooks tell the story of the progressive incorporation of nature and the harnessing of technology to meet human needs. Where they differ is in the degree to which they acknowledge the tensions that such capitalist progress creates between people and the environment, and between different social groups. In general, the textbooks opt for a vision of social consensus and stress the role of the state as the manager of change.

The Place of the Textbook

These brief discussions of the content of some school geography textbooks give a flavour of the types of representations of Britain on offer to students during the postwar period. Variations exist within the textbooks, and, in some ways, these texts simply mirror the larger stories that are told about social development. The textbook representations of Britain fit Harvey's (2001:231) observation that in much geographical writing, "natural and social phenomena are represented objectively as things, subject to manipulation, management and exploitation by dominant forces of capital and the state." The textbooks also exemplify MacDonald's (1976:223, 234) argument that textbooks have traditionally "helped to define the content and fix the limits of legitimate educational knowledge":

> In the positive aspect, knowledge is selected to emphasize certain values or a certain view of the world. Usually this is a view formed by wider and unexamined social demands—those, for example, of imperialism, industrialism, technocracy or bureaucracy. The negative aspect refers to the range of knowledge left out of texts, or out of the wider school curriculum. School children, as a result, are cut off not only from wide areas of knowledge, but also from many of the terms and ideas which could extend political dialogue.

Thus, during a period of important shifts in the economic, political, social and cultural geographies of Britain, students in geography were presented with representations of the nation that were essentially socially conservative and supportive of existing social, economic and environmental relations. Agnew (2002:2) points out that "regional texts" in geography fulfil this function: since they are concerned with

> recounting the official stories of the world-regional spaces they hope to describe, they rarely contradict or criticize the sociopolitical ideals associated with them, or consider how these ideals work out in practice. This is because regional geographies have been resolutely apolitical, avoiding any hint of explicit "bias" in measuring the empirical character of places against the political and social claims of the powerful institutions governing the spaces in which the places are located.

However, it might be useful to reread these textbooks in the light of recent discussions in human geography that stress that "[P]lace should be seen as a fluent, not a fixed, concept, not a settlement in the field of enquiry but a contested terrain" (Daniels 1992:314). One of the most striking features of recent debates within human geography is the way in which "places" can no longer be seen as common sense. Cresswell (1996) shows how place is implicated in the creation and maintenance of ideological beliefs. He discusses the ways in which how places are socially constructed is ideological. Places, landscapes and regions appear static and bounded. Hudson (2001:256) summarises much of the debate about the conceptualisation of place within geography: "For many years, places tended to be seen as bounded and closed territories, perhaps internally homogenous in respect to some characteristics, perhaps internally differentiated (for instance, by residential segregation within urban areas)."

More recent conceptualisations of "place" are based on two principles. First, places should be seen as constituted out of spatialised social relations, which not only lay down ever-new geographies but also work to reshape cultural and social identities and how they are represented. Places are to be conceptualised as open, discontinuous and linked to social relationships that are "stretched out" over space. Understanding places involves understanding the processes that come together to create them. The second feature of recent conceptualisations of place recognises the fact that "places are not 'out there' waiting to be discovered; they are our (and others') constructions" (Allen, Massey and Cochrane 1997:2). There are multiple ways of seeing a place; there is no complete "portrait of a region."

At root, these are issues of *representation*, about how we decide to tell stories about places. They involve asking the question: What types of representation are appropriate to the classrooms in which I teach? For geographers (and geography teachers) to ask such a question is not a sign of weakness. Instead, I think Short (2001b:18) is right when he suggests that the confusion over what we understand by the terms "space" and "place," "rather than showing a conceptual fuzziness, represents the way our picture of the world, our spatial awareness and our place sensitivity has shifted and changed as material practices transformed how we see the world and our place in it."

These arguments about how place should be conceptualised have had little impact on geography education at school level in Britain, despite the concern of government advisory bodies to reassert the importance of the study of "places" within school geography. This is due in large measure to models of curriculum planning and teaching that rely on the idea that there is a "secure" subject knowledge that teachers need to be in a position to "deliver." However, as I suggest in the final part of this essay, such debates are important where geography teachers are charged with the task of teaching about places in the contemporary world.

Conclusion

By way of conclusion, I want to return to the question of the specific role that school geography plays in processes of social reproduction. My analysis of school textbooks on the geography of Britain has suggested that they are a curious mixture of inherited tradition, piecemeal responses to contemporary geographical change and more or less explicit educational beliefs. Taken together, they present a picture of a relatively stable and coherent nation where, despite problems and issues, people generally live harmoniously and the state acts to ensure that people's lives are fairly tolerable. The textbooks present material about Britain and its place in the world to future citizens in a packaged format acceptable to the powerful vested interests in society.

These books are important because, through school subjects, a definition of "our" society is created and an identity is presented for the learner to put on. As taught to children in Britain, school geography offers a "narration of the nation." However, as Goodson (1994) has argued, when we talk about a national curriculum, it is important to ask whose nation we are talking about, since a curriculum is always an act of social prioritizing. Thus, it would be possible to offer representations of the geography of Britain that explicitly link it to the idea of being European. Similarly, it would be possible to stress the importance of regional or local identities. Indeed, the National Curriculum's requirement that pupils study their "locality" might offer opportunities to forge such identities. More radically, geographies of Britain could be used to interrogate claims of inclusiveness along lines of class, gender and ethnicity.

Debates about how to conceptualise "places" in a period of rapid economic, political and social changes that have been played out in geography have their educational corollary. For example, in 1996, Nick Tate, the chief executive of the Qualifications and Curriculum Authority, addressed the Geography Association—the organisation that represents geography teachers in schools in Britain—and exhorted them to teach a distinctly "British" geography. He suggested that while school geography lessons should encourage a global sense of identity in relation to environmental issues, this should not prevent pupils from developing their sense of national identity. This may be read as a deliberate attempt to challenge the efforts of geography teachers to offer alternative, less ethnocentric representations of the world.

More recently, the British government made "citizenship" a compulsory part of the school curriculum (Lambert and Machon 2001). Such debates about citizenship education are taking place in the context of broader political and cultural debates about the status of "Britishness" (or, more narrowly, "Englishness") in the light of processes of "globalisation." Gilbert (1997:73) has noted how the history of citizenship education has been bound up with the nation-state as the site of civil and political power: "Promoted as they are by nation-states, and historically grounded in such a strong tradition of grand narratives of progress through the story of the nation, programs in education for citizenship will surely find the concept of world citizenship difficult to accept and even more difficult to reconcile with the nationalist agenda."

In light of these arguments, it is possible to suggest that in recent years, school geography has been the site of a struggle over how to

represent Britain to students. That is, in a period during which questions of economic change, political and social order and national
identity have come to the fore, geography as a school subject has been
concerned with providing resources to help students locate themselves
in the national space. Though this essay has argued that popular geography textbooks used in schools have presented conservative images
of social, spatial and environmental relations, there is nothing inevitable about all this. Though curriculum texts and textbook interpretations
are written so as to give the impression that they offer a transparent
"window" on reality, they are, in fact, cultural productions and are
capable of being read in different ways. School geography classrooms
are one space in which social relations are represented, negotiated and
contested. The question of how these texts are read and interpreted in
the context of school geography lessons remains an area for further
study.

References

Agnew J (2002) Introduction. In J Agnew and J Smith (eds) *American Space/American
    Place* (pp 1–11). Edinburgh: Edinburgh University Press
Ahier J (1988) *Industry, Children and the Nation.* London: Falmer Press
Allen J, Massey D and Cochrane A (1997) *Rethinking the Region.* London:
    Routledge
Anderson B (1991) *Imagined Communities.* London: Verso
Apple M (1979) *Ideology and Curriculum.* London: Routledge
Apple M (1988) *Teachers and Texts.* London: Routledge
Ball M, Gray F and McDowell L (1989) *The Transformation of Britain: Contemporary
    Social and Economic Change.* London: Fontana
Ball S (1994) *Education Reform: A Poststructural Approach.* London: Routledge
Beddis R (1985) *A New Geography of Britain.* Oxford: Oxford University Press
Blaut J (1998) *The Colonizer's Model of the World.* New York: Guilford Press
Bourdieu R and Passeron J (1977) *Reproduction in Education, Society and Culture.*
    London: Sage
Bowles S and Gintis H (1976) *Schooling in Capitalist America.* London: Routledge and
    Kegan Paul
Coulby D (2000) *Beyond the National Curriculum.* London: RoutledgeFalmer
Cresswell T (1996) *In Place/Out of Place: Geography, Ideology and Transgression.*
    Minneapolis: University of Minnesota Press
Daniels S (1992) Place and the geographical imagination in education. *Geography*
    77(4):310–322
Flint C and Flint D (1989) *British Issues in Geography.* London: Collins Educational
    Press
Gibson-Graham J K (1999) Queer(y)ing capitalism in and out of the classroom. *Journal
    of Geography in Higher Education* 23(1):80–85
Gilbert R (1984) *The Impotent Image: Reflections of Ideology in the Secondary School
    Curriculum.* London: Falmer Press
Gilbert R (1989) Text analysis and ideology critique of curricular content. In S De
    Castell, A Luke and C Luke (eds) *Language, Authority and Criticisms: Readings on
    the School Textbook* (pp 61–73). London: Falmer Press
Gilbert R (1997) Issues for citizenship in a postmodern world. In K Kennedy (ed)
    Citizenship Education and the Modern State (pp 65–81). London: Falmer Press

Goodson I (1994) *Studying Curriculum: Cases and Methods*. Buckingham: Open University Press

Hall D (1990) The national curriculum and the two cultures: Towards a humanistic perspective. *Geography* 75(4):313–324

Harley J (1992) Deconstructing the map. In T Barnes and S Duncan (eds) *Writing Worlds* (pp 231–247). London: Routledge

Harvey D (2001) *Spaces of Capital: Towards a Critical Geography*. Edinburgh: Edinburgh University Press

Harvey D C, Jones R, McInroy N and Milligan C (eds) (2002) *Celtic Geographies: Old Culture, New Times*. London: Routledge

Henley R (1989) The ideology of geographical language. In F Slater (ed) *Language and Learning in the Teaching of Geography* (pp 162–171). London: Routledge

Huckle J (1985) Geography and schooling. In R Johnston (ed) *The Future of Geography* (pp 291–306). London: Methuen

Hudson R (2001) *Producing Places*. New York: Guilford Press

Kirby D and Robinson H (1981) *Geography of Britain: Perspectives and Problems*. London: University Tutorial Press

Knapp B (1988) *Britain in Today's World*. London: Unwin Hyman

Lambert D and Machon P (2001) *Citizenship through Secondary Geography*. London: RoutledgeFalmer

Lee A (1996) *Gender, Literacy, Curriculum*. London: Taylor and Francis

MacDonald G (1976) The politics of educational publishing. In G Whitty and M Young (eds) *Explorations in the Politics of School Knowledge* (pp 223–235). York: Nafferton Books

Maddrell A (1996) Empire, emigration and school geography: Changing discourses of imperial citizenship. *Journal of Historical Geography* 22:373–387

Marsden W (1978) *The Changing Geography of Britain*. London: Oliver and Boyd

Marsden W (2001) *The School Textbook: Geography, History and Social Studies*. London: Woburn Press

Mohan J (1999) *A United Kingdom?* London: Arnold

Phillips R (1997) *Mapping Men and Empire: A Geography of Adventure*. London: Routledge

Ploszajska T (2000) Historiographies of geography and empire. In B Graham and C Nash (eds) *Modern Historical Geographies* (pp 121–145). London: Prentice-Hall

Radcliffe S (1999) Popular and state discourse of power. In J Allen, P Sarre and D Massey (eds) *Human Geography Today* (pp 219–242). Cambridge, UK: Polity Press

Rawling E (2001) *Changing the Subject: The Impact of National Policy on School Geography 1980–2000*. Sheffield: Geographical Association

Ross A (2000) *Curriculum: Construction and Critique*. London: Falmer Press

Sharp J (2000a) Refiguring geopolitics: *The Reader's Digest* and popular geographies of danger at the end of the Cold War. In K Dodds and D Atkinson (eds) *Geopolitical Traditions: A Century of Geopolitical Thought* (pp 332–352). London: Routledge

Sharp J (2000b) Towards a critical analysis of fictive geographies. *Area* 32(3): 327–334

Shields R (1991) *Places on the Margins*. London: Routledge

Short J (1991) *Imagined Country: Society, Culture and Environment*. London: Routledge

Short J (2001a) *Representing the Republic: Mapping the United States, 1600–1900*. London: Reaktion

Short J (2001b) *Global Dimensions: Space, Place and the Contemporary World*. London: Reaktion

Simmons I (2000) *An Environmental History of Great Britain: From 10,000 Years Ago to the Present*. Edinburgh: Edinburgh University Press

Sinfield A (1997) *Politics and Literature in Postwar Britain*. London: Athlone Press

Smith N (1993) Homeless/global: Scaling places. In J Bird, B Curtis, T Putnam, G Robertson and L Tickner (eds) *Mapping the Futures: Local Cultures, Global Change* (pp 87–119). London: Routledge
Stephenson K (1984) *Geography of the British Isles.* 4th ed. Poole: Blandford Press
Tolson A and Johnstone M (1970) *A Geography of Britain.* Oxford: Oxford University Press
Walford R (ed) (1990) *A Geography of Contemporary Britain.* London: Longman

Chapter 2
Indigenous Professionalization: Transnational Social Reproduction in the Andes

Nina Laurie, Robert Andolina and Sarah Radcliffe

Introduction

> The challenge in these times of modernity and the era of globalization … is precisely to transform history.… I believe this is everyone's task; it isn't only [the task] of the indigenous people for the indigenous people, of the students for the students, or [of] academics for academics.… *In indianizing this America* [en indianizar esta América], I am not referring to the fact that everyone has to put on a hat, a poncho and let their hair grow and make a little ponytail and [thus] the problem is solved. When I say Indianize America I think that we [indigenous people] are saying that we absolutely have to overcome [discrimination] in the political, in the economic, in the cultural and in the social [worlds]. (Luis Macas,[1] an indigenous leader of the Confederación de Nacionalidades Indígenas del Ecuador [CONAIE]; emphasis added).

Access to and achievement in education is one of the most widely used development indicators. In Latin America, it frequently highlights indigenous poverty, indicating that indigenous people have the lowest levels of education in the continent (Psacharopoulos and Patrinos 1994). This essay illustrates how indigenous education plays a key role in approaches towards both nation-building and development. In particular, it focuses on the contribution of indigenous professionalization[2] to these agendas. Examining indigenous professionalization as a set of multiscalar practices, this essay examines the transnational social reproduction involved in "becoming indigenous" in the Andes. Here, we understand social reproduction in terms of the shaping of local, national and international development policies through social interactions between development actors. We argue that the position of these actors in development hierarchies and their differential access to political space are contingent on specific representations of social roles and relations, including those based on ethnicity. In this essay, we examine the social reproduction of indigenous identities in relation to development agendas through transnationally constituted higher education spaces.

In recent years, new indigenous professional careers have been forged in political and development administration, as people are recruited and trained for careers in governmental and nongovernmental organizations (NGOs) and international donor agencies and to assume advisory and leadership positions in indigenous organizations that are increasingly transnational in scope. While indigenous careers exist in conventional professions and applied technical fields,[3] more general careers as social development and environmental advisers/program managers are emerging as novel forms of indigenous professionalization. Thus, although all the higher-education programs under consideration in this essay (see Table 1) share an "intercultural orientation," some provide training for conventional careers (such as agronomy and teaching), whilst others are more interested in training development technocrats operating at a range of scales. Still other programs are more motivated by the desire to open a space for critical and political debate that critiques technocratic understandings of development.

These new careers reflect prevailing paradigms of social development and provide opportunities for the consolidation of indigenous subjectivities in development discourses. These subjectivities are particularly pertinent in the "development with identity paradigm," in which culture is seen as an asset to development, rather than an impediment, as was previously the case in economically driven modernization paradigms. We argue that development with identity is an adapted neoliberal social-development policy, offering poverty-alleviation elements in combination with multicultural frameworks and responding to transnational political networks around indigenous development concerns. In the Andes, a combination of strong indigenous rights movements, recent state reforms around multiculturalism and stringent neoliberal structural adjustments have brought into stark relief the nature of transnational connections around neoliberal development and culture. The new social development policies forged in this context have also gained exemplary status for multilateral and bilateral development agencies, thus acquiring a resonance and significance that transcends the immediate area. Molded through neoliberal paradigms, indigenous development has been co-produced by social-development provision for participation, targeted programs and institutional strengthening (Nederven Pieterse 2001). Neoliberal social development policy emphasizes the strengthening of civil society organizations, social inclusion, recognition of social diversity (gender, ethnicity, age, cultural, economic characteristics) and participation in decision-making and

Table 1: Higher Education Programs in Development with Identity in Ecuador and Bolivia

Place	Origins	Course	Funding	Aim of the Courses	Student Profiles	Neoliberal/ Governance Discourse Used in Publicity/Interviews	Transnational Classroom and Curriculum
Andina University, Ecuador	1987 Interculturalism program started	Masters in Interculturalism Open short course in local development	PRODEPINE	Train consultants Train university lecturers	Indigenous and *mestizo*[a] (mixed race) Some international students from the Andean region, including Bolivians	Human resources Aimed at the periphery Pioneering Social compensation Generate ability Teaching transversal themes	One full-time lecturer—nationality USA One lecturer has taught in Canada One lecturer teaches in CEIDIS (Bolivia) Teaches Bolivian local development

Table 1: Continued

Place	Origins	Course	Funding	Aim of the Courses	Student Profiles	Neoliberal/ Governance Discourse Used in Publicity/Interviews	Transnational Classroom and Curriculum
FLACSO, Ecuador	One of a number of FLACSO institutions in Latin America	Diploma in Indigenous Affairs; about to become a Masters'	PRODEPINE, Hans Seidell Foundation, Belgian funding	To train people for them to return to their communities	Indigenous and *mestizo*, Andean regional international students, including Bolivians	The new (pluricultural) institutionality, New frameworks, Ethnodevelopment, Positive discrimination, Strengthen local capacity, Citizenship	Director has taught in Spain, Uses Bolivian materials and case studies to deliver a comparative course

Table 1: Continued

Place	Origins	Course	Funding	Aim of the Courses	Student Profiles	Neoliberal/ Governance Discourse Used in Publicity/Interviews	Transnational Classroom and Curriculum
Indigenous University, Ecuador	CONAIE's idea in 1988. Revitalized in 1998. Currently is only a proposal; not yet validated	Three careers: indigenous law, bilingual intercultural education, agroecology	CODENPE; Northern universities	To take the university to the community; To validate indigenous knowledge	Indigenous students	Ethnodevelopment; Intercultural development; Indigenous framework; Resources or capital	Northern lecturers teach; Northern universities validate degrees; A series of universities to be developed across the region
La Salesiana University, Ecuador	Started in 1994, but a background in language education for teachers from 1991	Undergraduate programs in: applied anthropology, local development, social communication	PRODEPINE; Catholic funds; Hans Seidell Foundation; GTZ; CODENPE	To train people for them to return to their community; To link themselves to local	Indigenous and *mestizo* students	Sustainable development; Pioneering; Equality; Excluded sectors; Human resources; Institutional strengthening	GTZ has linked this program to Bolivian ones. Sees itself as an exemplar in Latin America

Table 1: Continued

Place	Origins	Course	Funding	Aim of the Courses	Student Profiles	Neoliberal/ Governance Discourse Used in Publicity/Interviews	Transnational Classroom and Curriculum
CEIDIS, San Simón University, Cochabamba, Bolivia	New relationship between CENDA (NGO) and CESU postgraduate school

Regional consortium, with Peru, Chile, Argentina | Diploma in Indigenous affairs since 1999

Converted to Masters in 2001 | Kellogg Foundation

DFID/British Council | Critical engagement with interculturalism and Bolivian reforms as a political project

To reflect on interculturalism globally | *Mestizo* and some indigenous students

Some international students—from Latin America and Europe | Develop critical tools

Generate analytical ability | International lecturers, including some from Ecuador

Historical links with Ecuador via CENDA and Bartolmé de las Casas in Peru

Lecturers doing postgraduate studies in the UK, Spain, Mexico and Ecuador |

Table 1: Continued

Place	Origins	Course	Funding	Aim of the Courses	Student Profiles	Neoliberal/ Governance Discourse Used in Publicity/Interviews	Transnational Classroom and Curriculum
PROEI-BANDES, San Simón University, Cochabamba, Bolivia	Began in 1995; built on staff experiences in Puno in bilingual education	Masters in intercultural bilingual education	GTZ	Share the Bolivia reform experience Train professionals (mainly teachers) working in communities with indigenous languages	Mainly indigenous; some *mestizo* Many indigenous international students	Human resources Interdisciplinary gaze Academic exchange Collaboration between indigenous peoples	Lecturers from the Andean region, Latin America, Europe and North America Satellites in other countries Latin American countries to recruit Very high profile internationally

a Data for this table was collected through a combination of interviews, student questionnaires and critical reading of Web sites and promotional material. In the questionnaires students were asked to identify their ethnicity. This data comes from these sources.

project execution. According to culturally appropriate development paradigms, cultural distinctiveness is compatible with good governance practices and economic productivity.

Our analysis is informed by a confluence between indigenous professionalization and these development agendas. Specifically, we focus on how indigenous politics and multicultural neoliberalism have created contexts for indigenous people's professionalization. In turn, professionalization is producing a transnational curriculum on indigenous development that informs higher education.

Education to become a professional has represented one of the few strategies for overturning discriminatory social hierarchies that militate against the upward social mobility of indigenous people (de la Cadena 1998, 2000). Obtaining professional status forms the basis of individual social ambitions and influences family and generational economic strategies. Such personal and family ambitions often rest upon the "whitening" effect that professional education has on social status (de la Cadena 1998; Weismantel 2000) and reflect the racist geographies of nation-building that have traditionally labeled indigenous people as "rural" and "backward."

Both the state and international donors set the parameters for inclusive education. Currently, international funding addresses social inclusion at the two extremes of the formal education system, primary education and higher education, while states are largely only investing in primary education in Latin America.[4] While much attention has been paid to primary education, little research has focused on the higher-education sector. Internationally, in the North and the South, few attempts have been made to examine the role that transnational practices play in intercultural/multicultural education in specific contexts. Nor has there been much focus on the ways in which international processes intersect with those of state nation-building agendas. One of the few exceptions to this is Katheryne Mitchell's work on elite Hong Kong immigrant communities in Richmond, Vancouver, Canada (Mitchell 2001). Her argument is that despite the power of the Hong Kong diaspora in Seattle and its challenges to established "Canadian" understandings of "good education," multicultural discourses and practices are still contained by the neoliberal state's adherence to democracy within a nationalist, rather than transnationalist, framework.

In this essay, we also examine the interface between state and transnational practices by offering a contrasting example from a very different context. In our analysis, the key transnational actors are not individual migrants with high levels of financial capital, but transnational donors with specific development agendas supported by significant institutional funding mechanisms. We argue that while the Ecuadorian and Bolivian states have set the legislative context for pro-indigenous educational reform (with the support of international donors), indigenous professionalization is currently being forged through transnational practices and forms of social reproduction that, in turn, circumscribe state/indigenous-movement relationships. Diverse donor interventions target a wide range of state agencies and indigenous movements involved in professionalization in Bolivia and Ecuador, with key donors such as the German Technical Assistance (GTZ) and the United Nations Children's Fund (UNICEF) operating programs with a range of actors.

The convergence between indigenous and international donor interests is currently being negotiated in transnational educational spaces that provide higher education in development with identity in Ecuador and Bolivia. We argue that these spaces are new in terms of the scale at which they operate, the ways they have become institutionalized, the networks they mobilize and the transnational curricula and personnel they deploy. They are also new in terms of the actor-led transnational indigenous subject they project and represent.

Below, we argue that struggles over representations of indigenous people and notions of culturally appropriate development in these programs attempt to accommodate different—and, in some cases, incompatible—political traditions of education within a (neoliberal) social-capital framework. These spaces constitute sites where transnational definitions of "good" development are produced and contested. The essay is divided as follows. First, we analyze the relationship between neoliberal development paradigms and the increasing focus on enhancing the human and social capital of indigenous groups. We analyze the indigenous subject represented in donor professionalization funding and indigenous demands for culturally appropriate education. Second, we examine the emergence of the paradigm of interculturalism and go on to describe state reform in education in Ecuador and Bolivia, specifically examining pro-indigenous legislation in the context of the creation of pluricultural states. Finally, we highlight the specific transnational practices underpinning the promotion of indigenous professionalization, examining the creation of a transnational classroom and a transnational curriculum. We question the extent to which indigenous professionalization can be mainstreamed into existing education structures, arguing that indigenous professionalization constitutes a space that directly engages with the state while at the same time creating and mobilizing networks that are able to bypass it.

Neoliberalism and Indigenous Education as "Capital"

In recent years, education policy in Latin America has been characterized by the state's emphasis on decentralization and privatization. Linked to increased school dropout rates and the further gendering and racializing of educational inequality in the Andes, these initiatives have been widely criticized (Laurie and Bonnett 2002;

Mujer y Ajuste 1996). While such neoliberal initiatives have gone hand in hand with the promotion of multicultural laws in Ecuador and Bolivia, the introduction of user fees has been particularly contentious. Indigenous movements assert that the privatization of education has further limited the access of indigenous people to higher education:

> The new constitution is favorable to us as, for example, collective rights are recognized in the new constitution. However, on the other hand, the privatization of education means that we can't go to university. We can't enter universities because everything has to be paid for over and over. (Interview, Vicente Chuma, head of the women's section of ECUARUNARI,[5] Quito, Ecuador, May 2000)

As the largest financial contributor to education and legislator of privatization measures, the state remains the most important education actor in Latin America. However, international donor funding is increasingly important in certain sectors and is profoundly affecting education strategies for poor and indigenous groups (Cortina and Stromquist 2000). Donor policy emphasizes the provision of basic education, suggesting that funds be diverted from secondary and higher education to primary schooling (Puiggrós 1999). There has generally been little international investment in higher education since the 1950s (Cortina and Stromquist 2000). However, donor interests in social exclusion have recently led to funds being targeted for higher-education courses specifically for marginalized groups. This funding is the primary source of support for indigenous professionalization programs (see Table 1—funding), many of which operate through hybrid development institutions that combine state and donor funding and often draw on personnel from indigenous movements and NGOs.[6]

Indigenous movements have long demanded "culturally appropriate education" that reflects indigenous everyday realities and practical needs. A key emphasis in the indigenous demand for culturally appropriate education is the freedom to attend educational institutions without having to sacrifice cultural identity, as has been the case in the past:

> Indians could not go to school because they had to have money. They had to change their surnames [from indigenous language names to Spanish names] and if they [boys] had ponytails in their hair they had to cut them off and if we [girls] wore *polleras* (homespun skirts) we had to take off the polleras and put on skirts. (Interview, Vicente Chuma)

For indigenous movements, culturally appropriate education is that which recognizes indigenous values and knowledge and seeks to strengthen existing indigenous political organization. The provision of this type of education equips indigenous communities to generate their own development projects based on their knowledge of their reality, without having to rely on outside experts and technicians (interview, Vicente Chuma; interview, Elena Ipaz, FENOCIN [National Federation of Indigenous Peasant Organizations], Quito, Ecuador, May 2000).

Indigenous movements' demands for culturally appropriate education prioritize a severely discriminated-against people, a subject marginalized in terms of access to education on financial and cultural grounds, whose knowledge has been devalued and for whom formal education has seldom fed into wider community political and development goals.

> We are trying to procure a university that can go to the community, rather than the other way round. The community, (the students) always have to come to the university. This is absolutely impossible, first because the students can't pay their costs in the city. Second, I believe that the university must engage with their reality [*pisar su realidad también*].... I believe that unfortunately our knowledge has been left out of scientific recognition. For all the results that it has obtained through thousands of years, in many aspects our knowledge definitely does not have the same scientific value [as Western knowledge]. I think that's precisely why we should revalue it; give it its own value, its own authenticity, the scientific value it should have. It should not only be cast simply as empirical knowledge. (Interview, Luis Macas, speaking in support of the proposal for an indigenous university, Quito, Ecuador, August 2000).

Donors are increasingly interested in addressing indigenous professionalization as part of wider social-development goals. A focus on human capital is rapidly becoming a hallmark of current development policy (Grindle 2000; Portes and Landolt 2000). While human-capital theory is not new,[7] it has taken on a new salience since the postadjustment 1990s, as social change has failed to keep pace with economic reform and inequality has persisted and, in many cases, worsened. Also important in the rise in popularity of human-capital-based policies has been the recognition of the success of politicians promoting social programs that claim to respond directly to citizen demands (Grindle 2000). Linked to a desire to replicate exemplars and cases of success globally has been a renewed focus on education in human-capital debates, following the positive role of education in welfare-enhancing reforms in East Asia (Grindle 2000). In the human-capital literature, the "socially excluded" are brought into development through education and full citizenship rights.

The networks that support the development of human capital are termed "social capital." The World Bank (2003b) defines social capital as "the institutions, relationships, and norms that shape the quality and quantity of a society's social interventions. Increasing evidence shows that social cohesion is critical for societies to prosper economically and for development to be sustainable. Social capital is not just the sum of the institutions which underpin a society—it is the glue that holds it together." While extensively criticized (see Fine 2001, 2002), the notion of social capital has been profoundly influential in the development field, offering a means to celebrate ethnic and cultural difference while often reducing it to fit formulaic policy frameworks. Moreover, the rise of development projects targeted at ethnically identified populations coincides with—and in part owes its existence to—a policy emphasis on the participation of ordinary citizens in the design of and/or decision-making about projects. Development funds intervene in the workings of livelihoods and institutions, as well as shaping the terms of debate and imageries about the actors involved in social change. Cultural politics thus intersect with material culture, shaping the institutions, actors and discourses in development. For Bebbington (2002:802), the concept of social capital acts as "a linguistic device" that enables a range of interest groups to communicate about the social dimensions of development and help shape prevailing under-standings of development orthodoxy.

The role that education plays in social-capital approaches has been critiqued by indigenous movements, development academics and those involved in the delivery of indigenous professionalization courses themselves.[8] Some academics involved in professionalization courses are wary of the role of targeted education in the context of neoliberal reform:

Education is always seen as a way to prepare people technically, to develop, to expand and to make their life better. There is an unstated connection between discourses of development and discourses of education.... It's like they [donors and governments] create a specific type of educational system that will prepare [people] for a specific type of development. That's what it is. Now indigenousness has replaced the sociology and development of rural areas and the discourse of indi-genousness has caught on, it's fashionable. It's a little as if governments like Germany and the Netherlands are following this trend in these neoliberal times. [Yet] what is being fought over is recognition not redistribution [and so] it is easy to talk about education without speaking about development. (Interview, Bolivian intercultural lecturer)

Despite critiques of the social-capital paradigm, however, the approach has become institutionalised in key funding agencies through social development units managing subprograms that attempt to introduce themes of ethnicity and gender transversally into other mainstream programs.[9]

Using a variety of definitions of indigeneity, the majority of higher-education programs on development with identity aim to attract indigenous students. Funders drive selection criteria and sometimes influence the definitions of indigeneity adopted in specific programs. For example, the Proyecto de Desarrollo de los Pueblos Indígenas y Negros del Ecuador (PRODEPINE—the Development Project for Indigenous and Black Peoples of Ecuador)[10] insists that a recommendation from local community organizations is very important. Other donors rely on language-based definitions, accepting students because they speak one or more indigenous languages. Most definitions, however, are contested because of the assumptions they make about markers of indigeneity. Language-based definitions are often particularly controversial:

> If I speak Spanish that doesn't mean I'm Spanish. If I'm the son of a plantation owner and I speak Quechua that doesn't mean I'm Quechua. So this thing about looking for people who speak indigenous languages is forcing things too much. (Interview, teacher in an intercultural master's program, Bolivia)

While the promotion of indigenous human capital and indigenous rights forms part of the social-development agenda, in practice the working out of these rights is complex. Clashes between donor investments in human capital—through the provision of scholarships to individuals, for example—and the promotion of more general social-capital goals are often difficult to accommodate. Although acceptance into scholarship programs usually requires letters of recommendation from local indigenous organizations, there is no guarantee that individuals on these programs display "social-capital criteria," such as a collective sense of cultural identity and community solidarity.

> It is necessary to do consciousness-raising with the students. [This is] an ideological task because, despite the fact that they are selected by their organizations, they do not have a social conscience, they don't have a commitment to the organization. The idea is to get them to do voluntary work with the organization ... the idea is to raise student consciousness to promote a cultural identity because we have noted some weaknesses there. (Interview, Ariruma Kowii, PRODEPINE, Quito, Ecuador, March 2000)

Transnational expectations of what constitutes "professional" behavior (ie full-time, life-time commitment to one specialization) are incompatible in some ways with the ongoing work required to maintain close involvement in the day-to-day activities of indigenous organizations and to secure what is commonly termed "a close connection with the bases." In Bolivia, for example, the implementation of pluricultural legislation placed divergent demands on community leaders, frequently taking them away from their communities for long periods and requiring excessive workloads over and above their own farming, familial and community duties. In Bolivia, the need for knowledge about pro-indigenous decentralization and the ability to implement it overstretched rotational models of community organization (Blanes 2000; McNeish 2001). The conflicts that resulted in these circumstances reflect the more deeply seated contradiction inherent in development models that seek simultaneously to invest in the human capital of individuals while promoting the social capital of a collective.[11]

Despite contradictions between human- and social-capital investments in indigenous professionalization and resistance on the part of indigenous individuals to a seemingly pro-indigenous agenda, the general demand from indigenous movements for culturally appropriate education has led to a variety of education initiatives. Many of these initiatives have found an intellectual and political home within interculturalism, as the following section outlines.

Interculturalism: Indigenous Education and Development

The promotion of multicultural education in the Andes is currently framed by the paradigm of interculturalism. A highly contested concept, interculturalism is defined in relation to education, culture, technology, society, forms of communication, the economy, politics, religion and global uniformity and local differences (COSUDE 2001). As a paradigm, interculturalism promotes a way of understanding the relationship between Western and indigenous (Amerindian) practices, spaces and knowledges in Latin America (Medina 2001).

Interculturalism's influence on education policy has been forged through periodic conflicts and negotiations over the politics of human-capital development and identity formation. With respect to indigenous professionalization, many interest groups focusing on culturally appropriate education—including indigenous movements, donors, NGOs and international NGOs (INGOs), the state and parents—have appropriated the paradigm. Consequently, the term "intercultural education" often means different things to different actors. While multiculturalism promotes "unrelated juxtapositions of knowledge about particular groups without any apparent interconnections between them" interculturalism is more proactive, because it implies "comparisons, exchanges, cooperation and confrontation between groups" (Cushner 1998:4). In practice, an intercultural approach requires the combination and convergence of different points of view in order to understand complex issues that cannot be understood through one approach alone (Kane 2001). In the context of Andean pluriculturalism, interculturalism requires not only that respect be afforded in equal part to indigenous and Hispanic cultures (and, where relevant, Afro-Latin Americans), but also that respect be established between various distinct indigenous cultures. In this way, interculturalism views the indigenous subject as an actor involved in the construction of a dialogue based on the location of indigenous people in discrete cultural spaces of mutual respect.

While indigenous issues have been studied as part of anthropology or linguistics degrees for many years, the interculturalism paradigm has increasingly developed a more interdisciplinary approach. Godenzzi (1996:569; translation by Laurie) suggests that interculturalism is both a strategy and a process, and that in the context of the "pluriform of reality" of Latin-American nations, it forms part of a call for democratization. The politics of interculturalism in Latin America were forged in the 1980s, when the emergence of intercultural bilingual education (IBE) coincided with processes of democratization in many countries and the growing awareness of indigenous people as social and political actors. University courses addressing the interface between development and interculturalism are emerging throughout Latin America; they are particularly evident in countries with a large politically organized indigenous movement. The individual histories of indigenous movements in the Andean region vary (Hale 1997). Ecuadorian and Bolivian organizations are considerably more organized and more powerful than those in Peru, where organized indigenous politics have been virtually invisible (Degregori 1998).

The histories and trajectories in Ecuador and Bolivia are also considerably different.[12] Bolivia's history was greatly influenced by the peasant movement after the 1952 revolution, and until recently indigenous demands have been largely articulated through local and national peasant-indigenous federations. In Ecuador, the discourse of indigenous "nationalities" has been important in challenging state-nationalist imaginaries and in asserting the pluricultural nature of the country. As a result, indigenous federations and confederations have become a driving political force in Ecuador, founded upon alliances between diverse indigenous groups, rather than on a generic peasant identity.

Although the indigenous movements in the Andes have diverse histories, they are united in their resistance to a language of minority rights, instead basing their citizenship claims on the politics of majorities (Laurie and Bonnett 2002). Despite interculturalism's nebulous nature, it has become an important concept in indigenous politics.[13] However, notwithstanding wide support from indigenous organizations and donors, interculturalism's position as the dominant paradigm is not fully consolidated. This is reflected in donor attempts to define and fix more clearly its relevance across an increasing range of topics.[14] There is also evidence that donor support for other approaches, such as antiracism, is competing with intercultural programs in some contexts (see Laurie and Bonnett 2002).

Thus, while interculturalism has provided a common language (see Table 1—neoliberal/governance discourse used in publicity/interviews) in which donors, indigenous activists and educators can engage in discussions of development, pro-indigenous curricula and education policy, it is also problematic. The local and national actors involved in intercultural debates are seldom comfortable allies, and interculturalism remains a contested transnational policy arena. As the following analysis of pro-indigenous education reform in Ecuador and Bolivia illustrates, different local and national interests are often reconciled only through the support of transnational actors.

State Reform and Indigenous Education

The constitutional recognition of Ecuador and Bolivia as pluricultural states[15] in the early 1990s framed an acknowledgement of the diverse educational needs and realities of the national populations. The wide-ranging introduction of pro-indigenous and socially inclusive laws in recent years has produced a legislative implementation gap; governments have been slow to act upon the new laws they have created (Van Cott 2002). While new legislation has, in theory, created opportunities for the recognition of indigenous self-determination through changing land ownership, natural-resource legislation and decentralization, the state seldom has the trained personnel necessary to put the new laws into practice. Many of the new ministries created across Latin America to carry out pro-indigenous reforms currently lack the expertise necessary to fulfill public expectations. Some donors suggest that investment in strengthening local leadership is needed in order to ensure that legislative changes are implemented in favor of poor and indigenous communities (interview, Hans Hoffmeyer, Danish Organization of Development Aid and Solidarity [IBIS]).

While the need for the professionalization of indigenous personnel is articulated at a local and national level by indigenous movements and donors, the demand for professionalization is also becoming recognized as a regional issue in the Andes.

> What can be recognized is that there is a real demand for postgraduate training for indigenous professionals in the whole region. I say this, for example, because in a conference that we had in Chile the people from the north of Chile, the Chilean Aymaras and the Mapuches, were really interested in the theme. In Bolivia it's the same and it's the same in Peru.... It's also the same with the Colombian indigenous people. The indigenous theme is beginning to be debated as a regional theme. (Interview, director of the Facultad de Latin America de Ciencias Sociales [FLACSO—Faculty of Latin American Social Sciences], Quito, Ecuador, May 2000)

NGOs and universities also play a role in the demand for indigenous professionalization. New courses are designed to meet the training needs of career consultants and the next generation of academics (interview, Fernando García, FLACSO, Quito, Ecuador, May 2000).

Our study plans have in mind training [two groups]. People who can become teachers in the university—in fact, ex-students from here are teachers in distinct universities in Quito and the interior of the country.... Then there's a group of people who can live from what they know under the name of consultancies and specific pieces of work, applied research. (Interview, director of intercultural program at Andina University, Quito, Ecuador, February 2000)

Thus, the political economic context of a (retreating) flexible state and new forms of development institutionalization are affecting the increased demand for development consultants.

Education reforms in the late 1980s and early 1990s adopted intercultural rhetoric in promoting new bilingual education laws. Ecuador was first to pass a program of bilingual intercultural education (DINEIB —Programa de Educación Intercultural Bilingue), in 1989; Bolivia's Education Reform Law, which introduced intercultural bilingual education, was not passed until 1994. Both laws, however, built on earlier experiences of state-led initiatives as well as NGO programs. Prior to receiving state funding, many early initiatives were financed by transnational donors. In Ecuador, the MACAC[16] government's indigenous-education program was financed by the GTZ in the first few years of its operation, before the government assumed a more direct role. The Bolivian Education Reform Law also drew on transnationally funded experiences of highland indigenous education, such as Quechua literacy classes in Raqaypampa, Cochabamba, which led to curriculum reform at a local level in this area. Directed by the community in partnership with a national NGO, CENDA, this program was funded by a diverse range of INGOs, including the Catholic Agency for Overseas Development (CAFOD) and the Inter-American Foundation. Controversy arose when the Raqaypampa communities themselves hired teachers to operate outside the official school system and organized a school calendar around labor needs at harvest time. UNICEF officials supported the Raqaypampa informal indigenous schools, promoting the experience in the development of the Education Reform Law. Their support influenced the importance that the law subsequently placed on decentralized community and parental control over schooling. Thus, transnational donors played an important role in legitimating local experience when it was scaled up in multicultural legislation (Regalsky and Laurie forthcoming).

Transnational involvement in Bolivian indigenous education also included the World Bank taking a leading role in the development of Bolivia's Education Reform Law. The Bank financed foreign consultants to develop the proposal for the reform through a unit called the Technical Support Team for Education Reform (ETARE). Subsequently, the implementation of the law itself was underpinned with loans from the Bank and the Inter-American Development Bank, while UNICEF sponsored the development and production of teaching materials.

The Transnational Social Reproduction of Indigenous Professionalization

Specialist courses with an intercultural focus have developed in both public and private universities in Ecuador and Bolivia, as Table 1 illustrates. In Bolivia, the main postgraduate programs are located in San Simón and at a state university in Cochabamba (the Consorcio de Educación Intercultural para el Desarrollo e Integración Surandino [CEIDIS] and the Programa de Formación en Educación Intercultural Bilingue para los Países Andinos [PROEIBANDES]). Additionally, intercultural modules and courses appear in other interdisciplinary centers and university programs. In Ecuador, postgraduate programs currently operate in the Andina University and FLACSO, while an undergraduate program runs in La Salesiana University. The Indigenous University is currently in the process of being launched by CONAIE. Core funding and scholarships for programs are available from a range of donors, including the GTZ, COSUDE, the Kellogg Foundation, Fundación Hans Seidell, and the World Bank through hybrid development institutions such as PRODEPINE and the Ecuadorian Council for Indigenous Nationalities (CODENPE).

Questions arise, however, over the extent to which indigenous development can be mainstreamed into higher-education frameworks. Recouping indigenous ways of learning, for example, is often difficult in courses based within existing university programs the curricula of which do not engage with indigenous knowledge:

> The challenge is that our projects, our academic programs institutionalize an intercultural perspective. At this moment, there is priority attention given to the indigenous student. The indigenous students get almost a sort of special attention. But our curricula design are not intercultural—they are monocultural. To give it a name, they are made from the perception of the rationality in Western logic. (Interview, lecturer, La Salesiana University, Quito, Ecuador)

Mainstreaming can lead to discriminatory classroom practices when members of the teaching staff are not familiar with indigenous conceptualizations.

> Look, let me tell you, it's not easy with a lot of teachers. There are two problems. [First] they [university faculty] have good human ways of treating [indigenous students], but they don't understand them. Indigenous logic is a different language. [Second,] there are cases of teachers we've had who treated them [indigenous students] badly; they didn't understand them and said they were stupid [*tontos*]. It isn't that they are stupid; the stupid one is the teacher who didn't

understand. But yes, there are problems like that, and an overall lack of understanding. (Interview, founder, La Salesiana University, Quito, Ecuador, May 2000)

In such situations, hierarchies of knowledge are produced and discrimination and racism reproduced. Knowledge hierarchies are compounded by a frequent emphasis in university programs on academic etiquette.

The course directors have the program in their own image. They really stress good writing and correct referencing. There are people that have hardly written in their lives, and they have much more difficulty. You notice that more and more people will resist, because obviously the "elite" student will do very well, in this elite academy [*a este academia de acun'a*]. It contrasts so much with the other extreme and with the people in the middle [range] of the course. (Interview, lecturer in a language-led intercultural program)

Not only is the distinction between indigenous and Western knowledge maintained by the actions and attitudes of teaching staff in established universities, but it is also drawn by students constructing a political agenda using a strategic discourse. Such a discourse offers political options and resources to certain actors.

Lecturer: The students really wanted to be indigenous. And the more indigenous [they are], the more resistant [they are] to academic work.... Those who read and write well are not [seen by the other students as] indigenous.

Interviewer: And the students reproduced that?

Lecturer: The students set it up that way. "Whiter students read and write well, we don't, we're oral. We don't write." ... "We indigenous are more oral." (Interview, lecturer in a language-led intercultural program)

Student distinctions associating particular forms of knowledge with specific groups of people reproduce seemingly essentialist ideas about the contrast between oral and written traditions as part of a political platform. The "political learning achieved by (indigenous) social movements" (Foweraker 1998:283) causes participants in the learning project to reflect upon the political nature of education and use the classroom to (re)produce different forms of indigenous politics and construct and contest definitions of identity and "good development."

The Transnational Classroom: Defining "Good" Development

Many postgraduate courses operate through classrooms that are transnational in terms of student and teacher composition. These classrooms

aim to mix students from a variety of countries and indigenous nationalities to ensure an exchange of experience.

> The enrichment that students experience with students from other
> countries is really interesting.... Each one brings their experience
> to the discussion; it's a good experience. (Interview, director of
> FLACSO, Ecuador)

In some cases, the transnational classroom is formed and reproduced through regional alliances, as the two Bolivian programs based
at San Simón University in Cochabamba illustrate. PROIEBANDES
operates out of a number of Andean countries with satellite nodes to
help in the selection of students. The students are mainly indigenous
teachers with future careers in high-level policy-making in NGOs and
government. There are approximately forty students split between two
master's programs.[17] GTZ core funding established and maintains the
program. The CEIDIS program has similar transnational origins.
It was founded as part of a consortium bringing together NGOs and
universities from Chile, Argentina, Peru and Bolivia to deliver a range
of activities, including postgraduate training on interculturalism. In
Bolivia, the members comprise the NGO CENDA, drawing on its extensive experience in popular education in Raqaypampa, and CESU
(Centro de Estudios Superiores Universitarios) the postgraduate
Social Science College of the University of San Simón, which has
wide experience in the delivery of specialist short courses and postgraduate degrees. The student body is smaller than that of
PROIEBANDES, with 17 students registered on the diploma course
in the first year.

The development of the transnational classroom owes much of its
impetus to the small transnational body of an intellectual elite who teach
modules and courses. Many programs draw on a pool of international
scholars and policy-makers. Most of this small group of scholars,
practitioners and activists are known to each other and move between
programs and countries for short periods. Hence, teachers based in
La Paz teach short modules on courses in both Cochabamba and
Quito, while others move from Ecuador to Bolivia. In some cases,
staff members also make more permanent moves across borders. In at
least one instance, another Bolivian institution purposely recruited an
individual based in a transnational program in Ecuador linked to one
Bolivian institution because, among other things, he had an intimate
knowledge of both systems. What both donors funding courses and
potential employers of the students who graduate prize about these
teachers is their ability to transfer real-life practitioner experience, academic work and policy knowledge across borders. While some Northern
scholars enter this circuit, most movements are made by Latin-
American- (often Andean-) based teachers travelling throughout the

region. In this sense, the transnational classroom is largely based on South-South connections. Such movements of teaching staff and mix of students quickly generates consensus around what the transnational classroom should provide and legitimates "accepted understanding" of what constitutes successful development with identity policy-making in the region.

Transnational Curriculum

Professionalization courses are characterized by the recruitment of indigenous students and the development of what we identify as transnational curricula, coalescing around ideas of interculturalism. The curriculum is transnational because it draws on examples of pro-indigenous development from across the region to develop course materials.

> Socialization occurs initially through various flows, let us say. One is to know certain foci that come from Bolivia and things that come from Peru. It seems to me that the things that come from Bolivia are not well known.... I wanted to give a course on the trajectory of the ethnic movements in Ecuador like in Bolivia because in Peru they have not made ethnic demands. (Interview, lecturer, FLACSO, Ecuador)

In Bolivia, the politics of engagement with the state also shapes the distinctiveness of professionalization programs on interculturality. Transnationally, within the region, the Bolivian legislative experience is well regarded. Seen by many to be innovative responses to citizen demands (see Grindle 2000), the suite of reforms introduced by the Sanchez de Losada government in the mid 1990s[18] is an important element of professionalization degrees elsewhere in the Andean region.

> Principally we have taken international experiences for discussion themes.... From Bolivia we have taken the theme of participation, of participative planning, [and] the law of popular participation in Bolivia, which is the innovative effort which characterizes the Bolivians with respect to the indigenous population. (Interview, lecturer, Andina University)

The role of these types of comparisons in the transnational curriculum is to disseminate and share "best practice." For academics, the transnational curriculum is an opportunity to analyze comparative tendencies in indigenous politics and its engagements with the pluricultural state. For the indigenous movement, it is also about sharing tactics and strategies of engagement with a range of actors. The organizational structure of CONAIE in Ecuador is analyzed and discussed in Bolivian curricula. It is framed as an example of best practice in intercultural alliances between diverse indigenous (lowland and highland) and

Afro-Ecuadorian groups. It is acclaimed for playing the role of a protagonist in law-making and for promoting development with identity.
The new Bolivian reform laws in education and popular participation
are widely disseminated in courses in Ecuador as examples of innovative legislation that recognize—and thus strengthen—indigenous,
collective decision-making and identity. Thematic issues such as protest
strategies, water and land politics, leadership training and indigenous
knowledge are treated within a comparative framework, and specific
political strategies are analyzed with a view to learning lessons across
borders.

Transnational Network Practices and the State

Transnational practices associated with indigenous professionalization
frame the way in which indigenous agendas engage with state
approaches towards pro-indigenous education. The production and
reproduction of professionalization programs illustrate the ways in
which pro-indigenous networks both engage directly with the state
and mobilize transnational connections to bypass it. These processes
involve the contestation and validation of examples of best practice
that figure in the transnational curriculum. While the transnational
curriculum validates the Bolivian experience of state reform outside
of Bolivia, the two main programs on interculturalism in Cochabamba
itself, CEIDIS and PROEIBANDES, have taken distinct positions
vis-à-vis the reforms. From CEIDIS's perspective, the PROIEBANDES
program is too close to the government's Education Reform Law.

> We want to work the theme of interculturalism more as the political
> aspect of intercultural education. [We want to work on] the most
> political components. So from the start we [CENDA and CESU
> staff] were agreed that while PROIEBANDES was a more functional
> thing—more operative, let's say—ours needed to be more analytical
> [and] critical [and] provide more critical tools. Overall [it needed] to
> train [students] to investigate the reality, not to generate technicians
> who afterwards could incorporate themselves into the Education
> Reform Law. (Interview, co-director of CEIDIS, Cochabamba, Bolivia,
> January 2000)

These different programmatic emphases point to the diversity of
indigenous politics and to the distinct positions occupied by different
groups. They also indicate that understandings of interculturalism are
evolving dynamically in academic and policy terms in response to this
diversity. They highlight the fact that the closer relationship that has
been forged between pro-indigenous networks and the state through
new education legislation is actively contested.

    While wide debate over development with identity is stimulated as
professionalization programs provide spaces for direct engagement

with specific state initiatives, support for these programs is also able to mobilize transnational networks to bypass the state. Proponents of CONAIE's Indigenous University seek autonomy from the state education sector because they doubt that the state will fund a radical initiative that aims to break with the tradition of established universities.

> We are dedicated to creating the Indigenous University with Luis Macas.... Here the state will never give a chance to the Indians.... What we have done is [to] create a chance with the other universities —for example, with Arizona [and two Swiss universities]. They are going to sponsor us. The university is going to select three careers, three academic areas; one is indigenous law, the other in bilingual intercultural education and the other is agroecology. (Interview, Isidoro Quinde, CODENPE,[19] Quito, April 2000)

Although CODENPE receives funding from the Ecuadorian government and is heavily involved in supporting indigenous development through local government, its position as a hybrid development institution allows it to adopt a critical stance vis-à-vis state practices, discourses and institutions where they impinge on indigenous development.

While the Indigenous University proposal seems to be an alternative to supporting the public state university system with indigenous scholarships, its independence from the state is being established by drawing on another set of transnational linkages: it is being supported by Northern universities in order to ratify degrees and help provide university teachers.

> We [now] have other strategies. We are not going to wait for the legalization of the university [by the Ecuadorian government]. Instead, we have said, "Let's speak with universities, with the universities from abroad that are our friends so that they can sponsor us through an agreement." ... That is to say, they are always going to come. A body of teachers will come at least for a workshop each year. It's the same with the University of Arizona; teachers will be here from that university. So above all, in this way it guarantees the seriousness [of our university]. These universities will voluntarily take responsibility to give recognition to the qualifications. It wouldn't be possible any other way. It's not because they don't trust us—they do, we have an understanding—but there will always be university teachers who come from these universities present. That is to say, in that sense, we guarantee the seriousness of the university. (Interview, Luis Macas)

The alliances surrounding the proposal for an indigenous university reflect the sometimes-positive ways in which transnational connections have opened up opportunities for indigenous movements to bypass the state. Outside qualifications are nearly always valued more than national ones in the academic and development consultancy worlds (Silva 1998). Thus, it is quite possible that, by being allied with the academic community in Europe and North America, qualifications issued by the Indigenous University will have more "cultural" capital than those issued by the existing national universities.

Conclusion

This essay has highlighted how the social reproduction of indigenous professionalization empowers and circumscribes diverse actors enmeshed in complex networks. Development with identity frames indigenous actors, while also establishing the spaces in which those same actors contest the paradigm, its meanings and examples of best practice. The indigenous movement mobilizes a discourse of exclusion and racism and emphasizes the need to recognize indigenous knowledge as something more than informal, unscientific, empirical and local. Donors, on the other hand, are most interested in leadership training and investment in indigenous human and social capital to fulfill a good governance agenda. For many donors, interculturalism represents a way to contain the contradictions of neoliberal social inclusion, whereas for indigenous organizations it is primarily a rallying call to "Indianize this America." This essay argues that questions about the extent to which those agendas are compatible remain at the heart of indigenous professionalization, shaping its outcomes, success stories and failures.

Our analysis has suggested that social reproduction takes place in a range of professionalization spaces, including the transnational classroom and curriculum as well as conferences and meetings. While transnational networks help to maintain these spaces, adherence to different understandings of the politics of interculturalism by different network actors helps to challenge them. As a consequence, although interculturalism has emerged as the framing paradigm for higher-education programs and education reform, its position as a political and policy strategy remains unconsolidated.

Transnational actors influence the climate that welcomes seemingly pro-indigenous education, and are mobilized, at times, to pressurize or bypass the state. Yet it is ultimately state institutions that implement and manage the reforms, which, in turn, are funded and monitored in association with transnational actors. The state, therefore, plays a crucial role in the transnational networks and forms of social reproduction associated with indigenous professionalization. While transnational definitions of good local and national development have a complex relationship with locally embedded constructions of indigeneity, the exportation and contestation of "national" best practice examples of development with identity dynamically influences what is accepted as "good" development, locally, nationally and internationally.

As many students currently undertaking professionalization programs aspire to future careers as experts in development with identity in local and national government, (I)NGOs and multilaterals, state-transnational-indigenous networks have within them the potential to shape pro-indigenous reform well into the future. The success of current professionalization programs will be measured over coming years by the extent to which future graduating "professionals" displace the current need for outside support by shaping the trajectories of transnational academic, development policy and indigenous communities themselves.

Acknowledgments

The authors would like to thank the many individuals and organizations in Bolivia and Ecuador who collaborated with this research. Special thanks are owed to Pablo Regalsky, Maria Ester Pozo, Pamela Calla, Patricia Oliart and the students at CEIDIS who helped shape the arguments and gave unstinting support. The research was funded by the Economic and Social Research Council (ESRC grant #L214 25 2023: "Now We Are All Indians? Transnational Indigenous Communities in Ecuador and Bolivia") and also supported by the DFID/British Council gender and development link between Newcastle University and CESU, Cochabamba. Finally, we would like to thank the anonymous reviewers.

Endnotes

[1] Luis Macas is one of the main supporters of the proposal by CONAIE (Confederación de Nacionalidades Indígenas del Ecuador—The Confederation of Indigenous Nationalities of Ecuador) for an indigenous university in Ecuador. He spoke these words at a plenary address during the Seminario Andino: Conflictos y Políticas Interculturales: Territorios y Educación, Cochabamba October 1999 (available on CD from CEIDIS, http://www.ceidis.com).

[2] "Indigenous professionalization" is defined as the development of careers that focus on indigenous issues in development, including opportunities for indigenous people to train for professional jobs.

[3] There is a long history of indigenous professionalization, dating back to colonial times and often linked to the work of religious orders. Until recently, however, the openings in development planning for indigenous careers have been largely limited to the teaching profession and, to a lesser extent, minor positions in the military and the police force.

[4] See Aikman (2000), Cortina and Stromquist (2000) on the World Bank, the United Nations Educational, Scientific and Cultural Organization (UNESCO) and the United Nations Children's Fund (UNICEF) and Kane (2001) on Nicaragua.

[5] ECUARUNARI is a Quichua word meaning the awakening of Ecuador's Indians. It is the title of the confederation of peoples of Quichua nationality in Ecuador.

[6] See Radcliffe (2001) for a discussion of the role of hybrid development institutions in indigenous development.

[7] Human-capital theory became popular with economists in the 1960s, but became less influential in the 1970s and 1980s (Grindle 2000).

[8] See debates on the World Bank Group's PovertyNet Web pages (2003a) for and against the role of education in social development.

[9] The World Bank and the UK government's bilateral aid organization, the Department for International Developmoent (DFID), both operate active social-development units.

[10] PRODEPINE is a hybrid development organization funded by international donors, including the World Bank and the Ecuadorian government.
[11] This is not to negate the fact that indigenous leaders representing indigenous political parties, which support intercultural education, also call for leadership training in more conventional careers based on dominant forms of knowledge, careers such as lawyers and legal experts. Rather, the argument highlights the fact that donor and state understandings of human and social capital (expressed through scholarship schemes, for example) often see their investments as a panacea for strengthening indigenous leadership.
[12] See Andolina (1999) for a more detailed examination of the different trajectories in the Ecuadorian and Bolivia indigenous movements.
[13] This is exemplified in the quotation at the beginning of this essay, taken from a speech delivered at an international, intercultural education conference by Ecuadorian indigenous leader Luis Macas.
[14] See, for example, COSUDE (2001), the bilateral Swiss aid agency's annual report in Bolivia.
[15] See Seider (2002) for an explanation of the rise of pluriculturalism in the Andes.
[16] MACAC is the Quichua word for *guerrero*, meaning "war cry."
[17] In 2002, there were 44 students.
[18] These reforms include: the law of popular participation, which decentralizes power to local communities; land reform that recognizes indigenous territory; and education reform introducing a national curriculum based on extending bilingual, intercultural education.
[19] CODENPE is a state institution that oversees development projects for indigenous people and guides pro-indigenous laws through national congress. It has a committee in charge of it, with an executive director. In the past five years or so, CONAIE (the major national indigenous confederation in the country) has had a majority of seats on the committee, and its representatives have been executive directors.

References

Aikman S (2000) Bolivia. In D Coulby, R Cowen and C Jones (eds) *World Yearbook of Education 2000 Education in Times of Transition* (pp 22–39). London: Kogan Page
Andolina R (1999) "Colonial Legacies and Plurinational Imaginaries: Indigenous Movement Politics in Ecuador and Bolivia." PhD dissertation, University of Minnesota
Bebbington A (2002) Sharp knives and blunt instruments: Social capital in development studies. *Antipode* 34(4):800–803
Blanes J (2000) *Mallkus y alcaldes*. La Paz: PIEB-CEBEM
Cortina R and Stromquist N (eds) (2000) *Distant Alliances Promoting Education for Girls and Women in Latin America*. London: Routledge
COSUDE (Agencia Suiza para el Desarrollo y La Cooperación) (ed) (2001) *La Encrucijada Cultural: Anuario COSUDE 2001*. La Paz: Plural Editores
Cushner K (1998) Intercultural education from an international perspectivea: An introduction. In K Cushner (ed) *International Perspectives on Intercultural Education* (pp 1–14). London: Lawrence Erlbaum Associates
de la Cadena M (1998) Silent racism and intellectual superiority in Peru. *Bulletin of Latin American Studies* 17(2):143–164
de la Cadena M (2000) *Indigenous Mestizos: The Politics of Race and Culture, Cuzco Peru, 1919–1991*. Durham, NC: Duke University Press
Degregori C (1998) Ethnicity and democratic governability in Latin America: Reflections from two central Andean countries. In F Agüero and J Stock (eds) *Fault Lines of Democracy: Post-Transition Latin America* (pp 203–236). Miami: North South Centre Press

Deruyttere A (1997) *Indigenous peoples and sustainable development: The role of the Inter-American Development Bank*. Inter-American Development Bank publication no. 16 Washington, DC: Inter-American Development Bank

Fine B (2001) *Social Capital versus Social Theory: Political Economy and Social Sciences at the Turn of the Millennium*. London: Routledge

Fine B (2002) They f**k you up those social capitalists. *Antipode* 34(4):796–799

Foweraker J (1998) Social movements and citizenship rights in Latin America. In M Vellinga (ed) *The Changing Role of the State in Latin America* (pp 271–296). Boulder: Westview Press

Godenzzi J (1996) Educación bilingüe e interculturalidad en los Andes y la Amazonía. *Revista Andina* 14(2):559–581

Grindle M (2000) The social agenda and the politics of reform in Latin America. In J Tulchim and A Garland (eds) *Social Development in Latin America: The Politics of Reform* (pp 17–52). Boulder: Lynne Reinner Publishers

Hale C R (1997) The cultural politics of identity in Latin America. *Annual Review of Anthropology* 26:567–590

Kane L (2001) *Popular Education and Social Change in Latin America*. London: Latin American Bureau

Laurie N and Bonnett A (2002) Adjusting to equity: The contradictions of neoliberalism and the search for racial equality in Peru. *Antipode* 33(5):28–53

McNeish J (2001) "Pueblo Chico, Infierno Grande: Globalisation and the Politics of Participation in Highland Bolivia." PhD thesis, Goldsmiths College, University of London

Medina J (2001) Cultura, civilización e interculturalidad: Algunas definiciones básicas. In COSUDE (ed) *La Encrucijada Cultural: Anuario COSUDE 2001* (p 26). La Paz: Plural Editores

Mitchell K (2001) Education for democratic citizenship: Transnationalism, multiculturalism and the limits of liberalism. *Harvard Education Review* 71(1):51–78

Mujer y Ajuste (1996) *Ajuste Estructural Debate y Propuestas: El Ajuste Estructural en el Perú: una Mirada Desde las Mujeres*. Lima: Ediciones Mujeres y Ajuste

Nederven Pieterse J (2001) *Development Theory: Deconstructions/Reconstructions*. London: Sage

Portes A and Landolt P (2000) Social capital: Promise and pitfalls of its role in development. *Journal of Latin American Studies* 32(2):529–547

Psacharopoulos G and Patrinos H (1996) *Indigenous People in Latin America*. Avebury: Aldershot

Puiggrós A (1999) *Neoliberalism and Education in the Americas*. Boulder: Westview Press

Radcliffe S (2001) Development, the state and transnational political connections: State and subject formation in Latin America. *Global Networks* 1(1):19–36

Regalsky P and Laurie N (forthcoming) "This is our place": Negotiating the hidden curriculum and indigenous education in Bolivia. Working paper

Seider R (ed) (2002) *Pluricultural and Multiethnic: Implications for State and Society in Mesoamerica and the Andes*. Basingstoke: Palgrave Macmillan

Silva P (1998) Neoliberalism, democratisation and the rise of technocrats. In M Vellinga (ed) *The Changing Role of the State in Latin America* (pp 75–92). Boulder: Westview Press

Van Cott D (2002) Constitutional reform in the Andes: Redefining indigenous-state relations. In R Seider (ed) *Pluricultural and Multiethnic: Implications for State and Society in Mesoamerica and the Andes* (pp 45–73). Basingstoke: Palgrave Macmillan

Weismantel M (2001) Cholas *and* Pishtacos: *Stories of Race and Sex in the Andes*. Chicago: University of Chicago Press

World Bank Group (2003a) PovertyNet. http://www.worldbank.org/poverty/index.htm
    (last accessed 18 February 2003)
World Bank Group (2003b) PovertyNet: Social capital for development: What is
    social capital? http://www.worldbank.org/poverty/scapital/whatsc.htm (last accessed
    27 February 2003)

Chapter 3
Producing the Future: Getting To Be British

Jean Lave

Introduction

In a recent article, Katz (2001) argues that "[A]ny politics that effectively counters capitalism's global imperative must confront the shifts in social reproduction that have accompanied and enabled it." She insists that we must look at multiple facets of shifting practices of social life—political-economic, political-ecological, and cultural. Her call, and my research on the British port wine trade diaspora in Porto, Portugal, evoke studies of colonial elites during an earlier epoch of global movement of capital, culture, and people (eg Cooper and Stoler 1997; Stoler 1995). In the 1980s, Stoler and others explored domestic and sexual arrangements, reproducing labor forces, children of Europeans, and local populations seen as "a dangerous conduit of moral contamination and political subversion" (Cooper and Stoler 1997:24). The tensions of empire were such that "the otherness of colonized persons was neither inherent nor stable; his or her difference had to be defined and maintained," which required social engineering, education, and "civilizing missions" (Cooper and Stoler 1997:7). There were no simple boundaries between colonized and colonizers, antipodes and metropoles. The researchers concluded that "the historic turn in the social sciences … [has] played no small part in making colonial studies one of the prime sites where the political nature of cultural projects could be minutely explored, … and where the cultural embeddedness of political economy could be worked out" (Cooper and Stoler 1997:17).

Contemporary social, cultural geography is another such site. Marston (2000:235) writes about the transformation—economic, political, and spatial—at the turn of the 19th century "as new social—gender, race, class—relations were being wrought around an emergent form of mature industrial corporate capitalism." There was a

cultural consensus about the proper roles of men and women and public and private life. Ideally, men and women occupied separate,

naturally ordained, nonoverlapping spheres of influence and
operation: the public one men's and the private women's. In reality,
however, while bourgeois patriarchal ideology constructed a role for
women in the private sphere, the two spheres tended more to overlap
than to exist in isolation. (Marston 2000:235)

Marston argues that the division and enclosure of gendered spheres of
life-activity of a particular industrial capitalist variety was invented
and must be determinedly approached with questions about how this
was and is produced and sustained. That is, we must explore its contributions to the cultural embeddedness of political economy and inquire
into the political nature of that cultural project of gendered division.

Mitchell (2001) does this by looking closely at struggles over school
culture and its moral and political ethos, struggles between long-
term, mainly Anglo-British residents of British Columbia and recent
wealthy Chinese immigrants from Hong Kong. Canadian school
debates are preoccupied with colonizers, immigrants, and cultural
pluralism. She explores effects of "the accelerated flow of capital,
commodities, culture and people" on "conceptions of democratic
citizenship" (Mitchell 2001:52). The debates are not over precisely the
same issues and tensions that organize British factions and divide
British and Portuguese in the British enclave in Porto. But changes
in flows of capital, commodities, culture, and people are as important in Porto as elsewhere for understanding current struggles over
schools and community identities through which people seek to
fashion their futures.

Mitchell, Marston, and Katz all focus on the changing character of
practices of family, gender, race, and nationality as part of global political
economic changes. Stoler and Mitchell call attention to education
as a site of production of colonial (colonizers and colonized) transnational immigrant (and long-term resident) subjects.[1] Marston and
Katz question the reflexive way in which ideologies of public (men's)
and private (women's) lives have shaped and divided scholarship
in ways that unacceptably assume (a) a division between public and
private "spheres" (a geometric abstraction of space to which Lefebvre
would surely have objected (cf Lefebvre [1974] 1991:30), and (b) the
relative analytic (in)significance of "social reproduction" in our working understanding of the production of transnational fates.

The old British port wine merchant families have participated in
global political-economic transformations over two centuries through
their engagement in producing themselves, their lives, their enclave
in Porto, their futures, and their children's futures. They have also
participated in the (changing) production, marketing, and distribution
of port wine (Duguid forthcoming). In the last few decades, their lives
and labors have been transformed as Portugal and the British port

firms have opened their doors to multinational ownership and management. The old merchant families are gradually losing their economic base. The political economy and political-ecology of their situation, mediated as they are in everyday practice, probably never fit all that well: local political power articulates with political-economic forces and resources in an ill-fitting way and is always under contention (Holland and Lave 2001). In Porto in the mid-1990s, I found the British wine-merchant families dominating the social world of the 2000-strong British community in spite of their weakening fortunes. This led me to explore how multinational corporate managers and their families exert so little power over the enclave and its future, and old port merchants so much, given their rising and waning positions respectively in the production of port, shoes, and other products and forms of labor. In the course of my ethnographic research living in the enclave, taking part in community and family life, I found women, men, and children organizing and pursuing their futures as participants in multiple contexts that were neither essentially private nor public at the same time that they were both private and public. Enclave dwellers labored to produce hierarchical relations of nationality, class, and gender within and between those multiple contexts.

The enclave in Porto is the product of a transnational imaginary that brought British wine merchants to Portugal from the late 1700s on.[2] Long before the city—called Oporto by the British—became the industrial heart of Portugal, it was a center in a British trade diaspora (Curtin 1984) that stretched from the demarcated zone of small Portuguese vineyards on the slopes of the Alto Douro, 80 kilometers east of Porto, down the river to the port firms' warehouses in a tightly packed, demarcated entrepôt in Vila Nova da Gaia across the river from the British Factory House. There the young, fortified wine was aged, blended, and readied for shipment to corresponding merchants in London, Edinburgh, and elsewhere. As the British developed and partially controlled the port trade, they settled in Porto (mainly after the civil war of 1829–1832) and gradually built the institutional conditions of possibility for what even today is called "the British colony."[3] The three-story Factory House, with its dining rooms, ballroom, lounges, library, and billiards room, was built in 1790. The church and graveyard followed a few decades later, and the school at the turn of the 20th century. As they developed their enclave, the British in Porto also heavily influenced the history, architecture, and infrastructure of the city in the 19th century, though this is no longer the case.

The enclave is fashioned in spatial terms through daily rounds of activity concretely sheltered and made possible in those institutional settings that draw people together across broad reaches of the city. In the late 1800s, these stretched in a relatively compact north-south axis from the St. James Anglican Church and its graveyard to the British port firms' owners/managers' club, the Factory House, to the firms on the other side of the river (with names like Sandeman's, Dow's, Warre's, Graham's and Taylor, Fladgate, and Yeatman). In the 19th century, port families made an annual summer exodus to the ocean, the western boundary of the city. Foz is now the most common residential area for enclave members. The old north-south axis marks the easternmost reach of community institutions today. Moving toward Foz, one encounters the Oporto Cricket and Lawn Tennis Club (OC and LTC), the British Consulate, and finally the Oporto British School (OBS) in Foz, where the Douro River meets the sea. The city of Porto stretches well east, north, and south of this fairly circum-scribed area (see Figure 1).

Some especially powerful British port merchant families in Porto, exuding the entitlement of an old elite, command center stage today in the British enclave's institutions. They claim descent from early par-ticipants in the trade who came to set up and run branches of British wine import firms.[4] They and their allies insistently furnish the enclave with significance revolving around the noble wine and its long history —to do with manly mirages of empire, a privileged gentry, domestic women, vintage port (*with* cigars and *without* "ladies"). But getting to be British in Porto is also the more immediate product of political economic and cultural transformation in the 1970s. Much of the

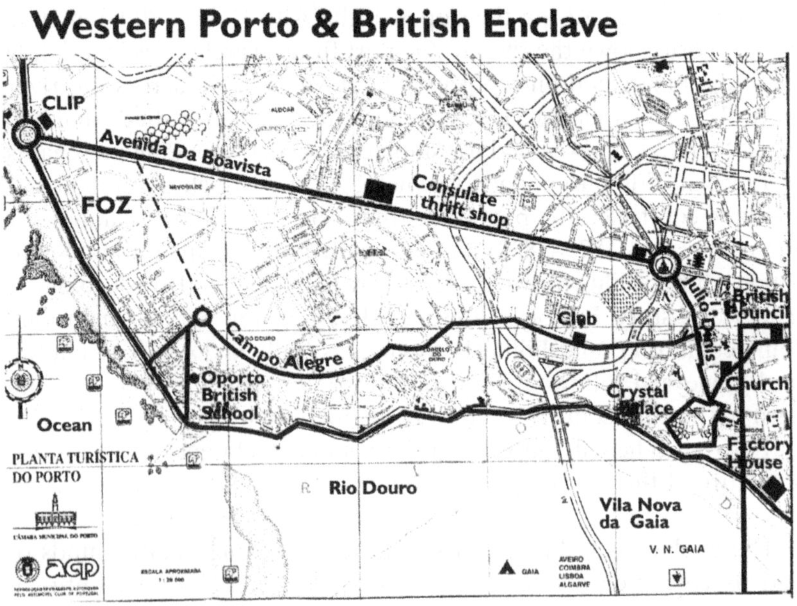

Western Porto & British Enclave

Figure 1: Western Porto and the British enclave

tension in the contentious practices around church, club, and school in Porto today can be understood as a local articulation of global political-economic struggles between mercantile and multinational corporate transnational imaginaries. Multinational, corporate political-economic forms and forces are in struggle with (contemporary versions of) older mercantile practices. The outcomes are uncertain. Different British citizens in Porto now fashion distinctive anticipations of future resolutions of the tensions that mark their lives while trying to provide for the next generation.

The children of port wine gentry families today are brought up to be British in families that are often described as "more British than the British." How they produce themselves and are produced—with what resources of "Britishness"—requires elucidation, for "getting to be British" may be a matter of nationality, but "more British than ... " is a transnational relation. Other participants in the enclave in Porto grow up British differently. For instance, British families from the United Kingdom who have come to live in Porto for a few years simply *are* British (for themselves) through social trajectories that produce them as such, without requiring them to make concerted, direct, and intentional efforts to produce those trajectories. Other British residents in Porto have come from long years—occasionally lifetimes—in former colonies, British and Portuguese, in southern Africa. Part of understanding what it means for the port wine gentry to "get to be British in Porto"—if in fact they do "get to be British"—is bound up in these heterogeneous life histories and social relations in the enclave.

Hall (1995:7) has insisted that we

not forget that retention characterized the colonizing cultures as well as the colonized. For if you look at the Little Englands, the Little Spains, and the Little Frances that were created by the colonizers, if you consider this kind of fossilized replica, with the usual colonial cultural lag—people are always more Victorian when they're taking tea in the Himalayas than when they're taking tea in Leamington—they were keeping alive the memory of their own homes and homelands and traditions and customs.

In Porto, the port families have not suffered the violent ruptures to which Hall points as constitutive of historical relations for the colonized (frightening though the 1974 revolution may have been). They "stayed on"—though what they stayed on "after" is not well defined. The British in Porto are both like and unlike "Caribbean people of all kinds, of all classes and positions, [who] experience the question of positioning themselves in a cultural identity as an enigma, as a problem, as an open question" (Hall 1995:8). From the point of view of the British port families, their nationality is not in question and should never, ever be seen by others as open, ambiguous, or doubtful. But the enormous effort it takes to produce themselves as "British" in their location in Porto surely changes the very meaning of their nationality and citizenship.

The rest of the essay is intended to lay out, however briefly, what it means for the port wine merchant families to be British in Porto—*in practice*. The differences (of nationality, class, and gender) they pursue help them define themselves as they help us dissect local meanings of "being British." The following two sections, on practices of exclusion and concession-making, present these differences and the ways in which they are established in daily life by port families in the enclave. At the same time, modes of exclusion and ambivalent and partial inclusion of various "others" are part of the "exclusive" stance that makes the port gentry families what and who they are. In the concluding discussion, drawing on my work with Holland (especially her reading of Bakhtin; see Holland and Lave 2001), I suggest why these practices are central to the changing transnational fates of the port families as they shape "other" fractions of the British community in Porto. The subsequent section on identity dilemmas extends the argument that whatever else it is about, the port gentry's ways of being British are not to be found in a shared ethos with others in the enclave, but in their different, sometimes clashing, interrelations (Holland and Lave 2001). Thus, even among the port gentry families, it is possible to identify three very different images of the trade, of the families, and, above all, of their futures in the trade. The next section explores clashes among the port gentry families, other British residents, and Portuguese families over what it means to be British as they struggle over what kind of school would best support their transnational lives and the imaginaries these embody.

Practices of Exclusion

It is not the apparently homogenous community identity as "the old British port merchant colony in Porto" but its constitutive divisions —its heterogeneous social fractions and their relations—that are crafted in day-to-day cultural practices in the British enclave. There are "leading" families with powerfully influential positions in port firms who still have strong claims on the privileges of autochthony. There may be two, a dozen, or perhaps two dozen such families, depending on the exclusivity of the criteria operating on a given occasion. These issues come to the fore in discussions and struggles around schooling and other institutional practices. In Oporto, at the time of my research, there were two key educational institutions of concern, the OBS and the Colegio Luso-Internacional do Porto (CLIP). Practices of inclusion and exclusion were also played out in other arenas, such as the OC and LTC and the church.

Who is not accepted? Portuguese children who applied to the OBS were given a cold reception until about 1960. Even then their parents were told without apology of the quota system, such that only after all British children were accepted would places be selectively available for Portuguese children.[5] The 1989 OBS Articles say that only British persons may vote on the sale of land or property, the amendment of the articles, or the disbanding of the association. The membership roll of the OC and LTC is divided into members (British) and associates (divided further into "other nationalities" and "Portuguese"). Associates pay equal dues but do not have voting privileges in the most serious decisions affecting the governance of the club. On the other hand, without the participation of Portuguese members, the club could not survive financially. So British members exercise polite tolerance along with visible exclusion, as they do towards the few Portuguese members of St. James Anglican Church.

If Portuguese families are merely tolerated, there are more subtle ways in which other participants in the British enclave (defined in terms of its spaces, organizations, and activities) are positioned in a social hierarchy between the most prominent and sought-after families and the Portuguese. There are two such categories of the unequal, both British. These are "pillars" and "manager families on contract."

The "pillars" are British citizens, high-level managers for British companies in and around Porto and their wives. In some cases, they arrived in Porto as adults to take up managerial positions in port firms. More often, they moved from southern Africa or other parts of the former British (or Portuguese) empire where their companies have offices. They expect to stay in Porto until they retire or even for the rest of their lives. They are respected, in part because of their positions and long-term residence, in part because of their colonial credentials. They organize civic life on behalf of the community, thus establishing substantial positions for themselves, though this is never sufficient to achieve full acceptance by the old port families. They are pillars of the community in one further sense, as they defend the identity of the enclave as a venerable and special one against the families of British managers of multinationally owned industrial enterprises in Porto. The "managers," on three-year contracts, are, on average, a bit younger than the pillars. Port families and pillars see the manager families as troublemakers, characterizing them, stereotypically, as people who just sweep in and then leave but, in the interim, want to change things without respect for those who have made the community what it is today.

In sum, while the old families exclude others, the pillars take a good deal of prestige from their fairly close association with them. The pillars translate for the old families, and in speaking on their behalf, appear to be of them. These highly respectable British men also do much of the community's "executive" work. But this work is financed largely by Portuguese residents and others, including manager families on contract. The pillars defend the old port families, and the manager families on contract give service to the community, seek friends there, send their children to the OBS, attend church, and depend on the OC and LTC for their social life.

Class relations, expressed in international terms, are urgent matters in the enclave. Divisions of gender are also deeply felt and practiced, if not subject to public struggle. Young British wives from the United Kingdom expressed privately to me their shock at expectations that they should devote themselves to raising children and doing most of the community's work. They are not able to seek employment in or out of the port trade, for they are expected to help create the illusion that the port firms are still family affairs as they assist in entertaining clients. They are explicitly excluded, according to a centuries-old rule of the Factory House, from attending the weekly luncheons held by the members.[6] Given starkly contrasting possibilities for women's life-paths in the United Kingdom and in the enclave in Porto, and given cultural resources for resisting enclave practices that exploit and disacknowledge women's contributions to the futures in which all have high stakes, it is surprising that struggles over gender inequality took no overt form in the enclave in the mid-1990s. No groups, no discussions, no critique surfaced in the social lives of the women I came to know well. This, too, was part of the struggles to get to be British in Porto.

Concessions

No matter how pervasive those practices of exclusion and their incorporation into the intimate identities of the British port merchant family members are, they are not uncontested, even in the practices of the British port families themselves. Instead, at least where nationality and class are concerned, they are tempered and muffled in contradictory relations by which concessions are made to those on whom the port merchant families long practiced more definite exclusions. British enclaves like the one in Porto purvey their class culture to the formerly—or, in this case, the informally—colonized in return for the opportunity to reproduce their own immediate social position and its social significance within the confines of antipodal enclaves. This can be seen in several ways. Concessions are implicated in what seems an unusual facility on the part of the British to continue reproducing their position as arbiters of class culture in the transnational ambience of Porto. Thus, in contentious local practice in the enclave, access to the OBS and to the OC and LTC have been gradually and reluctantly conceded to those whom the port merchant families have long struggled to exclude, but neither the agenda of activities nor control over these institutions has changed hands.

The British port families do an enormous amount of entertaining of business clients at the port houses and Factory House, as well as at the firms' *quintas* (field headquarters) in the Alto Douro. Their lavish hospitality is produced in such a way that it blurs lines between what, in many cases, had been family country homes but which since the 1970s have become small hotels/guesthouses. This productive confusion of the apparently private estate and the invisible public corporation allows them to extend specific concessions to marginal "others" on whom they must unwillingly depend if they are to conserve their way of life.

All of this helps to underwrite the position of the port shipping families in the enclave. They exude—and might be said to purvey— British class and cultural practices: by creating a common and vivid history; by asserting claims to the privileges of originating the wine, the trade, and the enclave; through contagion from the "noble wine" they make and sell (to hear community members talk); and through the attenuated but real effects of the (no longer formal) British empire on a global, international hierarchy of national class cultures. Further, the British in Porto have resources of connectedness with the signs of the British upper class—royalty, nobility, and influential politicians. They import those connections for consumption in Porto. Queen Elizabeth and Prince Philip visited the Factory House in 1957, and reminders of their visit are still prominently displayed. More recently, Margaret Thatcher opened the new building of the OBS, and John Major spent a holiday at one firm's quinta in the Alto Douro.

All of this helps to account for the resilience of the economically no-longer-salient British enclave in its present hierarchical and differentiated state. The continued participation of the Portuguese families is another facet of the same resilience.

Exclusions, Concessions, and Identity Dilemmas

Three prominent figures in the trade are fashioning, in practice, three different trajectories into the future of the enclave. One scion of an old port family and firm married an American woman and lived in the United States for many years as an employee of the multinational firm that bought the family firm from his father. He was sent to Porto by the corporation to head his family's former firm in 1990. His marriage at an end, he lived at the far end of Vila Nova da Gaia in a faceless new apartment block and had nothing to do with the social life at club, church, or school until he married a Portuguese employee of his firm. He appears to have joined his career with the corporation, having recently been seconded for a stint at its multinational European headquarters in Paris. But he seemed torn, claiming that his principal loyalty is to the family business.

The second scion twits the first about being merely a contract-manager interloper (perhaps as an ironic gesture towards his own family's "late" —19th century—arrival in Porto). The second port shipper's father bought several of the British family firms and fashioned a family holding company in which one male offspring of each male collateral in each generation is promised employment in the trade. They have prospered and are among the wealthiest in the enclave. The current head of the clan takes a central place in enclave affairs and maximal identification with and responsibility for it. He is married to a woman from a British family in Lisbon, and his adult children are deeply concerned with reproducing their trajectories for their children and maintaining the enclave as the old port families' fiefdom.

The third scion retired recently as manager of a major British family firm (now multinationally owned). He is dismayed by public opinion that attributes to Portuguese colleagues what he feels was his role in founding an imitation medieval fraternity designed to court prestigious patrons of port wine. He is married to a Portuguese woman, thinks the British are fools not to see the inevitable "Portuguese tide" washing over them, and is angry at the mismanagement and loss of historical records that might leave behind clearer traces of the British port family firms.

These three reflect in their lives and their outlooks alternative fates for the British enclave, as well as for their families and themselves. They and their children could try to become nondistinctive participants in new, global management trajectories. They could fight to sustain the enclave as it is, even if its boundaries are eventually reduced to those of the families themselves and it becomes something other than a community. Or they could succumb to that "Portuguese tide." Whatever their differences, these trajectories all involve a riveting focus on getting to be British—or not—in Porto. The stakes are wealth, position, precedence, and the pleasures of acting with a consciousness that one's actions have a historical significance beyond the immediate. The dangers include the possibility that they will be left behind as nothing but troglodytes (as one of their unrepentant offspring who lives in London dubbed them), only to find their identities of British privilege as "old wine gentry" dissolved one day.

None of these "futures" represents the possibility of "returning home" to the UK. Among other reasons, it would be difficult to do because of the incommensurability of class-cultural practices in Great Britain and Porto after all these years. The practical means demanded by struggles to be British in Porto anchor them in specific, practically situated ways. They *are* "at home"; they cannot *go* home. In this sense, long-occupied enclaves of colonizers who "stay on" are indeed diasporic societies (Hall 1995). The irony is that whatever they are peddling in the antipodes, it is not British contemporary upper- and upper-middle-class practice at the metropole.

Struggles over Enclave Identity and Futures

Of the three port scions whose future histories-in-person are outlined above, it is the second family head and his children, successfully in control of access to participation in their port companies for generations to come, who have invested energy in preserving the Porto British community as it is, was, or might have been. Other participants have a variety of other stakes in their children's future. Schools, then, are often key places in which struggles that inform all aspects of social existence surface as active debates over the imperatives of children's life trajectories. Some of these may be glimpsed in two events in the spring of 1994, and in excerpts from the brochure of a new school that styled itself as a rival to the OBS.

The first was a fight at the OBS—painful and unexpected, according to the new headmaster—at the school's annual general meeting. Parents of students in the school and the school governing committee argued over, then voted down the headmaster's appeal to change the name of the school to the Oporto British International School. He was surprised at the heat generated by such a small, obviously appropriate change that would reflect the changing student composition and new school priorities, for the OBS, after a decade of debate, had recently initiated the International Baccalaureate (IB) diploma. The disagreement was generated in intersecting, deeply related conflicts reflected more specifically in the examples that follow.

The second event begins to show how the school was caught up in ongoing struggles. After the school meeting, there was tense debate centered on the church between elderly members of old port families and the newly arrived manager of a British manufacturing plant in Portugal. He and his wife were energetic, responsible, and eager to take part in community activities. Both sang in the choir, and their children attended church with them. The debate was about moving the altar and changing the church service to make it less formal and more welcoming to children. The most vociferous opponent, the widow of the head of an influential family port firm, finally said, "I don't want it to change; I remember how church services have been all my life and I want them to stay that way."

At the club on a Sunday a couple of weeks later, I joined the elderly woman for lunch. In between greeting other churchgoers who were dining at the club, this woman described wrathfully a disagreement she had had with this same man during the hospitality hour that morning. The discussion was about whether children should be sent to boarding schools in England. The man had said he wouldn't dream of it. The woman exclaimed with indignation, "I asked him if he knew of [name of a public] school and he hadn't even heard of it," making it plain that she dismissed both his argument and his prospects for future participation in community leadership.

These conflicts within and about the school reflected the political-economic and cultural crosscurrents in which the British enclave in Porto is caught up in all aspects of its daily existence. At its founding in 1894, the OBS was embedded in relations of empire just as surely as were the mercantile practices of the port traders.[7] Even in 1994, it was the intentions of parents and the effects on children of being removed from their families to boarding schools in England (total institutions that have traditionally replaced personal roots in family with old-school loyalties of a more abstractly nationalistic sort) that principally expressed the peculiar concerns over life trajectories of old port family members. The port families viewed the OBS as a preparatory school for their children, who would attend public schools in England from the age of 13.

By contrast, managers in multinational firms with branches in Portugal who came to Porto for three years on contract (like the one who proposed changes in the church service) anticipated a peripatetic existence. These families favored a full international school with a curriculum available all over the world. The IB, a curriculum for a high-school diploma under international supervision and certification, had its origins, not in England, but in that center of capitalist neutrality, Switzerland. It is intended to make possible a continuous curriculum, at a coordinated pace, across international secondary schools, thus enabling transnationally migrating managerial families to secure a single, standard educational trajectory for their children without sending them to metropolitan boarding schools. It has been built on British educational traditions to a great extent, but if English is its most important language (it is offered in French and Spanish as well), the most compelling reason is its position as the global language of business, not its historical roots in late 19th- and early 20th-century relations of empire.

The headmaster at the OBS argued that the IB offered a high-standard educational plan from which students at the OBS could benefit greatly. The manager families sided with him. Old port families argued that putting resources into this project would take them away from the junior preparatory school.

The third glimpse into debates over children's futures comes from a Portuguese-sponsored, English-language international school in Porto that opened in 1986 with a Portuguese-American head. The school had a glossy brochure entitled "CLIP: Colegio Luso-Internacional do Porto"—reading from front to back in one direction, in Portuguese. Turn the brochure upside down and backward, and the English version is called "CLIP: Oporto International School." I learned in discussions with its author (the new head of the upper school, formerly in a similar position at the OBS) that a number of its claims were intended as challenges to the OBS. Consider the following quotes from the brochure, in the format in which they were boldly laid out there:

- The governance of CLIP is based on a democratic model for decision-making, as articulated in its Charter. CLIP recognizes the preeminent role of parents, teachers, and students in the educational process.
- Teaching methods and subject syllabuses are drawn from English-speaking educational systems, with careful note and consideration given to the programmes of work existent in the present Portuguese system.
- CLIP's pupils share the love of learning and intellectual ability so necessary to the attainment of academic excellence. They differ, however, in most other aspects. Coming from different national and ethnic backgrounds, and speaking a motley of languages, CLIP's pupils give to the Colegio the right mix for its success as an international school.

Criteria for admission include:

1. All applicants to CLIP will be considered regardless of their race, religion, sex, or national origin ...
4. A lottery system will be used when the number of candidates who have met the Standard of Admission exceeds the number of slots available ...
6. Prior knowledge of English, even though preferable, is not a condition for admission.

In 1994, CLIP was located in the restored former Porto trolley-line power station, at the opposite end of the oceanfront community of Foz from the OBS. The school commenced as the effort of a former OBS headmaster in collaboration with a group of Dutch and Scandinavian parents. Command of the project was soon taken over by a small group of Portuguese businessmen, each with professional training in the United States. CLIP's oppositional character surely had its roots, in part, in their experience with the OBS, whose multiply discriminatory practices eventually led them to withdraw their children and concentrate their efforts on the international school. The latter undercut OBS fees, paid its teachers higher salaries, and succeeded in hiring teachers away from the OBS. The school emphasized nationality-blind admissions, equality of pay and standing among all teachers, equal opportunity for all parents to participate, and above all its equitably international (rather than British) character.

The competitive, potentially life-and-death struggle between the schools helps to make visible contentious relations between the old port merchant families, contract managers, and Portuguese families with stakes in the British enclave. British expatriates were caught up in them in different ways and were engaged in different and changing relations with the Portuguese families who involved themselves in school and club, and who were themselves negotiating their stakes in the postrevolution political-economic transformation of Portugal. It seemed that the port families must capitulate, and the British enclave shed its identity as "the old port wine colony."

And yet, resistance, while it may be the weapon of the weak, is the weapon par excellence of the wealthy and the conservative. Port families continued to struggle to maintain the OBS in its old form. Their coordinated action carried the day into the late 1990s. A port family head (the second scion mentioned above) offered a desperately needed loan to the OBS in the mid 1990s—on condition that he be given control over appointments to the school governing committee for some years to come. There was then still strong resistance among the members to a more professional relation between the committee and the headmaster, who ordinarily would assume the day-to-day management of the school.

These are life-shaping endemic struggles that, in part, consist of their participants. They affect who participates in the port trade in the future and how, and with what kinds of views of their place in the trade, of national identities, and of relations between Portuguese and British farmers, firms, and multinational companies. Such struggles make clear the importance of continuity and tradition, however contrived. They affect intergenerational relations, as well. Exploring such struggles raises questions about whether and on what terms old British port families will continue to participate, and about what changes will emerge in the trade in years to come.

Discussion

"How do you get to be British?" is evidently a polysemic question: In one sense, it is about growing up—"becoming British." In another sense, it is about participation in daily practices—"being British" day by day. And in a third sense, it is about privilege: how is it that some are entitled to "be British," but not others? These questions should not be separated. Keeping them together is one way to refuse to draw a line between being British and learning to be British, between life trajectories that are part of everyday practice and the struggles of everyday life practices the contradictory complexities of which help to forge many varieties of lives (and identities) in the making.

There is a fourth meaning to the question of "How do you get to be British?" One could read into it uncertainty about the outcome. Porto is no longer a trade enclave in the age of empire—influential, confidently dominant, and strongly buttressed from "contamination" from "the natives." The enclave's problems are not those of wine merchants in an informal colony of Great Britain, going about their business with the arrogance of the self-affirmed "superior" and the support of political, economic, and diplomatic forces very much to their advantage. The descendants of those merchants live now as an enclave in a country with which they share membership in the European Union. The British "colony" has no official status, and the premises on which old British families in the enclave seem to operate are not so easily concealed or as acceptable as they might have been a century or even 50 years ago. Thus, getting to be British today in Porto is a privilege under challenge and imperiled.

For "old port families," two kinds of local processes of practical struggle—each with internal contradictions—reflect the precarious character of present arrangements, taking substance from the larger clashes between lingering merchant and aggressive multinational capitalist forces that are restructuring the port trade and the economic landscape of Portugal. The first local struggle, which creates the context for the second, is found in the families' attempts to grapple with potential fates of erasure and dissolution of their identity within a unique port wine community, of their place of privilege in a community defined to their specifications, and of their intimate sense of privileged and historically significant selves. These are fears of superannuation—of becoming irrelevant, of becoming fossils, of being dissolved, of being erased from history and memory, of being viewed as ridiculous or quaint. At the same time, there are palpable fears of pollution (perhaps just a different kind of fear of superannuation) through contaminating contact with Portuguese people of all kinds and a variety of differently but robustly British others.

The sites for this first struggle are surely those where futures are made—schools, principally, but club and church as well. Struggles to control the significance of social divisions and to dominate claims about social solidarities make such sites places where reifications of "community" are lived and believed and to which they accrete. Such sites are also the signs of a community—social congregations that are experienced as more than the sum of the families that compose them—at the same time that families, men, women, and children struggle to define and control them. They matter because capturing the flag of future community identity is so obviously a means of cultivating a place, a future, and even an honorable past for one's "own" (a more powerful stake than for "oneself" to patriarchal Porto-British men, women, and children). Producing the future in these ways stakes out advantageous grounds for ongoing enduring struggles.

Though on the surface they may be quite similar, struggles to escape superannuation and pollution are often at cross-purposes with one another. In concrete terms, there are various contradictory practices that involve gathering up allies while trying to avoid being overcome by them—simultaneously courting and rejecting "other" British and susceptible Portuguese families through practices of concession and practices of exclusion. So "old port family" exclusions of Portuguese and of contract managers' families are about staying uncontaminated, as well as about maintaining privileges that depend on exclusivity. Attempts to keep Portuguese children out of the OBS and their parents from intimate participation in the governance of school, church, and club, the dangers of speaking Portuguese too well, the avoidance and second-ranking of Portuguese club members and teachers at the school —all of these express, create, and sustain fear of contamination, or, ultimately, mistaken identity. In this transnational imaginary to be taken for Portuguese would amount to being taken for a native, an inferior.

It is possible to join the new managerial forces—to join the enemy —but still preserve the living edge of one's existence, and perhaps power and resources comparable to present ones. But then pollution is inevitable. To fight superannuation may entail trying not to compromise or recruit allies. Safe from polluting ties, one may be true to one's heritage, one's being, and one's way of life—and lose it. Or one may give up, accepting the (apparently) inevitable. The three scions' visions of the future reflect different varieties of these uneasy, unsatisfactory ways to resolve—but not solve—the dilemmas they all face. A few men may be successful at moving into multinational management, a way of accepting superannuation with cheering compensation. Comparatively less romantic, more humdrum possibilities await those who retire to become odd, antipodal residents in London or Edinburgh. Alternatively, there are a variety of trajectories, rare and more radical than geographic removal, for moving into Portuguese social spheres and family life. Though such trajectories are close and convenient (their danger), they involve cutting social ties and refusing British views of national, racialized inferiority. The various levels at which seduction and rejection operate together in concessions made by the British are ways of protecting the community from contamination under circumstances in which it is increasingly difficult to avoid contact, much less interdependence. Most common is uneasy and vaguely defeated exit by young men and women to the United Kingdom, where they try to blend in and plan to stay.

The second internally contradictory process concerns the unintended, paradoxical effects of *struggling* to get to be British in Porto. In this struggle, the meaning of "getting to be British in Porto" does not sit still: The old port families—and, to the extent that they control its popular identity, "the British community"—end up getting to be "more British than the British," which is definitely not the same thing. The local and relational character of processes by which intimate interiors are made in everyday social life comes into focus in the tensions, disagreements, and quarrels through which "the" British contend with each other. They are quite heterogeneous in class, life experiences, positions, and perspectives on being British in Porto. Those differences help to make each of them complexly "British." Interior dialogues surely involve a variety of confusing us/others with different claims on Britishness.

Various kinds of identifications and various kinds of voices (some present, some absent) contribute to the varied trajectories of the "old British." I have tried to show some of that variety—old port families, pillars, contract managers, British visitors from the United Kingdom, Portuguese workers who are "not British," upper-middle-class families who also do not make it as British, and so on. If the I-for-itself for long-term British residents in Porto is British-in-Porto, then the "not-I-in me" is, in part, "real British." There is deep uncertainty about the authenticity of that which they find most crucial to defend against all comers: that they are *not* Portuguese, but *British*. These uncertain dialogues of nationality in persons and in practice must contribute to the intensity with which national identity is in question in Porto, much more so than among UK-British.

Being "more British than the British" is usually considered a signature problem of transnational enclaves, which are seen as somehow falling into a frozen language, culture, or history. To repeat Hall's (1995:7) sketch of former colonists: "If you consider this kind of fossilized replica, with the usual colonial cultural lag—people are always more Victorian when they're taking tea in the Himalayas than when they're taking tea in Leamington." Some visitors to Porto would agree. But social fossils are surely made rather than left over, and these "Victorian" scenes are made in practical struggles. On the ground, being "more British than the British" seems to me a matter of present struggles concerning the future, in circumstances in which that future is in grave doubt. "Old port families" fight for their future by homogenizing a disparate past and claiming 300 years of continuity that are belied by the changing history of British participation in the port trade (see Duguid 1995; Lave 1999). I have argued that they are engaged in practical processes involving bartering a certain British class culture for a continued privileged position in the enclave. They make other complicated concessions as well—not to keep things as they were, but to produce the privileges of being British-in-Porto into the future.

Conclusion

Historical processes, the structuring of social practice, and the precipitates of social change emerge in enduring struggles that unfold in contentious local practices (Holland and Lave 2001). In this essay, I have tried to demonstrate ethnographically how global transformations of political economic relations can usefully be understood in terms of the articulation of forces that take on concrete instantiations differently in different local circumstances. I argue (along with other authors in this volume) that, taken by themselves, conceptions of political-economic global transformation are in danger of claims too broad, homogeneous, static, abstract, and deterministic. At the same time, I have tried to show that local contentious practice cannot be read off local practices alone. These practices, in turn, must also be understood as partly the concrete instantiations of far-flung and enduring struggles. The location of the enclave, and the spatial circuits produced by British (trans)national subjects in the port wine enclave in Porto as they produce their lives, surely matter as they try to keep (or take) control of their futures and instantiate them in the enclave identity. What appears to be inevitable re-production is, in fact, produced in complicated, culturally creative, improbable, and uncertain ways, as British citizens, many-generation residents in Porto, get to be British in Porto differently from one another in interconnected ways. There being no such thing as the unglobal local or the unlocal global, I am encouraged instead to concentrate on located historical struggles, trajectories of heterogeneous futures, and articulations of enduring struggles and contentious local practice.

Acknowledgments
The Luso-American Foundation for Development and the National Endowment for the Humanities generously supported my research in Portugal for a year and two subsequent short visits in the mid-1990s. I am grateful to my co-researchers, Paul Duguid and Shawn Parkhurst, and to Dorothy Holland, Susan Shepler, and Gill Hart as well for their perspicacious readings. Thanks also to Katharyne Mitchell, Sallie Marston, and Cindi Katz for crafting the project of which this essay is a part. This essay recontextualizes material from Lave (2001).

Endnotes
[1] Stoler focused on early childhood, ignoring the circulation of the older children of colonial elites through the boarding public-school system in England. In this exclusion she joined many other scholars. As Mangan (1986) points out, historians of empire on the whole do not touch on education, while historians of education rarely have focused on imperialism.

[2] As an example of centuries of transnational migration and the making of (trans)-national subjects, the Porto British remind us that the phenomenon is not new and not always to be addressed from the point of view of a powerful receiving nation. They remind us also that it is not always newcomers and the disadvantaged who are the vagabonds of globalization.

[3] In spite of their quite different composition and purposes, the practices of day-to-day life in the colony in Porto have precedents in the colonial enclaves at the antipodes of

the British empire, in colonial government enclaves, military outposts, merchant entre-pôts (or "factories"), and missionary stations (eg Allen 1976; Bailey 1976; Comaroff and Comaroff 1991; Farrell 1978; Orwell 1934; Scott 1977; Tanner 1964, 1966).
⁴ The grapes are grown in the world's earliest (1756) demarcated zone for wine production on the steep, terraced mountainous terrain along the Douro River east of Porto, stretching almost to the border with Spain.
⁵ The school charter of 1894 begins, "First Resolution re: Scholars, Clause I: That the School be exclusively for British subjects [meaning boys] of the age of six years and upwards provided they can read and write." As late as 1989, the first article of the OBS charter simply copied a declaration brought along through many official revisions of the charter:

> The Oporto British School is an educational association, formed by the members whose names appear in the corresponding register and whose object is to maintain a school to administer instruction and education to the children of British subjects, in order to prepare them for the entrance examinations to British schools, up to the 13-plus level. The principal, after consultation with the Board of Governors, may accept non-British pupils as long as the number of pupils from countries where the common language is not English does not prejudice the normal school programme.

The articles of the charter revised in 1957 stipulate that students who come from foreign countries cannot compose more than 20 percent of the students.
⁶ The Factory House was crucial in establishing the boundaries of the port gentry and anchoring major social divisions in the enclave (cf Lave 1999). The exclusion of women is one of these and has a history (at least) as old as the Factory House itself.
⁷ J A Mangan (1988:6) introduces an edited volume with the proposition that: "One fact emerges with great force[:] … the close and continuing association between British imperialism and the public school system."

References

Allen C (ed) (1976) *Plain Tales from the Raj*. London: Futura
Bailey J P (1976) "The British Community in Argentina." PhD dissertation, Department of Sociology, University of Surrey
Comaroff J and Comaroff J (1991) *Of Revelation and Revolution: Christianity, Colonialism, and Consciousness*. Chicago: University of Chicago Press
Cooper F and Stoler A (eds) (1997) *Tensions of Empire: Colonial Cultures in a Bourgeois World*. Berkeley: University of California Press
Curtin P D (1984) *Cross-Cultural Trade in World History*. Cambridge, UK: Cambridge University Press
Duguid P (1995) "Negotiating Change: Town-Country Relations in the Twilight of the *Companhia Geral*." Paper presented at the sixth annual International Conference Group on Portugal (ICGP) conference, Durham, NH, October
Duguid P (forthcoming) In vino veritas: The future and the past of global supply chains. In M F Kenney (ed) *Locating Global Advantage: Industry Dynamics in a Globalizing Economy* Stanford, CA: Stanford University Press
Farrell J G (1978) *The Singapore Grip*. London: Weidenfeld and Nicolson
Hall S (1995) Negotiating Caribbean identities. *New Left Review* 209 (Jan–Feb):1–14
Holland D and Lave J (eds) (2001) *History in Person: Enduring Struggles, Contentious Practice, Intimate Identities*. Santa Fe, NM: School of American Research Press
Katz C (2001) Vagabond capitalism and the necessity of social reproduction. *Antipode* 33(4):709–728
Lave J (1999) Re-serving succession in a British enclave. In J de Pina Cabral and A Pedroso de Lima (eds) *Elites: Choice, Leadership, and Succession* (pp 167–199). London: Berg

Lave J (2001) Getting to be British. In D Holland and J Lave (eds) *History in Person: Enduring Struggles, Contentious Practice, Intimate Identities* (pp 281–324). Santa Fe, NM: School of American Research Press

Lefebvre H ([1974] 1991) *The Production of Space*. Translated by D Nicholson-Smith. Oxford: Blackwell

Mangan J A (1986) *The Games Ethic and Imperialism: Aspects of the Diffusion of an Ideal*. Harmondsworth: Viking

Mangan J A (ed) (1988) *"Benefits Bestowed"?: Education and British Imperialism*. Manchester: Manchester University Press

Marston S A (2000) The social construction of scale. *Progress in Human Geography* 24(2):219–242

Mitchell K (2001) Education for democratic citizenship: Transnationalism, multiculturalism, and the limits of liberalism. *Harvard Educational Review* 71(1):51–78

Orwell G (1934) *Burmese Days*. New York: Harper and Brothers

Scott P (1977) *Staying On*. London: Heinemann

Stoler A L (1995) *Race and the Education of Desire*. Durham, NC: Duke University Press

Tanner R E S (1964) Conflict within small European communities in Tanganyika. *Human Organization* 23(4):319–327

Tanner R E S (1966) European leadership in small communities in Tanganyika prior to independence: A study of conflicting social and political interracial roles. *Race* VII (3):289–302

Willis P (1977) *Learning to Labour: How Working-Class Kids get Working-Class Jobs*. Farmborough: Saxon House

Part 2

Domesticity and Other Homely Spaces of Modernity

Chapter 4

Domesticating Birth in the Hospital: "Family-Centered" Birth and the Emergence of "Homelike" Birthing Rooms

Maria Fannin

Introduction

"Home away from home" is the catchphrase of modern hospital birth-center promotional literature. This sentiment of displaced domesticity reflects the recent transformations of birthing rooms in hospitals across the United States over the last several decades.[1] "Normal" birth no longer takes place in the "alienating," "sterile," and "stark" environment of the modern hospital room that was so criticized by natural childbirth and home-birth activists as indistinguishable in its brutalism from the wards of the physically and mentally ill. Hospital rooms have been transformed into "homelike" spaces, with hardwood floors, brightly colored bedspreads, rocking chairs, and carefully designed cabinetry that masks medical equipment (see Figure 1). Most of these rooms feature private bathrooms—perhaps even a whirlpool bath—and other amenities not usually available elsewhere in the hospital: accommodations for an overnight guest, a gourmet postpartum picnic basket. Laboring mothers are encouraged to bring videocassettes, CDs, and personal photos with them to the hospital for their short stay, and the birth-center promotional literature abounds with pronouncements of the individuality and uniqueness of birth. The newly "personal" environment of the hospital is offered as evidence of a transformed medical philosophy that no longer views childbirth as pathological. Birth is now so natural, these texts seem to say, that it belongs at *home*.

In this essay, I examine the emergence of the homelike birthing room in contemporary US hospitals for how this complex shift transforms understandings of the domestic and the reproductive body. Reading these new hospital birthing rooms as *landscapes* of birth conceptually links the production of homelike birthing spaces with the increasing

Figure 1: The birthing room in the Porter Memorial Obstetrics Unit, Denver, Colorado as a soon-to-be mother might see it on a tour of the hospital's obstetrics unit. Part of a $1,040,000 renovation in 1988. Source: American Institute of Architects (1988). Photographer: T John Hughes

pressures on the hospital to corporatize under the rhetoric of a competitive health-care market. Such a reading permits the analysis of both the material and the discursive production of spaces and identities at the scale of the hospital room, linking their mutually constitutive production and reproduction to the neoliberal economic logics that blur the boundaries between market, home, and hospital. The "domestication" of hospital space, theorized both as a response to demand by middle-class consumers of birth and as an attempt by hospitals to market a particular kind of birth, can thus be understood at the nexus of social reproduction and economic production. The cultural production of birthing spaces cannot be separated from the increasing economic pressures on US hospitals in the last several decades to market services to new "consumers" of birth, and these landscapes of cultural production are intimately bound to interpellations of new subjectivities around birth. As the landscape of the birthing room spatially reiterates the performance of birth as *domestic*, the consumption of birth in the hospital by middle-class, professional consumers is reinscribed as the norm.

Criticism of the "austerity" of hospital space has become quite commonplace, and the design literature speaks of "minimizing fear and discomfort"—of the "harsh clinical atmosphere" associated with "ominous-appearing high-tech medical equipment." The shifts toward more homelike birthing rooms in the space of the hospital are often linked to the idea that hospitals are becoming places of wellness, not illness. In order to attract well people, hospitals are being designed with residential criteria in mind (Mayer 1989). While hospital designers and architects are attempting to use space to create these new meanings, the extent to which these meanings (the hospital as a space of "wellness") circulate outside the hospital is uncertain. Yet the increasingly shorter postpartum stays in hospitals and the prevalence of outpatient surgery—or even separate surgical centers—mean that hospitals, once again, are not places where one remains to "get well." The environment of the hospital is described as "inevitably quite frightening," and, at the request of hospital administrators, designers attempt to make hospitals more "welcoming and comfortable" (Mayer 1989:235). The solution that many designers have employed is simply to attempt to hide the medical equipment behind paneled cabinets or fabric screens. This yields curiously hybrid spaces, provoking a host of questions. Why have hospitals changed their birthing rooms, and what sorts of *spatialities* do these rooms employ to marshal claims to being the "best of both worlds," or a "home away from home"? How do these centers shape women's notions of "normal" childbirth? What currency of meaning do hospitals attempt to create in a more "homelike" setting? And how are homelike birthing rooms negotiations of struggles over conceptualizations of *safety*, *control*, and *family*, and thus over the very meaning of birth itself?

Representations of birth are (always) spatial, yet, until recently, popular and academic works on birth tended to elide the significance of the changing spatiality of birth. As my research demonstrates, birth is a *spatial* as well as a *social* process, bound up with discursive and material representations that mobilize certain historically and geographically contingent spatial metaphors. I examine the mobilization of these spatial metaphors, such as the homelike hospital room, in order to interrogate the tensions between the political economic and the cultural significance of birth. Much of the scholarly and popular work on childbirth has tended to dichotomize the spaces of home and hospital. I argue that the idealization of these spaces works to mask their cultural and economic production. In what follows, I unpack some of the structuring dualisms that frame contemporary debates over the appropriate spaces of birth, and I argue for increased attention to the mutually constitutive processes of the cultural production of birth spaces and recent economic transformations in health care. Such attention is necessary for understanding how landscapes of social reproduction

are actively created, both discursively and materially, through processes of economic transformation and the cultural mobilization of
spatial metaphors.

Domestic Aesthetics and Medical Camouflage

In the early 1970s, as increasing number of hospitals across the nation
began to emphasize "family-centered care," the transformation of
birthing rooms materialized this shift in the status of birth as a family
event. These birthing rooms incorporated elements of the domestic
bedroom into the hospital: rugs, curtains, pictures, rocking chairs, and
—rarely—double beds. These changes were generally characterized as
responses to increasing pressure from parents' associations and birthing women themselves for more "humane" birthing experiences.
Activists of an alternative childbirth movement that emerged most
vocally during the 1960s and 1970s held out domestic spaces as "places"
with particular meanings for birthing women (Abel and Kearns 1991).
"Home" was posited as a site of autonomy and control, where familiarity
and continuity of care figured into decisions about where to give birth
(Abel and Kearns 1991:832). The transformations of hospital rooms,
which continued through the 1980s and 1990s, were often described—
particularly by advocates of home birth—as a co-optation of the home
birth movement (De Vries 1985; Ruzek 1978). Competition with home
birth was often the justification for changes in a hospital's management
of birth. In 1981, a survey of hospitals in the state of Washington
linked hospitals' shifts toward birthing rooms to the perceived incid-
ence of home births, even though home births have never been more
than 1% of total births in the US since the 1970s (Dobbs and Shy 1981).
Many home-birth advocates thus saw the hospitals' transformation of
hospital birthing rooms into "homelike" spaces as an appropriation of
the symbolic meanings of home that masked a continuation of medical
control and management and the persistence of a conceptualization of
birth and women's bodies as pathological (Sullivan and Weitz 1988:144).

The rhetoric of competition is evident in contemporary birthing-
room literature, as hospitals herald their newest transformation into
birthing centers in the hopes of attracting the middle-class consumer
of birth. For example, the administrators of Miami Baptist Hospital
wanted their Family Birth Center to be "the nicest place around for
having babies" (Gaskie 1990:98). Architects attempted to transform
the postpartum unit into a deliberately "nonclinical setting" with custom furniture, including armoires in each room that hide a television,
music equipment, and a refrigerator. The consumers of such custom
birth environments are often assumed to be the happy heterosexual
couples that grace birthing-center literature, for the rooms also feature
"oversize sleeper chairs that allow fathers to comfortably join mother
and babies overnight, and—of course—rocking chairs" (Gaskie 1990:

100). In an article describing the transformation of a Chicago hospital's labor/delivery/recovery/postpartum (LDRP) rooms to birthing "suites," the author writes that "Getting the woman out of the corridors meant bringing the medical equipment to her, and keeping it well out of sight except during the short time it is actually in use" (Davidsen 1990:192). The bulkiest equipment is hidden behind a folding fabric-covered wall. The bed covered in a quilt can be quickly converted to a labor table, then a delivery table, and then back to a bed. Like most of the newly designed hospital birthing suites, the room described is a kind of doubled space, bearing signs of both the domestic and the highly technological: "An upholstered headboard attached to the wall slides away to reveal outlets for oxygen, air, and suction vacuum for use in case of emergency. The nightstand houses blood pressure and fetal monitors. The examining light drops down from a ceiling recess on an articulated arm when needed" (Davidsen 1990:193). "Residential criteria" become important in the transformation of a hospital room to a "birthing suite." "Comforting aspects"—such as quilted coverlets and pillow shams, pastel paint, and rocking chairs—are featured prominently in the industry literature on LDRP renovations (Cohen 1991:116). The interior design of the rooms draws heavily on a middle-class aesthetic of domestic heterosexual and familial space, and thus marks a significant shift in the normative conceptions of birth.

The hospital's appropriation of domestic space places the *home* and the *hospital* in tension. This tension is evident in the discourses of safety and control that circulate in debates over the appropriate site of birth. Both home and hospital spaces are heavy with metaphoric connotations of safety, danger, alienation, and empowerment. In the hospital birthing room, this ambivalence over safety is reflected in the masking of highly sophisticated technology. For most women giving birth in homelike hospital rooms, however, the medical equipment will ultimately appear: fetal monitors, oxygen, perhaps an IV (see Figure 2). In the decades since the first appearance of homelike birthing rooms in late 1960s, technical intervention in hospital birth has increased. In 1965, less than 5% of births were delivered through Cesarean section; this rate increased steadily, to 17.9% in 1981 and 24.7% in 1988 (Eskew et al 1994:809). In 2001, the rate was 24.4% (Martin, Park, and Sutton 2002:3). Other interventions in birth have similarly increased over this period.[2] In 1989, 68% of women had electronic fetal monitoring at their births. By 2000, this number had increased to 84%. Ultrasounds increased from 48% in 1989 to 67% in 2000. Rates of induction and stimulation (the use of synthetic hormones to start labor or speed up uterine contractions) increased as well: induction rates increased from 9% in 1989 to 19.9% in 2000, and stimulation rates increased from 11% in 1989 to 17.9% in 2000 (Curtin and Park 1999:4; Martin et al 2002:13–14). This increase in

Figure 2: The same room during labor and delivery. Source: American Institute of Architects Press (1988). Photographer: T John Hughes

obstetric interventions occurred simultaneously with the emergence of a new rhetoric of birth that attempted to de-emphasize the technological nature of the hospital and emphasize birthing women's role as consumers.

In effect, the hospital's shift to homelike birthing rooms is an attempt to spatially mediate conflicts over the very meaning of reproduction through mobilization of the signs of the domestic. Placing birth in the homelike space of the hospital birthing room situates the birthing woman within both domestic and institutional space—equally ambivalent sites with respect to women's political agency. Likewise, the tensions between the economic pressures on hospitals to profit from complicated births and the uncomplicated nature of most births materializes in the masking of technological sophistication behind the mundane trappings of domesticity. The uncertainty over birth enacted in the hospital birthing room—at once homelike and highly technological—points to the very epistemological uncertainties around birth in the contemporary United States, in an era when the hospital's hegemony over birth is being challenged both by birth activists and by a climate of increasing privatization and competition for a decreasing number of middle-class births.

The Limits of "Home versus Hospital"

Many scholars of birth have documented the 20th-century shift in the place of birth from home to hospital, and have analyzed the effect of this spatial shift on the increasing interventions by medical professionals in the process of birth (see Leavitt 1986; Martin 1987, 1992; Oakley 1984; Rich 1976). Contemporary efforts to depathologize birth also have an explicitly spatial tack, as both home-birth and natural childbirth advocates foreground the importance of the *environment* of birth both to medical outcomes and to birth's "humanization" within a technocratic and profit-driven society. Until recently, however, much of the scholarly work on birth operated within the framework of dualisms that structure conventional or popular discourses around birth. Some authors, such as Barbara Katz Rothman (1982), link this geographical shift to the epistemological separation modern medicine mapped onto the mind/body dualism, enabling the very redefinition of birth as pathological (Rothman 1982). Rothman theorized the shift from home birth to hospital birth as a movement in which the private, woman-centered event of childbirth was colonized by a patriarchal society and moved into a public institution, with an attendant loss of women's political agency. Feminist scholars have noted the profoundly political implications of this movement of birth from private domestic space to the public institution of the hospital. Yet what emerged in much of the early literature on birth were two dichotomous spaces, mirroring the Cartesian separation of body and mind that Rothman and others would argue enables the very definition of birth as a surgical event.

Much of the early scholarship around childbirth thus explicitly reproduced a dualism: home is positive; hospital is negative. This binary mode of thinking forecloses the possibility of other understandings of these spaces, plotting a potentially rigid framework onto historically and geographically contingent spaces. Criticisms of the midwifery movement's emphasis on home birth and conceptualizations of the "natural" from women who are empowered by their experiences in the hospital point to the limits of such "sociospatial dualisms" (to borrow a term from Gleeson and Kearns 2001) for theorizing a more liberatory politics of birth. Feminist critics of midwifery's reliance on the dualism of medical/ natural have aptly demonstrated the limits of such binaristic thinking regarding women's reproductive capacities and the complicity with hegemonic understandings of childbirth that such dualisms create (Annandale and Clark 1996).

The homelike hospital room complicates the weakness of the moralistic dualism of home and hospital. Indeed, the homelike hospital room can be read as the "domestication" of a formerly public and institutional space that produces a *hybrid* space, ambivalently situated as a site of domestic comfort and technological sophistication. This ambivalence is evident in the concern many midwives express over the homelike hospital room's potential as "deinstitutionalized" space still firmly situated within an institution. The blurring of boundaries between home and hospital occurs in other arenas as well, as recent research on the growing industry of home health care makes clear. The transformation of the home into a health-care workplace (see Brown and Colton 2001) and the deinstitutionalization of many functions of the health-care industry (see Gleeson and Kearns 2001) demonstrate the increasing dissolution of divisions between home and hospital or institution and community.

More recent scholarly work has attempted to unpack the debates over "natural" versus "medical" and "hospital" versus "home." Geographers and other scholars have begun to query the significance of the spatiality of contemporary pregnancy and birth, in an attempt to map the cultural and political production of spaces and bodies.[3] Scott Sharpe's (1999) study of the discursive constructions of an alternative birth center in Sydney, Australia challenges the binary of home and hospital while placing the "territorial element" at the center of contemporary debates over childbirth. Sharpe (1999:94) argues that the representation of the hospital as patriarchal and home birth as wholly natural relies on static notions of the spaces of birth that obscure the ways in which "the debate itself constructs spaces and bodies." Thus, the terms of this debate reiterate potentially limiting discourses within which women can narrate a "successful" birth. Such narratives, Sharpe argues, are evacuated of historical or geographical specificity and leave little discursive space for narratives of "failed" home birth or empowering hospital birth.

Other critical work on the "territorial element" of birth points to the rhetorical uses of home and hospital within the literature on birth. Helena Michie's (1998:261) insightful article on the ways in which the "domestic" is employed by home-birth advocates and in feminist literature on home birth cites the numerous ways in which the popular representation of childbirth in the US is enabled by norms of class and gender identity, "deriv[ing] its power and its idiom from a deeply middle-class and heterosexual ideal of domesticity." Michie (1998:263) notes that the power of the narrative told and retold recounting birth's shift from home to hospital relies on the unquestioned "rhetorical status of home" as a site of security, safety, and autonomy. Michie argues that the complex meanings surrounding both "home" and "hospital" are never firmly attached to material spaces. Citing home-birth advocates' claims of the superior safety of the home compared to the potential dangers—interventive, infectious, psychic —of the hospital, she posits the home as an "unstable signifier," its meaning contingent on social, historical, and geographical specificities that produce "home" as an ambivalent space. The idealization of home is problematic, given its status as the site of both women's reproductive and productive labor. Home does not signify autonomy and bodily control for all women, nor is domestic space always the safest place for women (Michie 1998:262). Statistics on the higher rates of domestic violence against pregnant women point to the very real dangers of reifying the domestic as a site of women's empowerment (Fine and Weis 2000).

In the hospital's references to domestic space, the home functions as an "enabling fantasy as a place of free choice over one's body, a context safe for the exercise of will, body, and desire" (Michie 1998:261). This fantasy is historically specific and contingent on an understanding of a particular white, middle-class maternal subject. The literature on home birth also tends to assume an audience of upper-middle-class educated women, neglecting other women who give birth at home: religious or conservative women who view birth as a family-centered event in which the father's wishes are paramount; and poor or very young women for whom hospital birth is not an option (Michie 1998: 263).[4] The rural woman who cannot afford to travel to a distant hospital and the teenager who is hiding her pregnancy may both give birth at home, but under very different circumstances than the empowered maternal subject of much contemporary home-birth activism. Likewise, much of this literature posits the hospital as the site of either women's victimization or their false consciousness under a patriarchal medical system. The limits to these tropes of agency, or lack of it, are thus brought into tension when the *hospital* begins to mimic the *home*.

The domestic is reiterated as the "natural" site of women's agency, yet control of the body and of the process of birth in the hospital birthing room is often translated into control over the landscape of birth at its most superficial: the lighting, the choice of music, and so on. The narrative of home to hospital thus relies on a "revalencing of home and hospital with respect to safety and danger" that has been geographically and historically contingent, bearing different relationships to different women in particular times and places (Michie 1998:262). In the 1920s and 1930s, upper-middle-class women were among the most outspoken proponents of developments in anesthesia that promised painless birth in the hospital.[5] The contemporary struggles of poor women and women of color for fair treatment and access to medical care in the hospital complicate debates over home birth that focus solely on the rhetoric of safety and danger.

Complicating the well-worn tale of the shift from home to hospital, as another scholar of birth, Della Pollock (1999), writes, the home was not always the haven of private heteronuclear familial relations as it functions in the contemporary US. Rather, Pollock (1999:11) characterizes the move from home to hospital by the way in which "bodily life was disentangled from the social rites and economics in which it was traditionally enmeshed. Birthing, like dying, was removed from domestic public spaces. Domestic spaces, in turn, ceased to be public." Pollock cites urbanization and women's increasing mobility in the late 19th-century US for the breakdown of women's social networks, displacing birth from the web of social relations within which it had been located. Pollock locates this transformation within the larger context of industrialization in which hospital birth was imbued with value. The Enlightenment promise of technological and scientific progress made the hospital "seem not only a practical but a necessary alternative" to homebirth (Pollock 1999:12). Relying on notions of control that were shared by many birthing women, doctors claimed the relentless drive towards "modern" birth would reduce infant and maternal mortality and streamline the birth process and the birthing body under the model of industrial production.

Such close scholarly attention to the mutually constitutive cultural, political, and economic production of birth challenges the tendency to isolate birth from the context within which many scholars and activists have viewed the process. In the following section, I examine more closely the popular discourses of birth that link economic production with social reproduction. I highlight the ways in which birth was constructed as a "family" event in the hospital, "domesticating" birth both discursively and materially in the hospital. This shift in the conceptualization of birth is reiterated in the hospital through the mobilization of domestic metaphors that reflect the hospital industry's attempts to encourage middle-class women to become consumers of birth.

Industrial Reproduction and "Family-Centered" Birth

There's nothing natural about natural birth. (Smith 1979:118)

For most urban and suburban middle-class women in the United States, childbirth became an increasingly medical phenomenon through the 1940s and 1950s. In the South, "granny" midwives continued to attend the births of children born to poor black women, and in rural areas far distant from hospitals, midwives were a necessity if no doctor was available.[6] For the majority of women in the United States, however, medical birth was becoming the norm, and medical technology was often given credit for decreasing the maternal and infant mortality rate, due to increased sanitation, antibiotics, and other public-health improvements. By 1955, 95% of women in the US delivered their babies in hospitals (McQueen 1966:93). Hospital birth was often lauded as the scientific management of a spontaneous and unpredictable process, and hospital birth was reformulated as the "norm." Hospital birth also signified economic and social status. The mechanization of birth was its modernization, and, as such, was the enactment of difference between the middle-class suburban woman and the rural or inner-city poor. In the context of the idealization of middle-class women's domestic roles and the value attached to middle-class women's reproductive responsibilities, childbirth was framed both as a supreme act of womanhood and as the female citizen's duty to the nation (Strong-Boag et al 1999). This vision of motherhood, shaped around a white, middle-class, heterosexual ideal, served to exclude women outside those boundaries of race, class, and sexuality.

However, frequent medical interventions in a "natural" process within the hospital led some middle-class women to resist obstetric definitions of the body as abnormal until proven otherwise. The hospital was increasingly criticized for its mechanization of birth, the process likened to Fordist production. As one obstetrician commented in a July 1953 article in *Cosmopolitan*, "We handle patients with the same assembly-line technique that has proved so efficient in turning out motor cars. It is a sad commentary on our sense of values that we inflict this on sensitive young women going through the supreme emotional experience of their lives" (Pollack 1953:39). While expressing concern for the dehumanizing effects of "modern" birth, the paternalism explicit in this invocation of birth as the "supreme emotional experience" of "sensitive young women" reinforces the roles ascribed to middle-class women in the early 1950s. The "sensitive young women" giving birth in the hospital were expected to find their greatest sense of pleasure in their roles as mothers. The metaphor of the body as a machine, or "material object" of control, thus relied on and affirmed deeply held convictions regarding the seemingly inexorable process of industrialization that characterized the period from the late 19th to the mid-20th century (Pollack 1999:13). The unpredictable process of birth was streamlined in its shift to the hospital, and the model of assembly-line production that supported this shift reified birth as an event controllable by technological intervention and scientific rationality. The "scientific" assumptions of women's bodily processes as chaotic formed the underlying rationale for technological control.

In the 1940s and 1950s, a discourse of "family-centered" birth emerged that challenged the notion of the mechanized birthing body and put increasing pressures on hospitals to change their practices. Family-centered birth usually included the presence of the husband during an unmedicated or "natural" labor and delivery in a single room, with the "rooming-in" of the newborn with the mother after birth. Grantly Dick-Read's book *Childbirth without Fear*, an early exposition on "natural birth" published in the United States in 1944, attributed pain in childbirth to women's fear and tension over an unfamiliar process. Dick-Read's book gained popularity among middle-class women, even as obstetricians criticized it for its "unscientific" foundations on a "messianic vision of motherhood" (Caton 1999:177). Though much of what Dick-Read espoused was nothing new in the medical profession, early accounts of "natural" childbirth promoted it as the "child's birthright" and stated that "conscious motherhood is the supreme experience for a woman" ("A mother" 1948:86). This idealization of "natural," or drug-free, birth characterized the woman who asked for or received anesthesia as a failure. "Women should be ashamed of other kinds of birth," one early proponent of natural birth proclaimed (Anderson 1956:36). Women who accepted or requested anesthesia in the hospital were thought selfish, disregarding the potential effects of anesthesia on their babies, and in some instances were viewed as shirking their God-given responsibility to endure the pain of birth.[7]

The institutionalization of birth that the medical profession claimed had saved the lives of many women increasingly came under public criticism by middle-class women. Middle-class women interested in Dick-Read's methods often faced strong opposition from their doctors over employing techniques of "natural" childbirth within the hospital, and representations of the hospital in popular literature on birth during the 1950s were fraught with contradiction. One obstetrician's glowing overview of hospital birth in 1957 stated that "[N]ever before has there been a year like 1957, when birth is so devoid of risk, so free of pain, so perfect in result" (Guttmacher 1957:39). Yet the following year, the publication in the *Ladies Home Journal* of "Cruelty in the Maternity Ward," a letter describing the conditions under which many women gave birth in the hospital, sparked intense public debate over the modern hospital's medical management of childbirth (Schultz 1958). The hospital and the home were polarized in these emerging debates over the appropriate space of birth. The characterization of the hospital as "inhumane" constituted the space of the middle-class home as its potential alternative, and the "homelike" hospital room as a means to manage this crisis around birth.

As much as Dick-Read's methods challenged traditional obstetrics, the women who pushed for natural childbirth in the hospital did so within a paternalist, middle-class, and heteronormative understanding of women's reproductive roles (Sandelowski 1984). Indeed, many of the early public advocates of natural birth in the medical profession were male obstetricians. Robert Bradley, who popularized a set of natural birth techniques known as the "Bradley Method," encouraged husbands to "coach" their pregnant wives through pregnancy, labor, and delivery. He recommended husbands watch their wives while they slept in order to advise their wives of their most natural position and thus direct them through the birthing process (Yarrow 1982).

The surveillance of the birthing woman by her husband through pregnancy, labor, and delivery extended paternal authority from the home to the hospital, and birth, reconceptualized as a "family" event, affirmed the heterosexual couple as the primary participants in the process of birth. Conventional hospital birth separated husbands from their wives. The framing of this separation as a deviance from the "natural" served to naturalize the heterosexual married couple and reconfigure the heteronormative family as the appropriate relationship within which birthing women became mothers. In contrast with the circle of female friends and acquaintances that had accompanied birthing women in previous decades, or the triad of obstetrician, nurse, and birthing women that characterized early hospital birth, "family-centered" childbirth stressed the "natural" rights of the father to participate in birth.

Increasing numbers of hospitals in major metropolitan areas began to offer family-centered care in the late 1960s and early 1970s, particularly hospitals in the northeast and on the West Coast, although these changes came slowly (Giles 1973:76). Forced to reconcile and accommodate birth as a social as well as biomedical process, hospitals became the contested terrain on which definitions of normative childbirth and the normative family were negotiated and consolidated. The "domestication" of hospital space thus emerged at the same moment in which a specific ideal of the appropriate family materialized around birth in the hospital. The gradual redefining of birth's primary location within the heterosexual family eventually became synonymous with the material representation of the "home" in the homelike birthing room, and these changes in hospital birth practices naturalized the heteronormative family as the appropriate site of birth. "Family-centered birth" became the catchphrase for a set of changes in the philosophy and practice of birth in the hospital, and the homelike birthing room further inscribed birth as an enactment of domesticity in the space of the hospital.

These cultural shifts, reflected as birth moved from the home to the hospital and then to the homelike space of the hospital, were not simply effects of the consolidation of ideologies of gender in the family. They must also be considered in terms of the broader political economic transformations in the United States during the latter half of the 20th century.

Capital, Bodies, and Hybrid Hospital Space

The shift in birth from the home to the hospital reflected broader concerns over social reproduction, and the forms of that shift supported the societal transformations wrought by industrial production. The postindustrial landscape of early 21st-century health and medicine is intimately linked to the material shifts in contemporary childbirth and the discursive constructions of birth through the homelike hospital room. The growing *corporatization* of the hospital industry in the latter half of the 20th century, increasingly dominated by national and multinational firms, and its *proprietarization*—in which nonprofits begin to act more and more like for-profit firms—have led scholars to describe the contemporary period as one of increasing *privatization* of hospitals and of the health-care industry in general (McLafferty 1989:133).

The dominant discourse within the health-care industry in the 1970s and into the 1980s was cost containment, and the rhetoric of rapidly escalating health-care costs justified the privatization of health care and hospitals. The number of investor-owned (for-profit) hospitals grew dramatically, with the proportion of services provided by for-profit hospitals increasing by 50% in these two decades and the number of hospital beds owned by for-profit firms almost doubling between 1972 and 1983, from 57,000 to 94,000 (Schlesinger et al 1987:27). Between 1980 and 1995, 348 public hospitals converted to private, nonprofit status, while 231 converted to for-profit status (Hudson 1997, citing Needleman, Chollet, and Lamphere 1997). During this time, pressure on public and nonprofit hospitals to behave like for-profit hospitals increased, and for-profit firms began providing management and con-sulting services for these hospitals. These trends increased through the 1980s. By 1981, 278 hospitals were being managed by for-profit firms, an increase of 40% over the number in 1980 (Salmon 1990:65). In the 1980s, 698 acute-care hospitals closed, with the number of closures increasing in the latter part of the decade to a high of 88 in 1988 (*Hospitals* 1990).

Public hospitals were particularly susceptible to closure, as they served large numbers of uninsured patients whose care was subsidized by a shrinking number of privately insured patients. The closure of urban community hospitals through the 1980s and the transfer or "dumping" of poor patients from private hospital emergency rooms to public hospitals put severe strains on diminishing public resources (Whiteis and Salmon 1987). The number of public hospitals decreased 33% between 1980 and 1999, from 1778 to 1197, while the number of private hospitals decreased by only 7% during the same period, from 4052 in 1980 to 3759 in 1999 (Jaklevic 2001). The calculus of profit-ability and market-driven competition also justified hospital administrators' moves to downsize, with a 40% loss in hospital beds between 1975 and 1995 (*Health Care Strategic Management* 1999). Downsizing accompanied the trends towards converting acute-care hospitals (for brief but serious illnesses) into outpatient facilities and the divestiture of services with low profit margins—including wellness classes, rehabilitation, substance abuse, and mental-health services—in favor of investment in more profitable departments, such as neuro-surgery, organ transplants, cardiology, and oncology (Greene 1989:30).

These trends in privatization also represented shifts in the corporate control over health care. Large, for-profit, multinational firms grew rapidly in the 1970s and 1980s. By 1987, four major for-profit firms, Hospital Corporation of America, Humana, American Medical International, and National Medical Enterprises, operated almost 15% of all domestic hospital beds, and almost 70% of all for-profit beds (Berliner and Regan 1987:1280). The privatization of public-health services and the dramatic growth of large, for-profit firms in the health-care industry were justified by the rhetorics of decreasing profitability (particularly among hospitals with large number of uninsured patients) and increasing competition that reflected the increasingly corporatized nature of the US health-care system.

The competitive rhetoric that fueled much of the changes in hospital birthing rooms was attributed, in part, to decreasing enrollments in hospital obstetric units in the 1970s, as women's workforce participation increased and birth rates steadily decreased. In 1957, the birth rate had reached its peak, at 25.3 per 1000 people. Through the 1960s, the number of births steadily declined by an average of 2.2% each year, with a dramatic decrease between 1970 and 1973 of an average of 5.3% each year (Taffel 1977). By 1975, the birth rate had reached a then-historic low of 14.6 births per 1000 people (Martin et al 2002).[8] Hospitals' concerns about the decreasing numbers of births and the decline in deliveries—particularly at hospitals with small obstetrics units—fueled discussions of changes to traditional hospital practices (Anderson 1976; Shanklin 1972). These trends—combined with the low profitability of obstetrics, especially for uncomplicated vaginal births—were compounded by increasing resistance to the medical management of birth within the hospital by the very population upon which hospital revenues for patient fees depended: middle-class women.

Faced with decreases in their birth censuses, hospitals administrators' options were to eliminate obstetrics altogether, to specialize in high-risk obstetrics and establish neonatal intensive care units that would provide additional revenue, or to attempt to capture the majority of normal births by specializing in "normal" obstetrics and drawing women into hospitals with a "family-centered," homelike atmosphere (Sender 1977). Although homelike birthing rooms varied widely in terms of practices, marketing research demonstrated that single-room maternity care—an integral part of the homelike birthing room philosophy—was attracting women to hospitals where it was offered. In addition to the increased markets for birth, such single-room care also meant hospitals paid less for nursing and other labor costs. No longer would nurses specialize in particular aspects of nursing; instead, they would care for women and babies through every aspect of labor, birth, and recovery (Super 1987:128). While birthing rooms were rarely highly profitable, they introduced women—and, by extension, their families—to a hospital's services (Kingsley 1986:16). Although it can be seen as a response to birthing women's demands for more comfortable environments in which to give birth, the impetus for this shift toward homelike birthing spaces was also the potential for increased profits from accommodating satisfied consumers of birth who might later choose the hospital for more life-threatening—and profitable —procedures (Ngeo 1998:34; Wallace 1985:52, 56). The logic of this calculation by hospitals lies in women's roles as health-care "gate-keepers" or decision-makers in families. Emphasizing education and choice, health-care marketing targets women's traditional roles as nurturers, yet constructs the family's dependency on women as a source of empowerment.

The increasing corporatization of the hospital also brought about transformations in the discourse of birth, revalenced in marketing terms that figure natural childbirth as a "product in the obstetrics product line" (France and Grover 1992:32). In a sense, the homelike birthing room is the coalescence of conflicting tensions under the marketization of health care. On the one hand, the focus on "natural" birth and fewer interventions and the increase in midwifery care was one response to the impetus for cost reduction. Midwifery care is less interventive and thus less costly than obstetrical care. On the other hand, the hospital birthing room bears, behind its floral wallpaper and wood-grain cabinets, all the highly specialized instruments that support the increasing technologization of birth, increasing interventions, and increased capital flows into the hospital. This tension is visible in the contradictions of the hospital birthing room, as well as inherent in the production of the contemporary birthing subject as consumer.

The "naturalization" of birth in domestic space also proves problematic for feminist understandings of the reproductive body (Michaelson 1988). Contemporary medical and legal discourses around pregnancy posit the pregnant body as antagonistic to the fetus, now given the rights and legal status of a whole person. Lauren Berlant (1994:169) argues that the increasing distance between the woman and the fetus (enabled by technologies that make her transparent or "evaporate" her) is both a condition of technical irrelevancy and a *political erasure*, since all reproduction is now public. Representations of the womb as a container or an empty space reflect the profound unease the pregnant body poses to theories of a unified, singular subject. Iris Marion Young (1990:163) conceptualizes the pregnant body in explicitly spatial terms in her discussion of pregnancy's material manifestation of a fragmented and fluid subjectivity, "rendering fluid the boundary between what is within, myself, and what is outside, separate." The pregnant body possesses the fluidity and ambiguity of an embodied subjectivity that is both self and other, in which "the transparent unity of self dissolves" (Young 1990:161). In the domesticated hospital, it is the body of the baby, not the birthing mother—to paraphrase a caption of the interior-design literature—that is the "only physical evidence that anything particularly momentous has taken place in the peach and Wedgwood blue room" (Davidsen 1990:193). The discourse of choice and control that situates the birthing woman as a consumer of birth does not necessarily imply autonomy or embodied agency for the birthing woman in the hospital birthing room.

The tensions between neoliberal pressures to privatize, the creation of new subjectivities for birthing women, and the fluidity of identifications with domestic space produce the homelike birthing room as an ambivalent space. Birth in the latter half of the 20th century is increasingly domesticated *within* the hospital through the production of homelike spaces, reflecting and sustaining the privatization of the hospital under a neoliberal discourse of competition. Competitive pressures to cut costs thus enable the production of normative homelike birthing rooms, ideologically sustaining birth consumers' desires for more humanizing births. The "specter of the perfect birth" invoked in the homelike hospital birthing room is powerful; it is the tension between notions of safety and control that figure in both domestic and medical space that hospitals elide in the homelike birthing room (Michie 1998:260). The safety promised by the hospital's technological armamentarium cannot be found elsewhere, yet homelike hospital birth brings its own unique risks beyond those of unnecessary interventions. Highly publicized kidnappings from hospital nurseries have required sophisticated security systems; the increasingly common practice of babies "rooming in" with their mothers is seen as ensuring an even safer environment. Significant responsibility for the security of the baby in the hospital thus falls on the mother. In the hospital, women are instructed repeatedly by tour guides, nurses, and hospital literature to check the identification cards of anyone who asks for the baby, and to verify any request to take the baby out of the room.

Medical discourses of birth framed in terms of healthy "outcomes" often reflect hospitals' anxieties over potential malpractice suits. A 1986 article on the new homelike birthing suites in a Chicago hospital argued that "[N]ew birthing suites may curb maternity malpractice suits … [T]he pleasant surroundings and the easy-going attitude of the medical professionals might lessen the chances that a woman would sue because of the slightest complication … In these surroundings, the patient may be more understanding" (Carter 1986:48). Woman's docility is thus reinscribed in the domesticated space of the hospital, her anger over potential medical complications negated by the "pleasant surroundings." As Michie (1998:261), whose work I outlined earlier, argues, "[O]ne cannot escape the discipline of the body by invoking the site of that discipline." In other words, the home as the site of women's bodily disciplining cannot easily be reworked as emancipatory. The home as a potential site of gender and sexual discipline in general makes the valuation of domestic space in the hospital suspect.

Conclusion

The continuously shifting definitions of normative birth and appropriate spaces for birth suggest a fluidity of meaning that is often overlooked in ahistorical and despatialized invocations of home and hospital. The dualism of home and hospital in scholarly literature on birth leaves out the ways in which biomedical and economic imperatives of corporatization and privatization constantly constrain and create the subjects they regulate. Even to speak of a dominant paradigm in birth glosses over the struggles that ensue constantly over how to define what is "normal," "natural"—indeed, over what is "safe," what is "modern." Homelike hospital rooms repeatedly draw on notions of domesticity and the naturalness of nonmedicalized birth, masking their technological sophistication and capital investment behind floral curtains and wood-paneled cabinets. But this transformation of hospital space from medical to homelike is also a reconfiguration of domesticity. For the brief time that most women and their partners, friends, and relatives spend in the hospital (48 hours, for most uncomplicated deliveries), the domesticated space of the hospital reiterates norms of motherhood, the family, and the relationship between the birthing woman's body and medical technology. This association of the home with natural birth can serve to naturalize women's reproduction in terms of the domestic as well, neglecting the ways in which domestic spaces and reproductive bodies are also technologically mediated. Most contemporary professional midwives provide prenatal care that relies on laboratory tests and physical exams for risk screening. Most midwives assisting home births carry with them a significant amount of medical equipment, including oxygen, IV, resuscitation equipment, antihemorrhagic drugs, and suturing material.

The establishment of homelike birth spaces is posited as a response both to the competitive postindustrial market in which hospitals are compelled to compete and to the increasing pressures from birthing women to create more comforting spaces in which to give birth. The creation of these hybrid spaces cannot be wholly lauded as progressive, but must be interrogated for their deployment within an increasingly corporatized hospital system. Hybrid identities and spaces are not unambiguously liberatory, and the material production of hybrid identities and spaces under economic imperatives requires critical attention (see Mitchell 1997). The move by hospitals to construct "homelike spaces" demonstrates how potentially radical challenges to the mechanization and medicalization of birth within the medical system are subsumed into a rhetoric of cost-effectiveness, consumerism, and patient rights that ideologically supports the downsizing and deregulation of the US health-care system. The representation of home within the hospital points to both the possibilities and the limits of the design and discourse of "home," as contemporary political-economic and cultural shifts transform the modernized and medicalized birthing subject in the United States from a patient into a consumer of birth, and as the site of birth is privatized and domesticated within the homelike hospital.

As a hybrid space that attempts to replicate particular understandings of *home* within a clearly bound notion of the domestic, but that also enacts material change in the structure and practices of the hospital, the hospital birthing room both disrupts and reworks the medical paradigm surrounding "normative" birth. The changing practices and philosophies of birth in the hospital demonstrate how social reproduction and economic production are inextricably linked. In the hospital birthing room, the heteronormative disciplining of the birthing woman's body, the creation of identities of consumption, and the production of new domestic spaces are mutually constitutive. The spatiality of birth in newly domesticated homelike birthing rooms is created both through political economic processes of privatization, corporatization, and the marketing of birth and through cultural and symbolic processes, which produce new desires and subjectivities that reify and reinscribe hospital birth as natural and the domestic as ideal.

Acknowledgments

The insightful comments of Katharyne Mitchell, Robyn Longhurst, Robin Kearns, and Nancy Duncan added immeasurably to this essay. Many thanks also to Maureen Hickey, Matt Sothern, and Catherine Veninga for their insightful comments, and to Kim England, Michael Brown, and Katherine Beckett for their support of this research.

Endnotes

[1] Hospitals in the US fall into several categories: urban teaching hospitals, associated with university medical education and research; typically not-for-profit private hospitals that receive tax exemptions because of their nonprofit status; publicly funded federal, state, and local government hospitals; and for-profit hospitals, many of which are owned by national or transnational hospital chains. Salmon (1990) discusses in detail the rapid growth of proprietary or for-profit health-care chains, the increasing trend to operate not-for-profit hospitals under management contracts with investor-owned firms, and the contraction of public hospitals.

[2] Comprehensive data on other obstetric interventions was not available until 1989, when the US birth certificate was modified to collect information on obstetric procedures.

[3] See Robin Kearns' 1993 essay suggesting new avenues of inquiry for medical geographers, "Place and Health: Towards a Reformed Medical Geography," in *The Professional Geographer.* Mike Dorn and Glenda Laws respond to Kearns' invitation in their 1994

article, "Social Theory, Body Politics, and Medical Geography: Extending Kearns' Invitation." Dorn and Laws (1994) suggest that the insights of feminists and cultural theorists can further enrich studies of the body and the specificities of place. For research on the pregnant body in social space, see Robyn Longhurst's work on pregnant women: "'Going Nuts': Re-presenting Pregnant Women" (1997) in *New Zealand Geographer*; "'Corporeographies' of Pregnancy: 'Bikini Babes'" (2000) in *Environment and Planning D: Society and Space*; and *Bodies: Exploring Fluid Boundaries* (2001).

[4] See Pamela E Klassen's 2001 article, "Sacred Maternities and Postbiomedical Bodies: Religion and Nature in Contemporary Home Birth" for an excellent examination of the natural and sacred body among home-birthing women in North America. Klassen argues that some women's sacralization of "natural" birth can be read as a reclamation of autonomy through the body.

[5] See Richard Wertz and Dorothy Wertz (1989) and Donald Caton (1999) for discussions of the move by wealthy feminist and suffragette women from the 1910s through the 1930s to promote Twilight Sleep, a mixture of an amnesiac, scopolamine, and morphine.

[6] See Margaret Smith and Linda Holmes' engaging life history of an Alabama midwife (1996).

[7] Curiously, women who chose home birth were likewise regarded as selfish by the medical community for putting their "values" above the safety of their baby. In this medical estimation of safety, the increasing autonomy of the fetus from the pregnant and birthing woman places the interests of the mother and baby into conflict, when the mother's interest is defined solely in terms of the process of birth and the baby's "interest" solely in terms of outcome.

[8] The birth rate remained low through the 1980s, increasing slightly to 16.7 in 1990. Between 1990 and 1997, the rate decreased 13%. The birth rate for 2000 was 14.7 per 1000 people (Martin et al 2002).

References

"A mother" (1948) I had my 3rd baby without anesthetic. *Parents* 23:18–19, 86

Abel S and Kearns R A (1991) Birth places: A geographical perspective on planned home birth in New Zealand. *Social Science and Medicine* 33(7):825–834

American Institute of Architects (1988) *Health Facilities Review: 1988 Selected Projects.* Washington, DC: American Institute of Architects Press

Anderson J (1976) Alternative birth center gives parents a new option. *Hospital Forum* 19(2):4–5

Anderson M A (1956) The fresh look at natural childbirth. *Parents* 31:36

Annandale E and Clark J (1996) What is gender? Feminist theory and the sociology of human reproduction. *Sociology of Health and Illness* 18(1):17–44

Berlant L (1994) America, "fat," the fetus. *Boundary 2* 21(3):145–195

Berliner H S and Regan C (1987) Multinational operations of US for-profit hospital chains: Trends and implications. *American Journal of Public Health* 77(10): 1280–1284

Brown M and Colton T (2001) Dying epistemologies: An analysis of home death and its critique. *Environment and Planning A* 33(5):799–821

Butler J and Scott J (eds) (1992) *Feminists Theorize the Political.* New York: Routledge

Carter K (1986) Michael Reese's new birthing suites may curb maternity malpractice suits. *Modern Healthcare* 16:48

Caton D (1999) *What a Blessing She Had Chloroform.* New Haven, CT: Yale University Press

Cody L F (1999) The politics of reproduction: From midwives' alternative public sphere to the public spectacle of man-midwifery. *Eighteenth-Century Studies* 32:477–495

Cohen E L (1991) Burkett Building: A health-care facility for special services by Quantrell Mullins and Associates. *Interior Design* April:114–117

Curtin M A and Park M M (1999) Trends in the attendant, place, and timing of births, and in the use of obstetric interventions: United States, 1989–97. *National Vital Statistics Reports* 47(27):1–13

Davidsen J (1990) Birthing center: A hospitable hospital room by Loebl Schlossman and Hackl. *Interior Design* November:192–195

De Vries R G (1985) *Regulating Birth: Midwives, Medicine, and the Law*. Philadelphia: Temple University Press

Dick-Read G (1944) *Childbirth without Fear*. New York: Harper and Brothers

Dobbs K B and Shy K K (1981) Alternative birth rooms and options. *Obstetrics and Gynecology* 58:626–630

Dorn M and Laws G (1994) Social theory, body politics, and medical geography: Extending Kearns' invitation. *The Professional Geographer* 46:106–110

Eskew P N, Saywell R M, Zollinger T W, Erner B K and Oser T L (1994) Trends in the frequency of Cesarean delivery: A 21-year experience, 1970–1990. *Journal of Reproductive Medicine* 39(10):809–817

Fine M and Weis L (2000) Disappearing acts: The state and violence against women in the twentieth century. *Signs* 25:1139–1146

France K R and Grover R (1992) What is the health-care product? *Journal of Health Care Marketing* 12:31–42

Gaskie M F (1990) Making special care special. *Architectural Record* June:98–101

Giles C D (1973) It takes two to have a baby. *Parents* 48:42–43, 72–74

Gleeson B and Kearns R (2001) Remoralising landscapes of care. *Environment and Planning D* 19(1):61–80

Greene J (1989) A strategy for cutting back. *Modern Healthcare* 19(33):29–47

Guttmacher A F (1957) Birth fears are out of date. *Parents* 32:39

Hayden D (1981) *The Grand Domestic Revolution*. Cambridge, MA: The MIT Press

Health Care Strategic Management (1999) Hospitals downsize, continue trend of increasing profitability during past decade. 17(3):6–7

Hospitals (1990) Total hospital closures in the 1980s hit 698. 64(12):16

Hudson T (1997) "Faster. Stronger. Private?" *Hospitals and Health Networks* 71(13): 22–26

Jaklevic M C (2001) Hospital closure pace still high. *Modern Healthcare* 31:22

Kearns R (1993) Place and health: Towards a reformed medical geography. *The Professional Geographer* 45:139–147

Kingsley V (1986) Increasing market share through consumer marketing: A case study in obstetrics. *Health Care Strategic Management* 4(5):16–20

Klassen P E (2001) Sacred maternities and postbiomedical bodies: Religion and nature in contemporary home birth. *Signs: Journal of Women in Culture and Society* 26:775–809

Landes J B (ed) (1998) *Feminism, the Public, and the Private*. Oxford: Oxford University Press

Leavitt J W (1986) *Brought to Bed: Childbearing in America, 1750–1950*. New York: Oxford University Press

Lichty E (1950) Childbirth here and abroad. *Parents* 25:158

Longhurst R (1997) "Going nuts": Re-presenting pregnant women. *New Zealand Geographer* 53:34–39

Longhurst R (2000) "Corporeographies" of pregnancy: "Bikini babes." *Environment and Planning D: Society and Space* 18(4):453–472

Longhurst R (2001) *Bodies: Exploring Fluid Boundaries*. New York: Routledge

Martin E (1987) *The Woman in the Body*. Boston: Beacon Press

Martin E (1992) *The Woman in the Body*. 2nd ed. Boston: Beacon Press

Martin J A, Hamilton B E, Ventura S J, Menacker F and Park M M (2002) Births: Final data for 2000. *National Vital Statistics Report* 50(5):1–102

Martin J A, Park M M and Sutton P D (2002) Births: Preliminary data for 2001. *National Vital Statistics Reports* 50(10):1–20

Mayer R (1989) Hospitals under the knife. *Interior Design* February:234–235

McLafferty S L (1989) The politics of privatization: State and local politics and the restructuring of hospitals in New York City. In J L Scarpacci (ed) *Health Services Privatization in Industrial Societies* (pp 130–151). New Brunswick: Rutgers

McQueen R J C (1966) The obstetrical suite takes on new dimensions. *Hospitals* 40:93–97

Michaelson K L (1988) *Childbirth in America*. South Hadley, MA: Bergin and Garvey

Michie H (1998) Confinements: The domestic in the discourses of upper-middle-class pregnancy. In S H Aiken, A Brigham, S A Marston and P Waterston (eds) *Making Worlds* (pp 258–273). Tucson: University of Arizona Press

Mitchell K (1997) Different diasporas and the hype of hybridity. *Environment and Planning D: Society and Space* 15(5):533–553

Needleman J, Chollet D J and Lamphere J (1997) Hospital conversion trends. *Health Affairs* 16 (2):187–195

Ngeo C (1998) The first gatekeeper. *Modern Healthcare* 28:34

Oakley A (1984) *The Captured Womb*. Oxford: Basil Blackwell, Inc

Pateman C (1989) *The Disorder of Women*. Cambridge, UK: Polity Press

Pollack J H (1953) The case for natural childbirth. *Cosmopolitan* 135:38–43

Pollock D (1999) *Telling Bodies Performing Birth: Everyday Narratives of Childbirth*. New York: Columbia University Press

Rich A (1976) *Of Woman Born*. New York: Bantam Books

Rothman B K (1982) *In Labor: Women and Power in the Birthplace*. New York: W W Norton and Co

Ruzek S B (1978) *The Women's Health Movement: Feminist Alternatives to Medical Control*. New York: Praeger

Salmon J W (1990) Profit and health care: Trends in corporatization and proprietarization. In J W Salmon (ed) *The Corporate Transformation of Health Care* (pp 55–75). Amityville, NY: Baywood Publishing Company

Sandelowski M (1984) *Pain, Pleasure, and American Childbirth: From the Twilight Sleep to the Read Method, 1914–1960*. Westport, CT: Greenwood Press

Schlesinger M, Bentkover J, Blumenthal D, Musacchio R and Willer J (1987) The privatization of health care and physicians' perceptions of access to hospital services. *The Milbank Quarterly* 65(1):25–58

Schultz G D (ed) (1958) Response to "Cruelty in maternity wards." *Ladies Home Journal* 75:4, 58–59

Sender N (1977) Changing from orthodox to family-centered obstetrics. *The Journal of Reproductive Medicine* 19(5):295–297

Shanklin D R (1972) The birth rate, obstetricians, and primary medical care of women. *The Journal of Reproductive Medicine* 8(2):47

Sharpe S (1999) Bodily speaking: Spaces and experiences of childbirth. In E K Teather (ed) *Embodied Geographies* (pp 91–103). London: Routledge

Smith D G (1979) Viewpoint: Natural childbirth. *Glamour* 77:118

Smith M C and Holmes L J (1996) *Listen to Me Good: The Life Story of an Alabama Midwife*. Columbus: Ohio State University Press

Strong-Boag V, Dyck I, England K and Johnson L (1999) What women's spaces? Women in Australian, British, Canadian, and US suburbs. In R Harris and P Larkham (eds) *Changing Suburbs: Foundation, Form and Function* (pp 168–186). London: Routledge

Sullivan D A and Weitz R (1988) *Labor Pains: Modern Midwives and Home Birth*. New Haven, CT: Yale University Press

Super K E (1987) Single-room maternity care aiding hospitals. *Modern Healthcare* 17:128

Taffel S (1977) Trends in fertility in the United States. *Vital and Health Statistics* 21(28):3–4

Wallace C (1985) Women's healthcare spending new target of hospitals' ads. *Modern Healthcare* 15:52, 56

Wertz R and Wertz D (1989) *Lying-In: A History of Childbirth in America*. New Haven, CT: Yale University Press

Whiteis D and Salmon J W (1987) The proprietarization of health care and the underdevelopment of the public sector. *International Journal of Health Services* 17(1):47–64

Yarrow L (1982) Meet Dr. Bradley. *Parents* 57:60–64

Young I M (1990) *Throwing Like a Girl and Other Essays in Feminist Philosophy and Social Theory*. Bloomington: Indiana University Press

Chapter 5

Adolescent Latina Bodyspaces: Making Homegirls, Homebodies and Homeplaces

Melissa Hyams

Introduction

> The boys and the girls live in separate worlds ... My brothers, for
> example. They've got plenty to say to me and Nenny inside the
> house. But outside they can't be seen talking to girls ... Nenny is too
> young to be my friend ... And since she comes right after me, she is
> my responsibility. Someday I will have a best friend all my own ...
> Until then I am a red balloon, a balloon tied to an anchor. (Cisneros
> 1984:8–9)

In this essay, I explore the geographies of social reproduction as they
are comprehended and contested by young, US-born, low-income
Latinas[1] living in Los Angeles. The narratives of these young women
convey understandings of the local spaces and social relations in and
through which they negotiate coming of age. These are the spaces of
home and neighborhood, and of familial and friendship relations in
which they struggle for autonomy and affirmation.[2] Esperanza, the fictional character quoted above who is portrayed in Sandra Cisneros's
1984 novel, *The House on Mango Street*, conveys an experience of the
local, gendered "inside/outside" spatiality of power structuring the
day-to-day lives of these young women. Esperanza's self-identification
as an "anchored balloon" is an apt metaphor for the young women's
visceral experience of being tied, materially and discursively, to homely
spaces, while simultaneously struggling to "get out of the house."
They struggle against the discourses and regulatory practices that
allow them a sense of value and self-worth in the private, domestic
sphere, or "inside," but render them vulnerable in the public sphere,
or "outside."[3] Inside "homeplaces" and "homebodies" are constructed
and contested as autonomous, modest, ordered and safe, in a recur-
sive relationship to the making and resisting of "outside" urban

spaces and "homegirl"[4] subjectivities as dependent, indecent, violent and vulnerable.

The spatial ordering of Latina bodies and subjectivities must be understood in the context of Los Angeles' worsening "landscapes of neglect," attributable to the changing geographies of private and public investment in the city (Davis 1990; Valle and Torres 2000). Since the 1970s, changes in capitalist investment have bifurcated the Los Angeles economy, downgrading manufacturing jobs and skills and generating hugely disparate service-based employment opportunities and access to the means of securing and maintaining social reproduction (Brown et al 1998; Chang 2000; Sassen 1988, 1994; Trueba 1998). This economic restructuring mobilized a large number of Mexican migrants to move to Los Angeles in the 1970s and 1980s to take up employment in unskilled and low-skilled, low-wage manufacturing and service jobs. Many of these immigrants stayed to raise their families in LA, settling primarily in the eastside neighborhoods of the city and attempting to rebuild their homes and lives in these new locations. These immigrants are, for the most part, the parents of the young women whom I interviewed.

In this macro economic and social context, young Latinas are engaged daily in constructing and contesting shifting gender and generational divisions of labor in the material and symbolic reproduction of their homes. Where once they typically worked in the home *alongside* their mothers, adolescent women are now taking up positions as "homemakers" and as home-based child and health carers for younger siblings and infirm and aging adults as their mothers are increasingly drawn into the waged domestic-service economy (cf Chant 1987, 1991; Robson 1996, forthcoming). The older women are entering the labor force as resources for social reproduction are being withdrawn (cf Katz 1993, 1998). As a result of this labor-market shift, the adolescent practices of "going out" and "hanging out" of the house—always difficult for "good girls" to negotiate—are becoming more difficult for young women in poor neighborhoods. At the same time, disinvestment in safe public spaces for recreation or just "hanging out" is being combined with the increasing criminalization and surveillance of young people, particularly those who are identified as "nonwhite" (Lucas 1998; Valentine 1996a, 1996b).

Based on an analysis of the Latinas' narratives, I argue that this "inside/outside" dichotomy articulates the effects of heteropatriarchal power, both dominating and resisting power (Sharp et al 2000). Global processes of capitalist restructuring are inflected through local social and spatial inequalities, which, crucially, are worked out daily through the bodies of young Latina women (Foucault 1978). Young Latinas comprehend the dominant norms and materiality of an "inside/outside" dichotomy in bodily terms, and, in turn, places make or create the bodies of young women with certain skills, capacities and desires (Grosz 1994). The workings of dominating heteropatriarchal power are never complete. The continual juxtapositioning of places and bodies "untidy" the ordered dispositions of dominating power—if only momentarily—making other, resistant practices and meanings possible (Radcliffe 1999a). My research shows some of these resistant meanings by looking at Latina subjectivity formation at the scale of the body. The disciplining of the young women's bodies in terms of the "inside/outside" dichotomy, and their various forms of resistance to that disciplining, manifests the importance of thinking of spatial production at micro- as well as macroscales. The research offers insights into the highly contested nature of spatial production and social reproduction at the scale of the body, the home, and the neighborhood, where discourses of public and private, safe and oppressive, strong and vulnerable are struggled over with passion and have important material consequences. It also helps to render visible young peoples' material social practices, and the understandings they attribute to those practices, in coming of age in Los Angeles.

Social Reproduction, Embodiment and Entanglement

Public/private and mind/body are perhaps the most pervasive yet elementary binary configurations of sociospatial relations of power in the modern period of Western society. The relationship between gender divisions and these binary sociospatial divisions has been an ongoing focus of research among feminist geographers (see reviews of these literatures in McDowell 1993a, 1993b, 1999). Scholars have convincingly argued that the mind/body and public/private binaries are gendered and intrinsically spatial (Le Doeuff 1989; Pateman 1989; Rose 1993). Scholarly scrutiny has also revealed the myriad material linkages between the so-called public sphere of production and the private sphere of reproduction (MacKenzie and Rose 1983; McDowell 1983). At the same time, research has reaffirmed that the ideal of separate spheres continues to produce powerful embodied effects in the daily lives of women (see reviews of these literatures on fear in Pain 1991, 2000).

Increasingly evident in the literature is an understanding of the contingent nature of space constituted and contested as private and public: in other words, spaces are heterogeneous and not entirely one or the other. The early work of socialist and liberal feminists posited— albeit from differing perspectives—the public sphere as emancipatory, whereas the home was perceived primarily as a site of oppression for women (Oakley 1974). In this view, the work of social reproduction was generally portrayed as the site of drudgery and exploitation (de Beauvoir [1949] 1972; Walby 1986). Contemporary interpretations, attending to the differentiating power relations of

race, class, sexuality, gender, and age, offer more nuanced interpretations and insights into the heterogeneity of these sites. For
example, the multiple and sometimes counterhegemonic meanings
and processes constitutive of "public" and "private" spaces and
their substantive effects in everyday relations of social reproduction are evidenced in recent research conducted on women's
reproductive waged labor and the ways in which conventional
understandings of private and public are often sexualized and
racialized (Duncan 1996; Glenn 1992; hooks 1990; G Pratt 1998, 1999;
M Pratt 1992; Valentine 1996c).

An ongoing challenge for geographers is to make sense of the entangled relations of social reproduction by foregrounding the importance of a particularly *spatial* understanding of the multiple processes
that constitute the subject in everyday life. How can we conceive
of the relationship between what Cindi Katz (2001:711) describes as
the "the fleshy, messy and indeterminate stuff of everyday life" and
the "set of structured practices that unfold in dialectical relation with
production?" In analyzing the personal, spatial, *embodied* public/private
geographies of young Latinas, I flesh out the concept of entangled
power articulated by Joanne Sharp and her colleagues (2000). I also
draw upon and extend Elizabeth Grosz's (1994) conceptualization of
body image in an effort to interpret the entangled, *spatial* relations of
social reproduction in the lives of young Latina women.

A notion of entangled power draws on Foucault's conceptualization
of the "spaces of dispersion," in which he challenges the a priori
ordering tendencies or temporal sequencing of historiography (Philo
1992). In *Archaeology of Knowledge* (1982), Foucault argues that the
order, or "local, changing rules," in the spaces of dispersion resides
in the juxtaposition of events, people and phenomena themselves, as
opposed to an order derived theoretically from "outside" (Philo
1992:149). In the concept of entanglements, Sharp and colleagues
echo Foucault's juxtapositioning of places and bodies generative of
particular relations of domination and resistance. They (2000:24)
argue:

> [R]elations of power are really, crucially and unavoidably spun out
> across and through the material spaces of the world. It is within such
> spaces that assemblages of people, activities, technologies, institutions,
> ideas and dreams all come together, circulate, convene and recon-
> vene … and it is only as a consequence of the spatial entangling
> together of all of these elements that relations of power are
> established.

The spatial assemblage of a multiplicity of meanings, uses and
value of space and their mutual inscriptions of difference within and
between complex subjectivities generates fractures in power, both

dominant and resistant. The productive, but never total, workings of power in entanglements is on a continuum the sociospatial poles of which are characterized as resistance within spaces of domination and domination in spaces of resistance (Sharp et al 2000:28). Power in both cases is seen as transformative. Dominating power is the "ability to transform the actions of others ... [and r]esistance ... transforming the conditions under which one lives" (Cresswell 2000:264). In the processes and practices of embodiment, as Akhil Gupta and James Ferguson (1997:20) make explicit, "If one of the modes of operation of power is to attach identities to subjects, to tie subjects to their own identities through self-knowledge, then resistance serves to reshape subjects by untying or untidying that relationship."

In an effort to analyze the operations of dominating and resisting power to tie and untie subjects to identities through self-knowledge, I draw on Grosz's (1994) theorization of subjectivity, presented in her book *Volatile Bodies*. According to Grosz, human subjectivity develops over a lifetime through the continuous production and transformation of an individual's body image. Both pliable and amenable to change, a body image is constructed gradually from perceptions, sensations and movements of the organic body derived from biological and neuro-physiological inputs that are psychically invested. Lived experience and embodied knowledge are conceived as neither precultural nor only cultural. In a continuous interaction between a corporeal interiority and exteriority, body image is reshaped and reinscribed, enabling human beings to "develop a practical relation to objects in the world and a psychic attachment to [their] bodies and body parts" (Grosz 1994:91). Mediated through body image, places make bodies—that is, individual bodily meanings, desires and capacities. And, recursively, bodies reinscribe and reproduce their sociospatial environment, reflect-ing the forms and interests of the body (Grosz 1998:42; Hyams 2002; see Nast and Pile 1998).

Grosz's conceptualization of *body image* provides a way to account for the specific perspectives, insights, desires and intentionality of women mediated by multiple discourses in the continual juxtapositioning of bodies and places (cf Harrison 2000; Mehta and Bondi 1999). As embodied subjects, the pliability of body image offers the young Latinas the possibility of resisting or reworking the dominant norms and regulatory practices constitutive of private and public spaces and embodied subjectivities. The young women untidy the relationship between dominant binary conceptualizations of femininity/masculinity and inside/outside spaces through the *willful* performance of situated embodied subjectivities effected in and through the interplay of the social and sensuous in body image (Grosz 1994).

Outside: Making Homegirls and *Callejeras*

As I argue above, the local, changing rules of sociospatial categorization and the spatial ordering of young Latina bodies are integrally related to the changing geographies of public and private investment in production and social reproduction in Los Angeles. Despite his hyperbolic style, Mike Davis's (1990:227) description of the public spaces of Los Angeles best captures the disparities of wealth constituted in and through the geographies of investment in production and social reproduction:

> In Los Angeles, once-upon-a-time a demi-paradise of free beaches, luxurious parks and "cruising strips," genuinely democratic space is all but extinct. The Oz-like archipelago of Westside pleasure domes —a continuum of toy malls, arts centers and gourmet strips—is reciprocally dependent upon the social imprisonment of the third-world service proletariat who live in increasingly repressive ghettoes and barrios. In a city of several million yearning immigrants, public amenities are radically shrinking, parks are becoming derelict and beaches more segregated, libraries and playgrounds are closing, youth congregations of ordinary kinds are banned, and the streets are becoming more desolate and dangerous. (See also Valle and Torres 2000.)

Homegirls

Discussions about the neighborhood where the Latina girls live almost always begins with a statement about the prevalence of violent crime —in particular, gang-related violence. The violence they speak of is always and only located outside. Almost without exception, they can recount their own experiences and that of a family member and/or friend who has been the victim of violent crime (characterized by some degree of bodily harm). The danger, however, is presented as a matter of fact, and no one individual holds a singular and unconditional sense of the streets. Both the ambivalence and the matter-of-factness are captured in the following account:

> Monica: Where I live it's pretty good, but sometimes there's drive-
>   bys. But it's OK. It's quiet but not that much because I
>   live in front of the freeway, so it makes a lot of noise ...
>   And then, it's pretty good.
> Annelise: I like it ... Well, where I live, it's calm. But sometimes it
>   isn't. There's people that died on the street I live, but I
>   didn't hear the shots. It's OK.

Many of the young women express fearlessness and stoicism in discussions about their experiences in public spaces. Although they refer to the potential for being victims of violent crime—in particular, stranger rape or gang violence—they reject identifying themselves as *feeling* vulnerable outside to physical harm.

Pilar:	It don't frighten me. I don't know. Like two guys got shot in front of me.
Melissa:	And how did you feel?
Pilar:	How can I feel? It was right in front of me. I was just surprised it happened. 'Cause I been through that since I was small so I don't fear it no more. When your time's gonna come, it's gonna come.

The young Latinas resist dominant discourses that construct their neighborhood as a "war zone" and position gang members as indiscriminately dangerous and threatening. In social interactions with "outsiders" to Los Angeles, they themselves are often positioned as either gangsters—and, by implication, perpetrators of violence on the streets—or, conversely, needing to take care or stay inside. Nikki states:

> [My Mexican cousins] look at me and they say, "Oh, you live in L.A.? But you're not wearing black lipstick or you don't dress like gangster or anything." I go, "You don't have to!" They're all like, "Oh god. It's dangerous over there. Be careful!"

However, the danger and deviance with which young, urban, racialized people are often associated is embraced by the majority of the young Latinas. The violence, noise and other negative qualities of Los Angeles city life in neglected neighborhoods are not perceived as purely negative:

Michelle:	But I like living in wild places where there's a lot of things going on. Yah, I like it. When it gets quiet it's like, "Oh, there's no crime going on," but—
Melissa:	So you like the crime?
Michelle:	Well, I don't like it, but without it, it wouldn't be Los Angeles.

They are positioned by others and position themselves as worthy of respect and enhanced social status for being tough enough to live/ survive in Los Angeles:

Gloria C:	Like when I go visit my relatives or my friends from Texas, they're like, "Oh my god, you've been to L.A.? Oh my god, have you been shot?" They're serious. They're like, "Oh my god, wait a minute, you're not a gangster, are you?"
Melissa:	How does it make you feel when they do this?
Lucy:	I love it! Everything you see in the news is always gonna be something about L.A. getting drive-by'd or the riots and stuff like that … They expect all these torture-like adventures. So, what do you do? You give it to them … And everybody wants to be around you all the time.

In the process of resignifying the place, they also rework their subjectivity. Often positioned as "homegirls," the majority of young women reject a feeling of vulnerability and, instead, experience the danger associated with Los Angeles as exotic and special. Feeling exotic gives them a sense of daring which sets them apart, symbolically and bodily, from other people:

> Margaret: When we go to visit my cousins up north in Lindsey, it's
>   a little town ... They trip out on us ... Like, they're
>   afraid of you. If you compare yourself to them, they
>   make you look bad [cool]. You're daring.

These comments are representative of the mindset of the majority of the young people who acknowledge the dangers of living in Los Angeles while simultaneously asserting their "right to the carnival, intensity and even the risks of the city" (Wilson 1991:10). In their travels to elsewhere and their embodied performances with "outsiders," the young people engage in the negotiation of a collective, youthful, public and daring urban identity. For most, social inscriptions of corporeal vulnerability do not accord with their self-conscious bodily experiences of Los Angeles. They rework the terms of bodily vulnerability constituted in dominant discourses of a dangerous and disordered Los Angeles, and gain control over body image in expressing their desires and engagement in performances of tough and daring natives of the city. At the same time, they reconstruct the city as a youthful place, a "wild place where there's a lot of things going on." In appropriating and resignifying the meanings of Los Angeles, the young people assert a positively valued way of life, accrue power and prestige and subvert the social and spatial exclusionary effects of dominating power.

Callejeras

The Latinas' out-of-town experiences illustrate the ways in which young people negotiate affirmation and agency through multiple positionings as "devils" and "angels," and how the city is constructed as intrinsically unsafe for or made unsafe by young people (Valentine 1996a, b). Closer to home, however, outside spaces are gendered and sexualized. "Hanging out" on the street is forbidden (cf Matthews, Limb, and Taylor 1999, 2000). The gendered and sexualized norms of "the street" are captured in the iconic image of *la callejera*, described by Rina:

> [A] woman that likes to be out a lot, to have a "good time," if you get my drift. You are automatically marked as a street woman ... as someone who has "been around the block."

"Outside" spaces are gendered and sexualized in negotiations with parents to gain permission to "go out" to social events. Most young women report that they are not allowed to go out in the evenings with their friends to parties or the movies. At the insistence of their parents, they are chaperoned outside by older, often male family members or friends. In patriarchal societies, the seclusion in private space and/or close supervision and surveillance in public space guards women against the assertion of male passion and—as importantly—against the assertion of their own passion.

Parents are concerned with both the young women's sexual vulnerability and their desire. The young women are told they cannot go out unchaperoned, if at all, even though their brothers can, because "It's different 'cause they're boys"; "Nothing's going to happen, only to girls, 'cause they could get raped, you know." Alternatively, they are told "No, because you're a girl. You're going to be playing around and you're going to be acting dumb with the guys … doing this with the guys." Although their mobility in public space is extremely limited, only a very few assert that they are afraid of being victimized by violence or passion and should stay indoors and/or be chaperoned.

The everyday experiences of public spaces have less to do with concerns about vulnerability to bodily harm than they do visibility of bodies—that is, being stared at (Young 1990):

Nena: They let me go out but I don't want to. I prefer to go
           play with my friends. Probably we'll meet in some house
           and watch TV … Or outside in the yard. I feel more
           comfortable 'cause probably something's going to happen.
Melissa: Where is the place that's scary?
Nena: Outside, when you're walking alone and it's dark 'cause
           probably people are going to stare at you.

Fear of being *stared at* does not correspond with dominant conceptions of the dangers for women in the streets after dark. However, it is the visual mastery to which young people feel subjected in outside (read adult) spaces (Valentine 1996a, b), day or night, which compels them to stay indoors or feel uncomfortable enough to avoid certain places in the neighborhood:

Venessa: I don't go to the park. 'Cause there's a lot of ugly *nacos*
           there … those old men that look at you and stuff.
Regina: They're perverted too. As soon as you go to the park,
           they just look at you and they whistle at you.
Venessa: Yah, they're perverted. I'm not comfortable there.

The discomfort Venessa and Regina experience from being seen as heterosexual beings, communicated by adult male stares and gestures, transforms the park—one of the few outside spaces designated for children/young people—into an adult, heterosexual male space from which they feel excluded. Gloria C explains how this adult male space and their discordant bodily experience is reproduced more generally in the streets:

I hate it when like guys are with their girls or they have babies and they're like walking with them and they're like … looking over their shoulder at you. It sickens me because you know they shouldn't be doing that. Especially to a young girl and they're like 40 or something.

I suggest that their comfort or lack of it is mediated by body image and their control over claims to a particular identity—where, when, and how to be seen to be *young*, feminine, and heterosexual. Their control over body image is undermined by *nacos* in the park and adult men in the streets. Perhaps unsurprisingly, the generational relations of power that reproduce outside space as adult space and exclude unaccompanied young people are overlaid with gender and heterosexual social relations in which young women are (dis)positioned in and through the sexually objectifying *adult* male gaze. Moreover, the unemployed and casually employed men who dominate the daytime streets and parks in Los Angeles' neglected neighborhoods articulate the way in which gendered norms of social reproduction intersect classed and racialized relations of production in a restructured economy.

While the lack of control over body image constrains their mobility and autonomy in the outside spaces of the neighborhood, some young women resist their experiences of bodily discomfort in public places dominated by "perverted" adult heterosexuality in implicit claims to age-appropriate desire. In contrast to the experience in the park, Venessa and Sabrina articulate an instance of comfort and bodily accord in interactions with *young* men:

Melissa:	Are there any places in your neighborhoods which are "off-limits"?
Venessa:	Well right here, there's a bunch of *cholos* [gangsters]. They always hang around right there. But I act dumb sometimes and just go by. I'll go by, check some of them out.
Sabrina:	They're called *cholos* but they're really *chulos*.
Melissa:	What's a *chulo*?
All:	Really cute!
Venessa:	Some of them, some of them they'll turn back and they'll look at you or say a little comment. It's not like you don't like it.
Sabrina:	Sometimes you look at them like [wolf whistle].

These young women are flattered, not frightened, by the attention they get from the *cholos*. But they also challenge the *cholos'* visual mastery over them by objectifying them through gazing and whistling.

The spatial hegemony of adult heterosexual males in outside spaces, although formidable, is not total. As suggested above, there are spaces and times outside in/at which the young women exercise a degree of control over their claims to a specifically heterosexual female identity *and* control over public space in encounters with *young* men—if only

in brief encounters (James, Jenks, and Prout 1998). In expressing their
desire for young men—gangsters, even—they resist both the dominant discourse, which defines "good" girls as vulnerable (Epstein and
Johnson 1998) and the visual mastery men have over women, which
denies their control over body image and compels them to remain
indoors or to cover up (Koskela 1997; Wilson 1991).

The outside spaces of the neighborhood are constituted, materially
and discursively, as dangerous and position young women in public as
vulnerable, dependent, and sexually promiscuous. In their daily negotiations of mobility through the streets and affirmation of selfhood in
local outside spaces, the majority who are compelled to "cover up," be
chaperoned or remain indoors unwittingly reproduce the heterosexual
adult male hegemony of public space. A few gain control over both
space and body image. Through verbal and bodily performances, they
resignify discourses of "danger" and "deviance," rework the symbolic
value of place, and challenge their positionality as vulnerable, incom-
petent, and "out of place" in the city and outside spaces of their neighborhood. To a large degree, however, they, too, reproduce the dominant
heterosexuality of public space in their resistant claims to heterosexual
subjectivity and desire.

Inside: Making Home, Homebodies and Homeplace

In much of the research on the construction and contestation of
meaning and materiality of the home, the analysis has centered on
adult women as homemakers (eg Cravey 1997; England 1996; Hanson
and Pratt 1995) and domestic laborers (Hondagneu-Sotelo 2001;
Pratt 1998, 1999). Children and young people's participation in social
reproduction and the production of home is largely invisible (Myers
1991; Roberts 1998); when made visible, it is conceived innocuously
and naturalized as socialization (important exceptions include Katz
1993, 1998; Robson 1996, forthcoming). This analysis seeks to contribute
to opening up the home as a space productive of and reproduced by
young Latina females. The masculinized public spaces of the neighborhood and the city, normativized as disordered and threatening
to both the bodies of young Latinas and the heteropatriarchal social
body, are mutually constitutive of the *order* and *safety* of the feminized
home. In their daily lives, the young women are actively making home,
making homebodies, and making homeplace.

Making Home

All of the young women spend time—some of them a lot of time—doing
domestic work, which, I argue, is an engagement in co-reproducing
the household. A typical day after school and on the weekends is spent
inside their homes "doing chores," which include cleaning, cooking,
and childcare. As the following passages suggest, the home is constructed

as a space worked in by women in the service of others and constituted through a discourse of sexual restraint and female responsibility for orderliness. As Mae's and Sportie's experiences illustrate, this is accomplished by confining young woman to domestic spaces, relegating schoolwork as secondary to domestic work, and rejecting claims to other subjectivities. Mae explains:

> Like I asked her to go to the library this weekend to work on a project over here. And she's using my room, that it's a mess, as an excuse just not to let me go. And so I have to go and do it at my aunt's house by myself.

In Sportie's case:

> Sometimes I come home and I'm doing my homework and she tells me, "Sportie, go wash the dishes." "Homework comes first, mom," and then she goes, "Sportie, go wash the dishes." "But you always tell me put my studies in front of everything." And then I have to get up and go do the dishes and like sometimes I'll stay up late doing my homework. "What are you doing, doing your homework!" "You told me to do the dishes, I couldn't do my homework."

These expressions of resentment unambiguously convey the young women's feelings about the limitations and constraints on their mobility and time. The prevailing gender norms regarding homemaking are revealed in their shared perceptions and are constitutive of a collective identity as aggrieved daughters. However, only a few refuse to do the work expected of them, and the meanings they ascribe to homemaking and their positions as homemakers are ambiguous and varied.

In most cases, the adult female members of the young Latinas' households are employed outside their homes. The gendered division of labour and the preference among Latinas/os for kin to care for their children (Lamphere et al 1993) combine to charge the young women with the responsibility of both housework and childcare for their adult relatives (cf Chant 1987, 1991). In the following passage, Patti represents the tremendous amount of work she contributes to daily reproduction as "help" she provides her mother. The terms "help" or "help out" are repeated by others and convey a sense of ambiguity:

> But sometimes I, like I wish I did have a [special] place 'cause I get so frustrated at my house. It's like, because I have a sister that, she lives with us. She got pregnant when she was, like, 15. And now she's 23 and she has 3 kids, and she works. And when I get home, I have to help, you know, my mom take care of them, clean the house and sometimes I wish I could just leave anywhere, you know and get away for awhile.

Patti "has to help" her mother (and her sister), and expresses her responsibilities for orderliness and nurturance as a burden that constitutes her home as exclusionary. In contrast, Angelica suggests that "helping out" will allow her mother to pursue her personal goals for increased social advancement:

> And my sister and I, we share all of the things we have to do. One week and one week, she takes care of the dog. And we do that, I don't know. And my mom, my mom goes to school and we help her out with everything 'cause she wants to get a job.

In both of these examples, the young women are homemaking—that is, engaged in reproductive labor in the service of family members. However, these are not the housewives and mothers characterized in feminist critiques of the ideal of home as women who "serve, nurture, and maintain so that the bodies and souls of men and children gain confidence and expansive subjectivity to make their mark on the world" (Young 1997:134). They are daughters and sisters who are serving, nurturing and maintaining the bodies and souls of *women* and children. Yet Patti experiences homemaking as oppressive—that is, in providing for others, she is denied something she needs. In contrast, Angelica's experience of homemaking is positively valued, and her home may constitute a site of dignity, autonomy and resistance (hooks 1991; see also Young 1997) to the daily indignities experienced by Mexican immigrants.

Making Homebodies

The practices and discourses of heteropatriarchal power constitutive of "home" as female, ordered and safe are mutually productive of domesticated young female bodies. The acquisition and performance of homemaking skills is constructed as a source of pride and a measure of competence in the day-to-day embodiment of femaleness. Mae describes how she feels when her domestic skills are held up as an indication of potential competence outside, beyond the sociospatial boundaries of parental supervision and control:

> Lately, I've been asking like to go places with my friends, and I'll be asking my mom but then my dad will butt in and say, "No, you can't go anywhere because look at your room. If you can't keep your room clean, then that shows that you're not gonna be responsible out with your friends or at a party or anything." And one time I got so mad, I just told my mom, just to tell him there's a difference between cleaning your room and going to a party and getting, like, drunk or stoned.

The contingent relationship these young women's parents construct between the home and outside are experienced as constraints on their physical mobility and psychosocial autonomy in space. More significant, however, is the discursive and material production of domesticated bodies. In the argument with her parents, Mae expresses a sense of how her body is inscribed/ascribed as ordered and self-regulating in and through the acquisition and performance of homemaking skills. In denying the causal relationship between her "incapacity" to clean her room and a body she imagines as utterly incapacitated by drugs and alcohol, she resists this discursive and material construction of her body and capabilities as domesticated.

Although some of the young women speak with a measure of pride about their competency in homemaking, they angrily resist the naturalization of females as cleanly.

Sportie: The girls do all of it.
Nikki: When my brothers do the chores, they do the dishes, it's ugly! Pieces of things on the glass. So that's why I do them.
Sportie: Like when they Windex, there are streaks all over and—
Melissa: Do you think that because they don't do a good job then they don't get asked to do it again?
All: Yeah, uh-huh.
Sportie: If we don't do it right, then we have to do it over until it's done.
All: Not the boys.

In the social space of the home, boundaries of gender categorization are drawn between the young women and their male siblings: orderliness and cleanliness constitutive of and by embodied femininity are mutually productive of masculinity as dirty and disorderly (cf Sibley 1995a, b). Their brothers' "ugly" behavior, worthy of being *swept out of the house*, is better suited for the "dirty" work engaged in by working poor Latino males in Los Angeles' service economy. However, in voicing their doubts about their brothers' efforts to clean effectively, the young Latinas also resist the naturalization of males as slovenly.

Feminine orderliness and cleanliness are ritualized in the rites of passage to female heterosexual adulthood. Lilliana, Michelle, Gloria J, and Sandra collectively explain how this works.

Melissa: So part of being a *quinceañera* or growing up and becoming a woman is doing [chores] on your own. What else?
Gloria J: Like washing your own clothes. You have to take care of your little brother and—
Sandra: clean the whole house, like have everything clean when they get home—
Gloria J: And be responsible for your own self.
Lilliana: And then they start telling you, "And then when you get married, you'll know all these things."

Michelle:	They say, "Then when you get married, your husband's going to bring you back to me."
All:	(laugh)
Melissa:	So what do you say when people say these things to you?
Lilliana:	Well, "I ain't going to get married!"
Michelle:	My mom tells me, "I still clean your underwear," 'cause you know she still washes my clothing.
Melissa:	This is the expression, "I still clean your underwear," this is sort of an insult?
Lilliana:	Yah. And you feel like getting her and slapping her.
Melissa:	OK, so your reaction to being told these things is, "It doesn't matter. I'm not going to get married." Is that how you feel or do you just say that?
Lilliana:	No, I just tell her that! I hope I get married!
Michelle:	I tell her the same that I'm never going to get married. I don't want to get married. Never.
All:	[laugh at Michelle]

The dominant discourses and practices of domesticity mutually constitutive of embodied femininity and the "parental home" are also constitutive of the future "married home." The sociospatial transition from the embodied domesticity of the daughter in a "parental home" to the wife in a "married home" is signified in and through the ritual reference to "still cleaning your underwear." Suggestive of cleaning/changing diapers and cleaning babies' backsides, this condemnatory expression infantalizes the young women. They express resentment and even rage at being positioned as infants. However, Michelle's refusal of a progression to heterosexual female adulthood marked by marriage is censored by the others' laughter as a violation of the rules.

In or out of the context of doing chores, young women who assert their authority are threatened with never being able to "achieve" the mark of heterosexual female adulthood: marriage—or rather, a patriarchal marriage. When Brenda argues with her father, she is told:

> "Damn, I don't think you're ever gonna get married." "When you get married, your man, your husband's gonna be a *mandilón*." Meaning he's gonna be more like a housewife, you know. And I be like, "Hell, yes, you just better believe it!"

The social space of home, a heteropatriarchal home is constitutive of and constituted by a silent woman. Women who "go back at it" don't marry real men, but rather subordinated males who, tellingly, are represented as "housewives."

The boundaries between "inside" and "outside" are produced through the discursive dichotomies safety/danger, autonomy/dependency, order/disorder and modesty/promiscuity around gender and sexuality. Dominant discourses and practices of orderliness and cleanliness are mutually constitutive of a patriarchal home and a domesticated heterosexual femininity—that is, a tamed, constrained and trained female body. The majority of the young women neither practice bold walking outside (cf Koskela 1997), nor "walk away" from the domestic responsibilities in their homes. They do, however, often "talk back," sometimes refuse and even run away in resistance to the positioning and naturalizing of differences between themselves and their male siblings in ways that dis-able and disadvantage them.

Making Homeplace

bell hooks' (1990) characterization of homeplace has become paradigmatic of the home as a haven of resistance to dominating power. In writing about her childhood experience of her grandmother's home and homemaking amidst American racial apartheid, hooks articulates the way in which a grandmother's care and nurturance of black families was an act of resistance against daily dehumanization and exploitation by patriarchal white supremacist society. Homeplace—constituted through the willful, sometimes risky practices of social reproduction—provided a space in which African Americans "could strive to be subjects, not objects ... be affirmed in ... minds and hearts ... [and] restore ... the dignity denied ... on the outside in the public world" (hooks 1990:44). hook's conception of homeplace offers a useful way of understanding the experiences and meanings of "home" for young Latinas, people marginalized by multiple social relations of power as well as positioned as both carers for family and cared-for family members.

For the majority of young Latinas, both the outside and inside spaces in their daily lives are constituted by and constitutive of male entitlement and female dis-ability—that is, constraints on their movements, capabilities and senses of self. The young women rarely feel free from the daily corporeal experiences of invasive stares, uncomfortable looks, censorship of their attitudes and behavior and vulnerability to harassment and harm. However, when specifically asked to describe a "special place," many of them articulate the experience of a place in which they can feel "in control" of bodily information. Those who are able to carve out spaces of control do so in their homes, the place most accessible to them. A small number of young women convey an experience of their homes and the relationships among family members characterized by dignity, autonomy and affirmation. Sabrina explains why she is comfortable at home:

> Because you know everybody there and you know they won't make fun of you. They know how you dress. They know how you act, so why are they going to make fun of you?

Much more typical, however, are the experiences conveyed below of carving spaces of dignity, autonomy and affirmation out of the dominating spatiality of home and familial relations. The bedrooms of adolescent girls have been advanced in cultural studies as spaces constitutive of autonomy and resistance for young women (McRobbie and Garber 1976; Griffiths 1988; cf Lees 1986). For some young Latinas who have their own bedroom, it is designated a special place in which they experience a sense of autonomy, as Carmen does: "Yeah, it [the bedroom] makes me feel free 'cause I just go in there, do my homework, play music, or I don't know, like do whatever I want in there." In overcrowded homes, among the majority who do not have their own bedrooms, some negotiate a degree of autonomy in other spaces inside their homes. Mae, for example, has to carve out a space of control in the dining room:

Mae: A place I spend most of my time is up on my bed.
Melissa: Up on your bed.
Mae: Well, it's not really a room. I have to share it with the
            whole house. It's the dining room, 'cause we made a
            bedroom 'cause we don't have a big enough house. And
            I sleep right there and then they, my brothers go and
            they eat in there. And they just go in there just to bother
            me so I can't do my homework.

Gloria's special place is her bedroom closet. In contrast to the spaces of home constituted in and through the needs of others, Gloria's closet provides her with a space to feel bad and care for herself:

Melissa: Why is your closet special?
Gloria J: Because it's really dark in there and it has a window
            with a curtain. I go in there sometimes when I'm really
            stressed or depressed. I just go in there and I read a
            book or I write a letter to my friends.

A few young women can only secure a sense of control or, at least, escape from oppressive conditions in spaces of the mind. Venessa describes her special place thus:

My thoughts and mind because that's my place where my thoughts are open freely without criticism. I don't have to worry about what people think about my thoughts.

Valentine (1996a, b) makes the point that teenagers who seek refuge from the gaze of parents can find the autonomy and affirmation associated with "private" *inside* spaces in the streets after dark. By so doing, they transform the "public" space of the street into a "private" space of refuge and, conversely, the "private" space of the home into a "public" space of exposure, thereby inverting the normative associations of these spaces. For the young Latinas who are confined in the "public" spaces of their homes, the "private" spaces of refuge are more elusive, constituted and contested as they are in the continuous juxtapositioning of bodies and places.

Conclusion

This essay has presented an analysis of the workings of heteropatriarchal power reproduced in young Latinas' narrative accounts of the "fleshy, messy and indeterminate stuff" of cleaning house and coming of age in the context of Los Angeles' worsening landscapes. Within and through this political-economic context, local, changing power effects are shaped by and give shape to the very fleshiness, messiness and indeterminacy of social relations and spaces of reproduction. I suggest that these local, changing power effects are best captured in a spatial analysis of entangled power.

In the continual juxtapositionings of bodies and places, outside and inside, the sensual and social, dominating discourses of danger and vulnerability and practices of homemaking combine to domesticate young women's bodies and tie their subjective senses of self, competence, and autonomy to homemaking. In the same juxtapositionings, moments and spaces are created in which the young women untidy the naturalizing and dis-abling relationship between dominant norms and materialities of local places and embodied self-knowledge. Through practices of bodily labor and performance and the resignification of body image and place, the young women engage in both willful contribution to reproducing their households and equally willful resistance to domestication. In parodic performances of "homegirl" identities, through strategic expressions of heterosexual desire, and in engagement in domestic "chores" and confinement to domestic spaces, the young women gain access to and carve out spaces of control, spaces in which they feel safe, trusting, competent, and autonomous.

Their local spaces, however, are heterogenous, neither singularly "safe" nor "unsafe." I suggest that bodily experiences of inside and outside places can contribute to a reconceptualization of the public/private binary. In general, the young women experience as "public" places in which they feel exposed to invasive stares, uncomfortable looks, censorship of their attitudes and behavior and harm. By contrast, "private" places are those in which they feel relatively safe, trusting, competent and autonomous. Sometimes the two overlap. For many women in some circumstances, there is a feeling of being exposed outside. Others experience affirmation and security inside their homes. In many cases, however, a tension exists between the ideologies of gender, sexuality, and age and the dichotomous public/private spheres and their lived experience.

Acknowledgments

I am indebted to the young women who participated in this research project and to my advisor, Sarah Radcliffe, my family and Sue Passler for their total support. I am grateful to the Economic and Social Research Council for their support; this research was funded by award number R00429734503. Earlier versions of this essay were reviewed by Katharyne Mitchell, Sarah Holloway, and Stuart Aitken, to whom I am very grateful for comments and suggestions.

Endnotes

[1] The young people with whom I worked used a number of ethnoracial and panethnic terms ("Mexican," "Mexican-American," "Latina/o," "Hispanic") interchangeably to identify themselves. I use one of these terms, "Latina/o," to refer to them, the majority of whom (all but three first-generation) are second-generation (US-born) or 1.5-generation (resident and educated in US from early childhood) and of Mexican descent.

[2] The data suggest that the social space of school is also a critical site in and through which the young women negotiate coming of age. The research was conducted in a low-income Latina/o neighborhood of Los Angeles over a six-month period in 1997–1998. I solicited volunteers in the neighborhood high school and brought together eight friendship groups from among a total of 46 young people. The principal method of data collection was five weeks of consecutive, in-depth group discussions held in a private room on campus, during which members discussed their experiences and understandings around the open-ended themes I presented regarding places and spaces in their day-to-day lives. Group interviews were supplemented by individual follow-up interviews and on-campus observation. I interpreted and analyzed the discussion data through the development of grounded theory. Each week's general theme and questions were modified and refined based on the experiences and meanings that emerged in the previous week's discussions, permitting the participants' agendas to guide me. Through repeated readings of the verbatim transcripts, I identified categories and related subcategories of shared and/or significant experience, as well as the dissonant, marginal or contradictory experiences that emerged.

[3] The terms "inside" and "outside" are my own. They are used to broadly represent the spatial binary structuring the young peoples' lives and to avoid the normative assumptions of the terms "public" and "private." "Inside" includes their homes and the homes of extended family members. "Outside" refers to the neighborhood's open public places, such as the street or the park, where people "hang out" with friends. Friends' homes and semipublic places, such as school, shopping malls, cinemas and so on, are not consistently one or the other.

[4] "Homegirl" refers to a female gang member.

References

Brown E, Wyn R, Hongjian Y, Valenzuela A and Dong L (1998) Access to health insurance and health care for Mexican-American children in immigrant families. In M Suarez-Orosco (ed) *Crossings: Mexican Immigration in Interdisciplinary Perspectives* (pp 227–247). Cambridge, MA: Harvard University Press

Chang G (2000) *Disposable Domestics: Immigrant Women Workers in the Global Economy*. Cambridge, MA: South End Press

Chant S (1987) Family structure and female labour in Quéretaro, Mexico. In J Momsen and J Townsend (eds) *Geography of Gender in the Third World* (pp 277–293). Hutchinson: State University of New York Press

Chant S (1991) *Women and Survival in Mexican Cities: Perspectives on Gender, Labour Markets and Low-Income Households.* Manchester: Manchester University Press

Cisneros S (1984) *The House on Mango Street.* New York: Vintage Books

Cravey A (1997) The politics of reproduction: Households in the Mexican industrial transition. *Economic Geography* 73:166–186

Cresswell T (2000) Falling down: Resistance as diagnostic. In J Sharp, P Routledge, C Philo and R Paddison (eds) *Entanglements of Power: Geographies of Domination/ Resistance* (pp 256–268). London: Routledge

Davis M (1990) *City of Quartz: Excavating the Future in Los Angeles.* New York: Vintage Books

de Beauvoir S ([1949] 1972) *The Second Sex.* Harmondsworth: Penguin

Duncan N (1996) Renegotiating gender and sexuality in public and private spaces. In N Duncan (ed) *Bodyspace: Destabilizing Geographies of Gender and Sexuality* (pp 127–145). London: Routledge

England K (ed) (1996) *Who Will Mind the Baby?* London: Routledge

Epstein D and Johnson R (1998) *Schooling Sexualities.* Buckingham: Open University Press

Fine M and Weis L (1996) Writing the "wrongs" of fieldwork: Confronting our own research/writing dilemmas in urban ethnographies. *Qualitative Inquiry* 2:251–275

Foucault M (1978) *The History of Sexuality: An Introduction.* Harmondsworth: Penguin

Foucault M (1982) *Archaeology of Knowledge.* New York: Pantheon Books

Glenn E N (1992) From servitude to service work: Historical continuities in the racial division of paid reproductive labor. *Signs* 18:1–43

Griffiths V (1988) From "playing out" to "dossing out": Young women and leisure. In E Wimbush and M Talbot (eds) *Relative Freedoms: Women and Leisure* (pp 48–125). Milton Keynes: Open University Press

Grosz E (1994) *Volatile Bodies: Toward a Corporeal Feminism.* Bloomington: Indiana University Press

Gupta A and Ferguson J (eds) (1997) *Culture, Power, Place: Explorations in Critical Anthropology.* Durham, NC: Duke University Press

Hanson S and Pratt G (1995) *Gender, Work and Space.* London: Routledge

Harrison P (2000) Making sense: Embodiment and the sensibilities of the everyday. *Environment and Planning D: Society and Space* 18:497–517

Hondagneu-Sotelo P (2001) *Doméstica: Immigrant Workers Cleaning and Caring in the Shadows of Affluence.* Berkeley: University of California Press

hooks b (1990) *Yearning: Race, Gender and Cultural Politics.* Boston: South End Press

Hyams M (2002) "Over there" and "back then": An odyssey in national subjectivity. *Environment and Planning D: Society and Space* 20:459–476

James A, Jenks C and Prout A (1998) *Theorizing Childhood.* New York: Teachers College Press

Jones O (2000) Melting geography: Purity, disorder, childhood. In S Holloway and G Valentine (eds) *Children's Geographies: Playing, Living, Learning* (pp 29–47). London: Routledge

Katz C (1993) Growing girls/closing circles: Limits on the spaces of knowing in rural Sudan and US cities. In C Katz and J Monk (eds) *Full Circles: Geographies of Women over the Life Course* (pp 88–106). London: Routledge

Katz C (1998) Disintegrating developments: Global economic restructuring and the eroding of ecologies of youth. In T Skelton and G Valentine (eds) *Cool Places: Geographies of Youth Cultures* (pp 130–144). London: Routledge

Katz C (2001) Vagabond capitalism and the necessity of social reproduction. *Antipode* 33(4):709–728

Koskela H (1997) "Bold walk and breakings": Women's spatial confidence versus fear of violence. *Gender, Place and Culture* 4:301–319

Lamphere L, Savella P, Gonzales F and Evans P (1993) *Sunbelt Working Mothers: Reconciling Family and Factory.* Ithaca, NY: Cornell University Press

Le Doeuff M (1989) *The Philosophical Imaginary.* London: Athlone Press

Lees S (1986) *Losing Out.* London: Hutchinson

Lucas T (1998) Youth gangs and moral panics in Santa Cruz, California. In T Skelton and G Valentine (eds) *Cool Places: Geographies of Youth Cultures* (pp 145–160). London: Routledge

Mackenzie S and Rose D (1983) Industrial change, the domestic economy and home life. In J Anderson, S Duncan and R Hudson (eds) *Redundant Spaces and Industrial Decline in Cities and Regions* (pp 155–200). London: Academic Press

Matthews H, Limb M and Taylor M (1999) Reclaiming the street: The discourse of curfew. *Environment and Planning A* 31(10):1713–1730

Matthews H, Limb M and Taylor M (2000) The "street as thirdspace." In S Holloway and G Valentine (eds) *Children's Geographies: Playing, Living, Learning* (pp 63–79). London: Routledge

McDowell L (1983) Towards an understanding of the gender division of urban space. *Society and Space* 1:15–30

McDowell L (1993a) Space, place and gender relations. Part 1: Feminist empiricism and the geography of social relations. *Progress in Human Geography* 17:157–179

McDowell L (1993b) Space, place and gender relations. Part 2: Identity, difference, feminist geometries and geographies. *Progress in Human Geography* 17:305–318

McDowell L (1999) *Gender, Identity and Place: Understanding Feminist Geographies.* Cambridge, UK: Polity Press

McRobbie A and Garber J (1976) Girls and subcultures. In S Hall and T Jefferson (eds) *Resistance through Rituals: Youth Subcultures in Postwar Britain* (pp 209–222). London: Hutchinson

Mehta A and Bondi L (1999) Embodied discourse: On gender and fear of violence. *Gender, Place and Culture* 6:67–84

Moore D (1997) Remapping resistance: "Ground for struggle" and the politics of place. In S Pile and M Keith (eds) *Geographies of Resistance* (pp 87–106). London: Routledge

Myers W (ed) (1991) *Protecting Working Children.* London: Zed Books

Nast H and Pile S (eds) (1998) *Places through the Body.* London: Routledge

Oakley A (1974) *The Sociology of Housework.* London: Martin Robinson

Pain R (1991) Space, sexual violence and social control: Integrating geographical and feminist analyses of women's fear of crime. *Progress in Human Geography* 15:415–431

Pain R (2000) Place, social relations and the fear of crime: A review. *Progress in Human Geography* 24:365–387

Pateman C (1989) *The Disorder of Women.* Cambridge, UK: Polity Press

Philo C (1992) Foucault's geography. *Society and Space* 10:137–162

Pratt G (1998) Inscribing domestic work on Filipina bodies. In H Nast and S Pile (eds) *Places through the Body* (pp 283–304). London: Routledge

Pratt G (1999) Geographies of identity and difference: Marking boundaries. In D Massey, J Allen and P Sarre (eds) *Human Geography Today* (pp 151–168). Cambridge, UK: Polity Press

Pratt M B (1992) Identity: Skin blood heart. In H Crowley and S Himmelweit (eds) *Knowing Women: Feminism and Knowledge* (pp 323–333). Cambridge, UK: Polity Press

Radcliffe S (1999a) Popular and state discourses of power. In D Massey, J Allen and P Sarre (eds) *Human Geography Today* (pp 219–242). Cambridge, UK: Polity Press

Radcliffe S (1999b) Embodying national identities: Mestizo men and white women in Ecuadorian racial-national imaginaries. *Transactions of the Institute of British Geographers* 24:213–225

Roberts S (1998) Untitled manuscript. Delivered at Geographies of Young People and Young People's Geographies Workshop. San Diego, CA, 11–15 November

Robson E (1996) Working girls and boys: Children's contributions to household survival in West Africa. *Geography* 81:403–407

Robson E (Forthcoming) Hidden child workers: Carers in Zimbabwe. *Antipode* 36

Rose G (1993) *Feminism and Geography: Limits of Geographical Knowledge.* Cambridge, UK: Polity Press

Sassen S (1988) *The Mobility of Labor and Capital.* Cambridge, UK: Cambridge University Press

Sassen S (1994) *Cities in the World Economy.* London: Sage Publications

Sharp J, Routledge P, Philo C and Paddison R (eds) (2000) *Entanglements of Power: Geographies of Domination/Resistance.* London: Routledge

Sibley D (1995a) *Geographies of Exclusion.* London: Routledge

Sibley D (1995b) Families and domestic routines: Constructing the boundaries of childhood. In S Pile and N Thrift (eds) *Mapping the Subject: Geographies of Cultural Transformation* (pp 123–137). London: Routledge

Skelton T (2000) "Nothing to do, nowhere to go?": Teenage girls and "public" space in the Rhondda Valley, South Wales. In S Holloway and G Valentine (eds) *Children's Geographies: Playing, Living, Learning* (pp 80–99). London: Routledge

Trueba E (1998) The education of Mexican immigrant children. In M Suarez-Orosco (ed) *Crossings: Mexican Immigration in Interdisciplinary Perspectives* (pp 253–275). Cambridge, MA: Harvard University Press

Valentine G (1996a) Angels and devils: Moral landscapes of childhood. *Society and Space* 14:581–599

Valentine G (1996b) Children should be seen and not heard: The production and transgression of adults' public space. *Urban Geography* 17:205–220

Valentine G (1996c) (Re)negotiating the "heterosexual street": Lesbian productions of space. In N Duncan (ed) *Bodyspace: Destabilizing Geographies of Gender and Sexuality* (pp 146–155). London: Routledge

Valle V and Torres R (2000) *Latino Metropolis.* Minneapolis: University of Minnesota Press.

Walby S (1986) *Patriarchy at Work.* Cambridge, UK: Polity Press

Wilson E (1991) *The Sphinx and the City: Urban Life, the Control of Disorder and Women.* Berkeley: University of California Press

Young I (1990) Throwing like a girl: A phenomenology of feminine body comportment, motility and spatiality. In I M Young (ed) *Throwing Like a Girl and Other Essays in Feminist Philosophy and Social Theory* (pp 141–159). Bloomington: Indiana University Press

Young I (1997) *Intersecting Voices: Dilemmas of Gender, Political Philosophy and Policy.* Princeton, NJ: Princeton University Press

Chapter 6
Of Fictional Cities and "Diasporic" Aesthetics

Rosemary Marangoly George

R K Narayan is revered by Indians like me who come from the lower-middle-class, run-of-the-mill milieu ... Swamy, the little boy of Malgudi, continues to epitomize average Indian boyhood despite the intervening decades between Narayan's fictional creation and 21st-century India.

Swamy holds the same charm for most ordinary Indians that Tom Sawyer and Huck Finn might hold for the average American (or Anglicized Indians like Mr. Varadarajan).... The "spare prose, simple tales, unvarying vocabulary and no obvious philosophy" that Mr. Varadarajan derides is precisely what is so appealing about Mr. Narayan's writing because it does capture the essence of the life and attitudes of ordinary Indians who live next door, around the corner and across the street in small-town India.... R K Narayan needs neither the Nobel Prize, nor the "literary affirmative action" of American academia. He is respected where he truly belongs: in India. (Anil Sivakumaran, letter to the editor, *Wall Street Journal*, 2001)[1]

When Indian author R K Narayan (1906–2001) died of heart failure at the age of 94, his passing was mourned in India and by diasporic Indians all over the globe. As the author of 15 novels (published at regular intervals from 1935 to 1993), five nonfiction books, seven collections of short stories and three books of mythology, Narayan was undoubtedly the most prolific and the most widely read Indian author writing in the English language in the 20th century. Over his lifetime and in most obituaries, Narayan was honored as the quintessential "Indian" writer, whose work spanned a whole era in Indian history, from the preindependence days of his early novels to the final essays written at the close of the 20th century. In recent years, negative assessments of Narayan's literary work by Shashi Tharoor and Tunku Varadarajan, New York-based members of the Indian intelligentsia who are also widely published in English-language newspapers in

India, have been met by a barrage of letters from readers from all over the globe who self-identify as "ordinary Indians," despite the globally dispersed locations from which their letters are sent (cf Tharoor 2001; Varadarajan 2001). For these admirers, what makes Narayan a great Indian writer is precisely that the "artlessness" of his work speaks directly to them and confirms what they believe is the essential India.

There is a noteworthy marshalling of national geography and national identity in Sivakumaran's letter to the editor. On the one hand, there is the conventionally understood geographic India, which is held in contrast to the geographic United States. Narayan, Sivakumaran insists, is respected *there*, in *that* geographic India. On the other hand, there is the India of Narayan's first novel, where the nine-year-old protagonist, Swamy, and his childhood in the fictional small town of Malgudi "epitomize average Indian boyhood." This is an India that extends to all locations where Narayan is respected (including New Jersey), but does not extend to disdainful "anglicized Indians"— the characterization that Sivakumaran assigns to New York critic Varadarajan.

I begin this essay about "diasporic" aesthetics and imaginary cities with this letter to the editor because it replays some of the supple ways in which cultural texts (novels as much as letters to the editor), produce subjects who, despite their dislocation from a strictly geographically understood India, are nevertheless actively involved in their own cultural reproduction as "Indian." Social reproduction is usually studied through considerations of institutional sites, such as the family, education, religion or workplace, and read within social, economic and political parameters. In this essay, I consider the work of social reproduction as it unfolds within the *cultural* realm in both national and diasporic contexts. I consider the creation and circulation of literary and visual cultural forms that work in tandem with *and sometimes against* the disciplinary dictates of these kinds of institutional sites to produce subjects with identities and affiliations that are equal to the challenges and demands of everyday life.

As migrants traverse across national borders, they create and re-create potent visions of home, and thereby sustain their sense of belonging to a specific social group. Within the cultural texts produced in such circumstances, these representations of home spaces summon forth an active and imaginative reordering of geography and a creative use of the many places and spaces of the past, present and future. National subject/citizens who are in the process of formulating or reformulating a new national identity for themselves and for fellow citizens culturally create and recreate home as vigorously as do diasporic peoples. Much of the *cultural work* of social reproduction in both national and diasporic locations is conducted in the creation, circulation and consumption of cultural products and practices that provide the material and sensory pleasures of cultural identity and belonging.

In this essay, I examine the work of three "Indian" cultural producers —two working in the South Asian–American context of the late 1980s/early 1990s and one in the subcontinent in the preindependence British India of the 1930s—whose work attempts to map alternative articulations of the spaces of home and community, with varying degrees of success. I trace the multiple affiliations in the work of two first-generation South Asian Americans, novelist Indira Ganesan[2] and painter Arijit Sen,[3] as they create fictional and visual spaces that are hospitable to a hybrid, seemingly idiosyncratic and yet familiar understanding of place and community. As an analogy to this examination of Sen and Ganesan's "imagined locations," I begin by offering some comments on the work of Narayan, paying special attention to his creation of Malgudi, the fictional Indian small town in which all of his novels written between the 1930s and the 1990s were set. I find this seemingly odd analogy useable despite the geographic and chronological distance between these literary projects because, in his work written in the 1930s and early 1940s, Narayan was creating a cityscape and a community outside the framework of the independent nation but very much inspired by the idea of autonomous, culturally (if not politically and economically) independent nationhood. In considering these works together, I break them out of their usual classification as diasporic/immigrant cultural products (Ganesan and Sen) and postcolonial national fiction (Narayan). Despite fulfilling the terms of its usual classification, Narayan's position in the preindependence years was, I argue, not unlike *an aesthetic position occupied by contemporary diasporic writers*. In the early literary works set in Malgudi (*Swami and Friends* [1935], *The Bachelor of Arts* [1937], *The Dark Room* [1938], and *The English Teacher* [1945]), Narayan carefully crafted a viable small-town ethos that produced and satisfied the need for an *Indian* childhood and domestic life triumphant in its daily negotiations with the British colonial presence. As with contemporary immigrant fictional texts, Narayan built a sense of home and belonging, (re)producing social relations, individual performances of identity and a feel for the navigations of everyday life by his characters, with a degree of authorial skill and readerly complicity that rendered it immediately authentic and true to life. Thus, prior to India's establishment as an independent nation in 1947, Narayan's Malgudi produced a viable *Indian* hometown ethos (a sense of the local), which was consciously carved out of and against an imperial era of British global dominance.

This essay urges reconsideration of the perceived gap between national and diasporic cultural reproduction by focusing on these three specific renditions of fictional hometowns, each with its own spatial and chronological logic and splendor. The aesthetics of imagining hometowns in these contexts is patterned quite similarly through an idiom of authenticity established via a sustained play with hybridity. In these cultural texts, both authenticity and hybridity are carefully constructed and can be challenged at every turn of a page and/or street corner. Despite the different circumstances in which national and diasporic subjects live their everyday lives, I argue that at some moments in a national cultural production, the governing aesthetic is what I will call a "diasporic" aesthetic. Further, and just as routinely, diasporic cultural production operates with an immense debt to *national(ist)* imaginings of home. Thus, the term "diasporic aesthetics" is used in this essay in a metaphoric sense, by which I mean to signal the work of imagining that operates from *outside* a comfortable national framework and yet is *shaped* by forces of the nation-state(s). I use the term "diasporic" for want of a more suitable word that would better convey this aesthetics of straddling nation(s), migration, nostalgia, plans for the future, the imagined and the real. "Diasporic" aesthetics thus describes the imaginings that take place outside of, but are overwritten by, the idea of nation in the past, in contemporaneous time or, as in the case of Narayan, in the future. What I explore in this essay through the paintings and fiction of Narayan, Sen and Ganesan are the ways in which hegemonic ideas of home and nation, as well as their corresponding cultural and national identities, are reproduced and contested in spatially ordered representations of "hometowns." Both space and time are crucial pivots in the "diasporic" aesthetic, especially in matters of imagining home. This essay will trace the kinds of spatial affiliations that are attested to when writers and artists create fictional and visual cityscapes that attempt to imagine home and belonging for (and from) locations that are not yet homelike.

In the scholarly and mainstream discourse on migrants, immigrants and diasporas, such peoples are commonly understood as "trapped" by essentialist narratives of origin, of blood, of return to or rebuilding of a homeland. As individuals, they are disciplined by a vigilant maintenance of cultural purity even as they must daily navigate unfamiliar territories. According to David Eng, Sau-Ling Wong and others, spatial considerations of Asian America are fraught with anxiety and yearning, since Asian America is, to quote Eng (1997:31), a "siteless locale with no territorial sovereignty" (see also Wong 1995). Eng (1997:31) argues that "suspended between departure and arrival, Asian Americans remain permanently disenfranchised from home, relegated to a nostalgic sense of its loss or to an optative sense of its unattainability." In their aesthetic productions, however, the two Asian Americans I study in this essay do not remain wishfully or wistfully "suspended" between spaces, but instead suspend (as in architectural suspensions) imagined structures that satisfy this yearning for home. And, as I demonstrate in this essay, in fabricating such cultural representations of "hometowns," Sen and Ganesan embroider and alter the fabric of the seemingly more "rooted" fiction of Malgudi.

Social reproduction, Cindi Katz (2001:718) argues, is "precisely not 'revolutionary,'" because it "is focused on reproducing the very social relations and material forms that are so problematic." Hence, as is true for social reproduction in most contexts, cultural work in the immigrant or migrant context and in the context of national struggles for independence often does not radically alter the hegemonic social and economic relations that are already in place. Yet sometimes, in the cultural realm, especially when texts are situated in the gap between the national and the diasporic, there are spaces and times in which the reproduction of the usual order of things is disrupted by cultural products and practices. Here, one catches glimpses of a territory where national identity and social relations could be imagined differently. This essay attempts to catch glimpses of that territory in the work of R K Narayan, Indira Ganesan and Arijit Sen.

Malgudi Days

As Stuart Hall (1994), among others, has advocated, "diaspora" must be interpreted as a broad term. In his important essay, "Cultural Identity and Diaspora," Hall (1994:402) writes:

> I use this term metaphorically, not literally: diaspora does not refer us to those scattered tribes whose identity can only be secured in relation to some sacred homeland to which they must at all costs return, even if it means pushing other people into the sea ... The diaspora experience as I intend it here is defined, not by essence or purity, but by the recognition of a necessary heterogeneity and diversity: by a conception of "identity" which lives with and through, not despite difference: by *hybridity*.

My use of the term "diasporic aesthetic" for Narayan's early writing, as well as for Ganesan's and Sen's work, is a gesture toward this widened understanding of the term. However, Hall's notion of a "diasporic identity" as one that foregrounds hybridity is, in the specific context of the Caribbean diaspora in Europe, a reproduction (albeit with alterations) of what is commonly accepted (and acknowledged by Hall) as an "essential" feature of Caribbean culture. While hybridity, in the terms described by Hall, is an equally "essential" feature of culture in other parts of the globe (including India), in kind if not in degree, it is not generally the most readily summoned aspect of "homeland culture" that is manifested in nationalist discourse. Thus, Narayan's Malgudi, when viewed as a microcosm of an ordered, socially hierarchical, *Hindu* India that quietly flourishes despite the

details of political rule, is anything but hybrid. Instead, in the preindependence days, Malgudi held out the possibility of an "authentic"
India that predated the colonial era and would postdate it simply by
the power of its aura of timeless authenticity and the seeming naturalness of its hierarchies of caste, gender and class.[4]

From his first novel *Swami and Friends* (1935) to his writings in the
late 1990s, all of Narayan's novels and most of his short stories are set
in the imaginary South Indian city of Malgudi. In *Swami and Friends*,
the story revolves around the antics of nine-year-old Swami and
his classmates in the Albert Mission School. The novel focuses on
the ways in which Swami spends his days: memorizing maps of Europe
and Africa, dodging the blows of teachers, resisting Christian scripture
lessons by the devout convert Ebenezar, setting up the Malgudi Cricket
club, evading his father's surveillance, being spoilt by a doting grandmother with an unending fund of Hindu mythological tales, impress-
ing his friends, running through the streets of Malgudi, relaxing at the
banks of the River Sarayu and generally enjoying a carefree childhood. From the very first novel, then, the contours of Malgudi are
lovingly prescribed. All Narayan's protagonists are, like himself, Tamil
Brahmins. All middle- and upper-class children—the class categories
to which all central protagonists of Narayan's novels belong—go
either to the Albert Mission School/College or to the Board High
School. All teachers, such as the protagonist of *The English Teacher*,
teach in one or the other of these two educational institutions. All
prosperous families live in Lawley Extension. All films are seen at
Palace Talkies. All road travel in and out of Malgudi is conducted via
the trunk road. Malgudi society is one that does not change under
outside pressure: over the sixty-odd years during which Narayan
wrote about Malgudi, the town and its inhabitants remained
essentially the same. In the "Author's Introduction" to *Malgudi Days*,
a collection of short stories, Narayan (1984:8) provides this discussion of Malgudi:

> I have named this volume *Malgudi Days* in order to give it a plausible
> geographical status. I am often asked, "Where is Malgudi?" All I can
> say is that it is imaginary and not to be found on any map (although
> the University of Chicago has published a literary atlas with a map of
> India indicating the location of Malgudi). If I explain that Malgudi is
> a small town in South India I shall only be expressing a half-truth, for
> the characteristics of Malgudi seem to me universal.

In the hegemonic Indian Hindu nationalist context, Malgudi does
indeed have universal appeal. Narayan's Malgudi functions as a cultural reproduction of a Utopian present and future India sketched from
the point of view of an upper-class/caste intellectual. It is the utopia of
a benevolent Hinduism—a model city the order and set patterns of

which cement a conservative, nationalist anti-imperialism through its confidence that Hindu India survives the assaults of outsiders.

In retrospect, it is quite logical that Narayan chose to construct this dusty small town, merging into the villages that surrounded it, as the setting for his stories that take place in the 1930s. Narayan's Malgudi skillfully reproduced the vision of a new India that was shared by Indian nationalist leaders and intellectuals of the time: a Gandhian notion of the pastoral rural as the heart of India. From the 1930s to the 1960s, Narayan's fiction served as a means by which upper-caste (or caste-observant), urban, Indian bourgeois readers, who were more comfortable in the English language and its literature and with city life, could recognize, experience and participate in what was otherwise not available to them in such an immediate and aesthetically pleasing manner—small town/village India. Malgudi, the small town, with its villages, forests and hills on hand, became the flexible space between urban and rural. For urban Indians, Malgudi bridged the gap between their own experience and what was promoted as the rural heart of India. In Malgudi, Narayan had worked out a quasiurban location necessary to support the kind of domestic fiction plot (childhood, the travails of education, young love, the everyday triumphs and failures of the middle-class householder, upper-caste domesticity, the educated housewife's daily troubles, the young schoolteacher's frustrations) that evoked a rich response from the English-reading Indian audience. Hence, his 1938 novel, *The Dark Room*, narrates the disruption that ensues when Ramani, the manager of the Englandia Insurance Company, hires the company's first woman insurance agent, Westernized outsider Miss Shanta Bai, and then promptly becomes infatuated with her. Clearly this is not a plot that could be convincingly set in an Indian village in the 1930s. However, later in the novel, when the plot requires Ramani's wife Savitri to walk out of her comfortable home in protest over her husband's extramarital affair, determined to live outside of masculine protection, the smalltown milieu of this imagined city ensures that she comes to no harm.

Narayan's minimal literary interest in depicting contemporary Indian national struggles for independence is read either admiringly or disapprovingly by literary critics as a measure of his apolitical, even simplistic worldview. But while Narayan's early fiction did not loudly proclaim its support for Indian independence or for social change, as some of his contemporaries' work did, his novels performed the more subtle task of imagining a viable—albeit casteist—"Indian" small town community, where the otherwise overwhelming fact of being under foreign, imperial rule was a minor detail.[5] This romance of the unspoilt small town or village, which supported a private, communal life nearly untouched by British rule, is visible in many of the films, fiction and early anthropological studies produced in India from the 1940s to the 1970s.

Consider, for example, M N Srinivas's many anthropological works, including *India's Villages* (1955) and *The Remembered Village* (1976), as well as the classic anthropological study, *Behind Mud Walls, 1930–1960* by William and Charlotte Wiser, the early films of both art cinema (Satyajit Ray's *Apu Trilogy Pather Panchali* (1955)) and commercial cinema (*Do Bhiga Zameen* (1953), *Mother India* (1957), *Naya Daur* (1957), and Rajarao's novel *Kanthapura* (1938). In these works, we see the very same recording of the mythologized, representative "Indian" small town or village, captured as it enters the threshold of modernity.

Upgraded from village to small town, Malgudi allowed for a discourse of the arrival of modernity and the domestic and social frictions it produced. In the postindependence era, it provided a literary alternative and solution to the difficulties of anthropological sojourns in the village that Srinivas captured so beautifully in his work (cf Srinivas 1955, 1976).[6] Whereas other nationalist public discourses lauded the processes of modernization reaching the Indian village and transforming agricultural production, Narayan was able to offer his urban Indian reader something they could identify with more easily, the arrival of an intellectual and cultural modernity—in sum, a comfortable sort of fiction for the newly awakened Indian national bourgeoisie.

Narayan's reward (or punishment) was that his Malgudi became solidified in the national imagination as more truthfully Indian than was any actual Indian city. Postindependence, the Malgudi milieu was one that the author could not or would not update: its simple pleasures, conflicts and triumphs became ossified by popular demand. It is not that places *like* Malgudi or childhoods *like* Swami's did not exist, but rather that Narayan offered his readership the chance to partake of a very particular experience as the heritage and legacy of *every* Indian, regardless of region, religion, caste, class or gender. To be socially reproduced as an urban, modern Indian was to accept this rendition of one's roots and to find complete satisfaction in Narayan's picture of a benevolent, caste-ordered Hindu world. Thus, from a projection into an idealized version of the present and future, Narayan's Malgudi became the map of a lovingly remembered and idealized past that was formative of "Indianness" the world over.

Hometowns

I now turn to the establishment of similar, substantially imagined locales in two novels by Indira Ganesan, *The Journey* (1990) and *Inheritance* (1998) and in cityscapes painted by Arijit Sen. In Sen's and Ganesan's work, the parameters of the imagined places are attentive to the domestic imperatives of both US and Indian layouts/cityscapes, even as the two locations (the US and India) are transformed into imagined cityscapes that first disrupt and then, paradoxically, refurbish the very notion of belonging securely in a location that has substantial spatial reference. Each of these texts creates a detailed and very specific location in which the "action" is set. Both the city-sites of Sen's paintings and "Pi," the imaginary island off the Indian subcontinent where Ganesan's novels are set, are imagined "at a slight angle to reality," to use the felicitous phrase Salman Rushdie coined to describe immigrant locations in his novel *Shame* (1983:24). And yet, throughout the works, several actually existing locations—in India, in the United States, in fiction (Indian and other), in television shows, and in architectural textbooks—are pulled into service in these projects.

For South Asian–American woman writer Indira Ganesan, no existing nation or island was adequate to the story that unfolds on the island of Pi: a story that references the US, Europe and India with equal ease but is suspended inside, outside and alongside these continents. *The Journey* opens with two teenaged South Asian–American sisters, Meenakshi and Renu, as they travel from New York, where they live, to Madhupur, their ancestral home. In *The Journey*, Ganesan (1990:17) provides the following history and geography for Pi:

> When a group of lost white explorers found shelter on the island in 1726, they though they'd stumbled onto paradise. The captain, a man smitten with Shakespeare, claimed it for Holland and named it Prospero's Island: ever since, it has been known as P.I. or Pi. To the surprise of the Dutch, who thought the island uninhabited, Pi contained prosperous cities built on citadels, the largest of which was Madhupur. Kings and queens, resplendent in jewels and silks, ate from golden plates while their darker-hued workers toiled on repairing heavily trafficked roads. In less than a century, however, with the arrival of the French and the English, the imperialist conquest was complete, and the power transferred from the rajahs to the Europeans, where it remained under colonial rule until 1947. That year, depleted of nearly all its natural resources and having undergone a cultural identity crisis made all the more severe because of the Island's small size, Pi was grudgingly granted independence. Imagine a chunk of India that is not quite India torn free to float in the Bay of Bengal—this is Pi.

Now this is, of course, not an impossible or implausible history. It is patterned on the contours of the usual postcolonial, nationalist historical narrative: the accounts of "prosperous cities built on citadels" and then the arrival of the Dutch, the French and the British colonizers, followed by independence in 1947, the year of Indian independence and the creation of Pakistan. Ganesan's version of this history is rendered plausible, not just because of the genericism of most colonial history when narrated in its broadest strokes, but also because it is an instantly recognizable history that we have encountered in the movies (Hollywood adventure films as much as in Bollywood historical films) and in popular fiction. Hence, the insistence that Pi is not quite India displays an authorial determination to revamp social relations and spatial ordering. However, what gets reproduced is "a chunk of India that is not quite India torn free to float in the Bay of Bengal—this is Pi." What we have here is a reliance on India—colonial and postcolonial India—that is at once presented and repressed.

In Ganesan's novels, the link to the Indian mainland is tenuous and yet very serviceable. For instance, all arrivals onto the island and all departures are mediated through India: quite literally in terms of travel arrangements, which require flying into Madras in South India followed by a boat ride to the island. A bridge to the mainland is under construction, but the Nigerian artist/architect who is in charge of this project has very shaky credentials for bridge-building, as nicely presented in this tongue-in-cheek passage from *The Journey*: "Ten years ago a Nigerian artist received a land grant to build an ash mound on Pi. He created a hill of shredded paper, glue, ash … But the rains came two days after the project's completion and reduced it to a pulpy mess.… Now the same artist was building a bridge to connect the mainland to Pi" (Ganesan 1990:16–17). A papier-mâché bridge is perhaps what is in the offing, but the narrative deadpans through this passage; the irony is very submerged. Toward the end of the novel, there is actually a celebration of the completion of this bridge. Yet we are offered no assurances that this bridge will be more substantial than the papier-mâché art that the artist has produced in the past. In offering the reader a "paper" bridge to the mainland at the conclusion to her novel, Ganesan toys with the readerly expectation of a realist ending to what has been a novel written in an ostensibly realist mode. What we get is a bridge that is suggestive of the kind of textual travel that the reader undertakes when she reads, or—even more alluringly —suggestive of the literary bridge that Ganesan's work suspends between two locations that are both fictionalized from a diasporic location: Pi and India.

It is significant that Ganesan's novels do not reproduce the usual postcolonial take on *The Tempest*, in that she does not exploit the Caliban/Ariel aspect of Shakespeare's famously recycled play. Instead, other interpretive routes are opened up in the wry use of "Prospero's Island" as a place that transforms all who step onto its shores.[7] Ganesan has noted that one of the major influences on her writing in terms of style and theme was Maxine Hong Kingston's *The Woman Warrior*. The idea of staging her story on an island came to her, she has noted, in Provincetown, the (almost island-like) East Coast town where much of *The Journey* was written during Ganesan's sojourn at the Fine Arts Work Center. The island staging was also inspired by the T.V. show "Gilligan's Island." Clearly, the author's late-20th-century US educational and intellectual formation is evident in the plot and plan for this novel. Thus, both Indian and US "vernacular" knowledge is harnessed to produce this imaginary hometown.

In her second novel, *Inheritance,* Ganesan once again sets her story on the island of Pi. In this novel, there is no sign of the Nigerian artist's bridge to the mainland. Perhaps it did not hold and was reduced to pulp, like his other rain-soaked artwork; perhaps it has not yet been built. Chronologically, the references to Western cultural icons suggest that *Inheritance* is set in the late 1960s/early 1970s—or, if we allow for a slight lag in the popularity of US pop icons in Madhupur, it could be the early 80s.[8] In *Inheritance,* the island is described in the following fashion:

> But this was Pi, not Madras ... The island was off the coast of India, not connected to the mainland, an eye, a tiny eye, to the teardrop that was Sri Lanka. It had been invaded and colonized so many times that it nonchalantly absorbed the morals of every culture that came to it. Castes intermarried, racial lines were blurred, and nearly everyone was an eighth something else. I was certain my family had both African and Dutch blood in it somewhere, but that was of course hushed up. Anthropology would prove me right, but religion remained an obstacle. Our family descended from pure-blooded priests, said my grandmother, firmly refusing argument. As such, we had our own codes for conduct and old traditions reigned. (Ganesan 1998:61)

Madhupur, we are told, is "not Madras" because here "castes intermarried, racial lines were blurred, and nearly everyone was an eighth something else." Could Madras be read through a similar racially "blurred" lens? History would support it—but would nationalist historians or literary crafters? Malgudi, we can be certain, does not allow for the blurring of caste and racial lines.

After the passage quoted above, the narrative in *Inheritance* goes into a description of the marketplace, with its own hybrid set of products— jeans, saris, books in several languages, with a Turkish vendor comfortably wedged between vegetable and betel-nut sellers. It is here that Sonil, the 15-year-old heroine, meets thirty-year-old American Richard, who soon becomes her "love interest." The passage continues: "I passed a foreign couple, Japanese, in a cuddle. All around me, people were cuddling—Indians, islanders, Pakistanis, Singhalese" (Ganesan 1998:63).

In Malgudi, there is no such casual mingling of people from around the globe. In the early Narayan novels, there are, of course, constant references to English literature, cricket stars (Australian Donald Bradman and British Maurice Tate are Swami's idols), British items of everyday use (pens, paper, perfumes, books, clothes, ties, cars, films) and so on. And yet, for all this swirl of British colonial culture through Malgudi, there is a very strict demarcation between those who belong and those who do not. Consider this passage that begins chapter 11, "In Father's Presence," in *Swami and Friends*:

> During summer Malgudi was one of the most detested towns in South India. Sometimes the heat went above a hundred and ten in the shade ... The same sun that beat down on the head of Mr. Hentel, the mill manager, and drove him to Kodaikanal, or on the turban of Mr. Krishnan, the Executive Engineer, and made him complain that his profession was one of the hardest, compelling him to wander in sun and storm, beat down on Swaminathan's curly head, Mani's tough matted hair and Rajam's short wiry crop and left them unmoved. The same sun that baked the earth so much that even Mr. Retty, the most Indianised of the "Europeans," ... screamed one day when he forgetfully took a step or two barefoot, the same sun made the three friends loathe to remain under a roof. (Narayan 1935:78–79).

The ability to bear the heat is one of the many subtle ways in which Narayan attests to Swaminathan and his friends' secure sense of belonging in Malgudi as fully enfranchised young boys. In their hesitant use of English, their confusion when faced with complex math problems, the fearful encounters with tough, low-caste boys, the pain of being caned by headmasters, the excitement of participating in a rampage through the school under the pretext of a nationalist strike and the thrill of breaking the head master's windowpane, Swami and his friends are local boys.

In Ganesan's novels, however, the young girl protagonists come to Madhupur from New Jersey and/or from Madras: they are not "local girls," but they are expected to live up to a moral regime that is not without its reference to high-caste Madras. "Our family descended from pure-blooded priests, said my grandmother, firmly refusing argument. As such, we had our own codes for conduct and old traditions reigned." Thus, Sonil, the half-Pi, half Anglo-American protagonist of *Inheritance*, is not a good Indian girl, but one caught in the snares of being "a good island girl." "Half-Pi" leads to yet another possible interpretation of Pi, as in mongrel, commonly used in Indian English, as in "pi-dog." This is an interpretation supported by the text: for example, Sonil's name, we are told, was chosen by her family precisely because it was "a name with no definite roots" (Ganesan 1998:8) What does one become if one is "half-Pi," or "half-hybrid"? Despite the insistence on a kind of "compulsory hybridity," as it were, the overlaps between Pi and India are so numerous that we are surprised by the differences— even though we should not be, because after all, Pi is not Madras.

Despite the trenchant and repeated assertions that Pi is not India, it would be futile to refuse any comparisons, or to underestimate the links to India or to Narayan's Malgudi. The narrative makes clear that Pi is not India (except when it is like India), and this ambivalence is quite deliberate. What is this India that Pi is and is not? The unviolated/ unviolatable India of the Indian upper-caste bourgeois nationalist fantasy, as much as of the diasporic imagination, is what Pi is measured against. But, one might argue, India is also not equal to the nationalist fantasy that is produced from within the Indian context, nor is it equal to the quite similar diasporic fantasy of the homeland. Against such impossibilities, Malgudi continues to serve as the best example of this serenely consumed fantasy.

Despite appearances, *pure* Malgudi and *hybrid* Madhupur are born of similar imperatives: both these "twin cities" (if you like) assume an ideal India that is a fiction and yet is so entrenched in the national and diasporic imaginary as to appear real. Malgudi, then, is the "real" India of Ganesan's fiction. The diasporic reading of time and space is such that sometimes a very "strict" notion of the national is, paradoxically, a diasporic stance in itself—hence the need for Pi, where variations on the ideal can be staged. The geographic and cultural proximity of this imagined island to (Tamil Brahmin) South India looms too large to easily allow for differences or alterations. Often these differences are read as "mistakes" in the home country, even as critics in the West commend Ganesan's work for its authentic recreation of "India." Hence, when *Inheritance* was reviewed in the highly influential *Indian Review of Books*, Kavery Nambisan (herself the author of a modestly praised novel, *The Scent of Pepper*) lambasted the novel in a review entitled "Disinherited." The review begins with a sentence that speaks volumes about the global economics of publishing and the envy created by the disparate value—perceived or real—assigned to books according to the location of the artist: "When the book you get to review is a Secker and Warburg publication and that too by an Indian writer (*expat but even so*), you had better sit up and get excited. More so when its price implies that her talent is worth its weight in gold" (Nambisan 1997:43).

Before I elaborate on Nambisan's critique of Ganesan's novel, I need to frame this review within a larger ongoing struggle being waged between Indian writers in English and those writing in other Indian vernacular languages. In brief, this "conflict" came out in the open with the provocative argument made by Rushdie (1997b:xiv) in the *New Yorker* in 1997 that, except for the work of the occasional writer such as Sadat Manto (Urdu), the best Indian writing since independence had been done in English. This arrogant assertion is underscored by the undeniable fact that the Indian literature that has garnered the largest royalties, as well as the most international literary awards, is written in English.[9] Regional-language writers of repute, such as U R Ananthamurthy (Kannada), Sunil Gangopadhyay (Bengali), Balchandran Nimade (Marathi), Dilip Chitre (Marathi), Rajendra Yadav (Hindi), Gurdial Singh (Punjabi) and others, were all quoted as having denounced Indian writing in English as "second-rate," "artificial Western flowers," "a third-rate serpent-and-rope trip," "removed from their own ethos" and "rootless" (Reddy 2002). Writers such as Shashi Deshpande, who writes in English, responded with astonishment and hurt at the degree of hostility expressed by vernacular writers. "We belong to the same world you did, all of us were part of the ocean called Indian Literature ... This is our home, as it is yours; we did not drop out of the skies when we started writing in English" (Deshpande 2002). In all these exchanges, the distinction/distance between IWE (Indian writers in English) from India and those writing in English from the diaspora is blurred by regional vernacular writers and insisted upon by India-based English language writers. Hence, Nambisan's specific disdain for the "diasporic" aspects of Ganesan's plot and characterization must be seen as a means of distancing her own writing—and the writing of other English-language, India-based writers—from the literary work produced in the diaspora.

In "Disinherited," Nambisan "forgets" her early noting that the book is set on the island of Pi and continues to read the novel as if it were attempting to reproduce a realist representation of domestic life in India. Note the dismissive synopsis of the plot Nambisan (1997:43) provides:

> The story is set in the imaginary island of Pi, which lies between India and Sri Lanka and is conveniently of no historic or cultural importance. Our fifteen-year-old protagonist Sonil (mother Tamil, father American) goes to Pi from Madras for a longish holiday with her grandmother. Sonil's mother, Lakshmi, has three daughters from three different genetic sources, but before you can spell "wow!" you read (in a single para) that Sonil's siblings aren't any less adventurous. One sister Shalini married Dan, an Irishman who schooled in Scotland and met her at the home of his parents in Mysore, and the other sister Leila married Petrov, a Russian who grew up in North India.

Even in India, I might insist, there are Shalinis who marry Dans (children of Scottish, Irish and English expatriates or missionaries), as well as, perhaps, Leilas who marry one of the many Russians who, in the postindependence years, were sent to various industrial cities in North India in the capacity of technical advisors, engineers, and so on to the many Indo-Soviet industrial and power projects. But this is *not* a mainstream Indian narrative of marriage, either in fiction or in other discourses. Hence, Nambisan declares that this is an unfeasible and overly "eventful" set of plot details. The review continues: "There are, scattered amongst the pages, little placards screaming that this is a book about the Indian Diaspora" (Nambisan 1997:44). Then Nambisan quotes a couple of passages from the book; interspersed between Ganesan's sentences are Nambisan's notations of "sic," which serve to illustrate the mistakes that "scream" the text's diasporic location and the corresponding "limitations" of the writer.

Granting Nambisan's right to find *Inheritance* wanting in literary merit, it is Ganesan's perceived inability (or disinclination) to perfectly reproduce the social ethos easily recognized as a "typical" South Indian (read, Tamil Brahmin) domestic world that seems to especially annoy the reviewer. Ganesan's protagonists are young girls and older Brahmin women, widows who live with their daughters in the US and visit Madhupur. Alternately, they are indolent Brahmin women, such as Lakshmi, in *Inheritance*, who has had one daughter in—and two daughters out of—wedlock with men with whom she refuses a more "respectable" or long-term affiliation. We are clearly not in the Malgudi of Narayan's *The Darkroom*, with its neat dichotomy between the virtuous Tamil Brahmin wife, Savitri, and the Westernized working woman, Shanta Bai, who comes from the big city and seduces Savitri's husband, Raman.

In *The Journey* and *Inheritance*, despite Ganesan's provocative attempts to alter *some* of the details of the usual representation of Tamil Brahmin domesticity, especially around the representation of upper-caste women, her work is unable to relinquish the class and caste privileges that accrue to such sites. Thus, in each of these novels, the drama unfolds around a familial tragedy that ultimately gathers up only those who are truly family. Ultimately, it is this return to the fold that undermines Ganesan's deliberate injections of "impurity" into her narrative about three generations of strong-willed Pi women. However, Nambisan is much too invested in dismissing the novel on the bases of its "diasporic mistakes" to appreciate Ganesan's attempts to fissure the terrain of upper-caste gender dynamics.

Accompanying and illustrating Nambisan's review is a remarkable cartoon by an artist with the pen name "Greystroke." The cartoon shows a man selling "Root-Nourishing Shampoo," and its punch line states: "Eh … I … don't know if there's … er … a special 'Expatriate Writer' version … sorry … " (Nambisan 1997:43). The cartoon is representative of some of the ways in which the expatriate writer is invoked in the home country as one in search of artificial, ineffective and superficial means of nourishment for her/his "roots." Narayan's early delineation of Malgudi was equally concerned with providing roots in the "real India" for an Indian clientele, and each subsequent work set in this city added nourishment to these roots. But because of the more conventional rules of classifying cultural products as either diasporic *or* authentic, the novels of Ganesan appear more readily diasporic, and thereby serve to consolidate Narayan's fiction as effortless, even artless, firmly grounded in reality: in a word, authentic.

Caught up in a complex discursive struggle over authenticity and language, the political economy of who gets to speak and from what material vantage point in the diaspora, Nambisan's review essay reveals much about the transnational dynamics of literary production and consumption. The review ends with this statement: "The *Sunday Times* has extolled this novel [*Inheritance*] as 'a book that glows with the magic of Indian childhood ... a quiet, intelligent novel.' It appears that the *Sunday Times* reviewer knows precious little about Indian childhood, and the author not much more" (Nambisan 1997:44). That Pi is not India is not taken seriously either by this Indian reviewer or by the (presumably Western) reviewer of the British *Sunday Times*. The many strands of history, experience and popular culture—all disparate vernaculars—that underwrite this fiction are not given equal attention. Diasporic writers are immediately pulled into one national frame or the other, in book reviews, on bookshelves, in catalogs and on syllabi. However consciously and carefully these "new" spaces are imagined, they are attached like phantom limbs to already existing narrations of domestic space within a national framework. "Diasporic mistakes," then, need to be read as "diasporic license," as a feature of a "diasporic aesthetic" that allows these works to elucidate the world in which they are produced (and the worlds they reproduce), even while they present detailed locations that cannot be found on ordinary maps.

Cityscape I, Cityscape II

Arijit Sen's paintings help to visualize some of these complexities of reproducing similar, though not identical, notions of home in both national and diasporic contexts. The cityscapes produced by the South Asian–American, Berkeley-based artist/architect offer a panoramic view of real and imagined city scenes to which all the landscapes of the places he has lived in (and/or imagined) contribute. I focus primarily on two paintings: "Cityscape I, 1985" and "Cityscape II, 1992."

"Cityscape I, 1985" is an aesthetic extrapolation depicting the view from the balcony of the artist's parents' flat in Calcutta, India (Figure 1). From here, Sen moves outward, but not into the Calcutta of easily identifiable landmarks, such as the Victoria Memorial, Howda Bridge or New Market. Nor does he move into the easily identifiable associations of Calcutta with Mother Theresa, or the hammer-and-sickle symbol of the communist state government. Rather, he expands this imagined cityscape into an abstract set of buildings and shapes that are suggestive of a dense urban cityscape. The banal Indianness of this urban scene is visible everywhere—in the *chhajas*, or small concrete awnings over the windows, the billboard that dominates its surroundings, the color and suggestion of dampness of the walls and the canvas tent in the foreground, of the kind typically used to cover ongoing telephone-line repair work in urban India. The buildings in the foreground meld into an abstraction of geometric shapes of varying size and color. Yet nestled among these shapes that signify urbanity is a

Figure 1: "Cityscape I, 1985." Reprinted with permission of the artist

carefully detailed cluster of six or seven huts, complete with thatched roofs, as suggested by the brush strokes and the shape and color of the same. Is this an aesthetically refined reference to the ubiquitous urban slum, or a gesture toward the mythologized Indian village that dominates the Bengali imaginary landscape—more forcefully, some would argue, than in any other region of the nation? In the Bengali Hindu bourgeois ethos (the Badhralok ethos, to be specific), the dominant reference for village India has been the powerful image of Shantinekatan, the center for the study of the visual and performing arts set up in a village-like setting outside Calcutta in the early 20th century. It was established by Rabindranath Tagore (1861–1941), the most feted of literary icons in 20th-century Bengali cultural history. In a cityscape that revels in its unreality, with its two-dimensional staging, this "hut" section of the canvas is presented within the careful "realist" mode supplied by the appropriate manipulation of depth and perspective. In this section of the canvas, in Sen's capitulation to the stark realist style, we see that very same national mythology of the Indian village. Yet, considering it as a part of the entire canvas as a visual representation of a "cityscape," what we have before us is an acknowledgement of this mythologizing in the midst of this reproduction of personal memory passing for a formalized view of the city. Sen effectively uses the visual rhetoric of architecture, of photography and of geometric model-building only to lay bare the constructedness of all of these mediums of capturing reality in scale.

One can see the pastiche of past and present places even more clearly in the autobiographical narrative, "Cityscape II, 1992" (Figure 2). The thematic and formal continuities between the work painted while

Figure 2: "Cityscape II, 1992." Reprinted with permission of the owner

in India and the one painted after the artist moved to the United States
are counterpoised by the differences in the two works. This painting
stitches together a very recognizable city from contributions made
by various buildings, streets and architectural details from the artist's
past. The Calcutta cityscape continues in the top left-hand corner of
the canvas. Several buildings from Iowa State University (to which
Sen went from India to study architecture) also appear in altered form
on this canvas, most recognizably Breardshear Hall, with its green
dome, and Mary Chapman Catt House; these are both apparent at the
top center of the canvas. San Francisco, Berkeley, New York City, rural
Bengal or Shantinekatan (see the pristine hut in the foreground), the
canals of Venice and the *chhajas* of Indian windows (or are they of
Berkeley buildings, owned, perhaps, by Indian landlords?) all present
themselves as an integral part of this cityscape.

In both these paintings, Sen plays with the viewers' expectations of
perspective. For example, the bottom left section of the 1992 painting
offers a view of stairs that lead "perfectly naturally" to a street or alley
in which the placement of street lights and of people (such as the
musician under one such light), violently distorts the expectations
of the viewing eye. The sudden switch to a two-dimensional
perspective disrupts a nostalgic understanding of the alley, with round
globes of light and a street musician, as the romanticized "real." On the
opposite side of the canvas, however, an embedded courtyard or city
square is presented in the precise visual diction of architectural plans,
with figures on the move, naturalized by the painstaking details provided
by the shadows and angles of the corners of buildings. The transitions

between the buildings, stairs and streets in this painting are not smooth or "natural," and yet we, as viewers, participate in composing these discrete parts of the painting into a cityscape. Sen's cityscapes both disrupt and assert the norms by which such spatial arrangements are represented. Yet, despite these disruptions, we are presented with a viable homescape: depth, perspective, geography and "the real," Sen's paintings suggest, are no impediments to spatializing home.

Conclusion

If, as the saying goes, the past is another country, then all memory is diasporic. In the imaginary cities created by Narayan, Ganesan, and Sen, the subject is cocooned in a hometown that seamlessly supports and is perfectly adequate to the narrative that unfolds within the text. In all of these lovingly imaged hometowns, nostalgia is managed, mixed with memory and desire and offered up for the pleasures of consumption for those who are "hailed" by the text. This imagining is evident in the much quoted-statement by Graham Greene that Narayan "wakes in me a spring of gratitude, for he has offered me a second home. Without him I could never have known what it is like to be an Indian." S Krishnan, the editor of *Malgudi Landscapes* (1992), ends his introduction to the collection with this quote by Greene, followed by this final sentence: "To which it can be added that even to Indians born and bred, he [Narayan] performs a similar service by revealing truths about ourselves we have not been aware of (Krishnan 1992:xiv)." Statements such as these confirm the power of culture in the task of social reproduction. "Diasporic" aesthetics, with its "mistakes," additions and subtractions, its nostalgic remembering and forgetting, provides avenues for the subject's flexing of cultural agency in the very manipulation of spatial sensibilities. The three topoi discussed in this essay all reproduce serviceable imaginary hometowns that both pay homage to and rebel against what has always passed for the real. In their spatiotemporal manipulations, these cultural texts demonstrate that desire, childhood, memory and fantasy are all at play in the processes of social reproduction.

Acknowledgments

I would like to thank Nicole King, Lisa Lowe, David Ludden, Katharyne Mitchell, Chandan Reddy, Kamala Visweswaran and Lisa Yoneyama for their comments on various versions of this essay. I thank Indira Ganesan and Arijit Sen for answering questions and for allowing me to recast their work within the interpretive frames I set up in this essay.

Endnotes

[1] This letter to the editor was written in response to Tunku Varadarajan's (2001a) article in the *Wall Street Journal* entitled "In Madras Once, A Writer Pauses, Visitors

Bear Gifts." See also Varadarajan's (2001b) article in the *Indian Express*, "In Chennai Once, A Sweet Talk with Narayan."

² Indira Ganesan came to St Louis, Missouri with her parents as a five-year-old child in the late 1960s. Ganesan did her BA at Vassar college and has an MFA from the Iowa Writers Workshop. She currently resides in Southampton, NY and is working on a third novel set in Pi (meeting with the author, 20 December 1999, Princeton, NJ; phone conversations, 11 March 2000 and 15 May 2001).

³ Arijit Sen was born in Calcutta, India in 1964. He studied architecture in Bombay and worked as an architect in New Delhi before coming to the US in 1989 to join the Architecture program at Iowa State University. Sen has a PhD in Architectural History and the Social Basis of Architecture from the University of California, Berkeley (phone conversation with author, 10 March 2000; meetings 3 May 2000 and 5 May 2001, Berkeley).

⁴ For more on this reading of Narayan, see George (1996:121–128, 134–135).

⁵ See for comparison, the overt nationalist, reformist message of Mulk Raj Anand's 1935 novel in English, *Untouchable*. (1935) New Delhi: Arnold Publications, 1981.

⁶ See Srinivas's *The Remembered Village* (1976) for a fascinating account of the attraction that village India held for patriotic, England-educated, urban Indian young men of the 1940s and the simultaneous sense of the difficulty of actually dedicating one's life to such places. Srinivas recounts his own romanticized expectations of village life even as he presents the trials of doing fieldwork in a village in south India in the late 1940s.

⁷ In a phone interview with the author on 11 March 2000, Ganesan stated that having studied the play at Vassar in the early 1980s, she found it compelling but saw no reason to identify with Caliban or Ariel, nor could she imagine any impediments to her choosing to focus instead on Prospero.

⁸ Subsequent references to the death of Indira Gandhi in the concluding section of *Inheritance* suggest that some of the events take place in 1984 (Ganesan 1998:161).

⁹ Most recently, the broad strokes of this battle were exposed by the exchanges between "IWE" (Indian writers in English) and writers in the vernaculars (regional languages) on the occasion of the first International Festival of Indian Literature (New Delhi, February 2002), as showcased in recent issues of Indian magazine *Outlook* (25 February 2002). I am grateful to Richa Nagar for bringing this particular set of articles in *Outlook* to my attention.

References

Chopra B K (1957) *Naya Daur*. Film

Deshpande S (2002) English's inter alia: An open letter to some fellow writers. *Outlook* 11 March. http://www.outlookindia.com/full.asp?fodname=20020311&fname=Column+Deshpandey+%28F%29&sid=1 (last accessed 17 February 2003)

Eng D (1997) Out here and over there: Queerness and diaspora in Asian American studies. *Social Text* 52/53:31–52

Ganesan I (1990) *The Journey*. New York: Knopf

Ganesan I (1998) *Inheritance*. New York: Knopf

George R M (1996) *The Politics of Home: Postcolonial Relocations and Twentieth Century Fiction*. Cambridge, UK: Cambridge University Press

Hall S (1994) Cultural identity and diaspora. In P Williams and L Chrisman (eds) *Colonial Discourse and Postcolonial Theory* (pp 392–403). New York: Columbia University Press

Katz C (2001) Vagabond capitalism and the necessity of social reproduction. *Antipode* 33(4):709–728

Khan Mehboob (1957) *Mother India*. Film

Krishnan S (ed) (1992) *Malgudi Landscapes: The Best of R K Narayan*. New Delhi: Penguin

Mishra P (1999) Little inkling. *Outlook* 15 November. http://www.outlookindia.com/full.asp?fodname=19991115&fname=pankaj&sid=1

Nambisan K (1997) Disinherited. *Indian Review of Books* 6(11):43–44

Nagarkar K (2001) The worlds of India. *Outlook* 12 March. http://www.outlookindia.com/contents.asp?fnt-20010312.archive
Narayan R K ([1935] 2000) *Swami and Friends.* Mysore, India: Indian Thought Publication
Narayan R K [1937] *The Bachelor of Arts.* London: T Nelson
Narayan R K [1938] *The Dark Room.* London: Macmillan
Narayan R K [1945] *The English Teacher.* London: Eyre & Spottiswoode
Narayan R K ([1972] 1982) *Malgudi Days.* New Delhi: Penguin
Narayan R K ([1974] 2000) *My Days: Autobiography.* Mysore: Indian Thought Publication
Narayan R K (1988) *A Writer's Nightmare: Selected essays 1958–1988.* New Delhi: Penguin
Narayan R K (1992) *Malgudi Landscapes: The Best of R K Narayan.* Ed S Krishnan. New Delhi: Penguin
Ram S and Ram N (1996) *R K Narayan: The Early Years: 1906–1945.* New Delhi: Viking Penguin
Ray Satyajit (1955) *Apu Trilogy: Pather Panchali.* Film. Produced by the Government of West Bengal.
Reddy S (2002) Midnight's orphans: How Indian is Indian writing in English? *Outlook* 25 February http://www.outlookindia.com/full.asp?fodname=20020225&fname=Cover+Story&sid=1 (last accessed 17 February 2003).
Roy Bimal (1953) *Do Bhiga Zameen.* Film
Rushdie S (1983) *Shame.* New York: Random House
Rushdie S (1997a) Damn this is the oriental scene for you! *The New Yorker* 23/30 June: 50–61
Rushdie S (1997b) Introduction. In S Rushdie and E West (eds) *The Vintage Book of Indian Writing, 1947–1997* (pp ix–xxiii). New York: Vintage
Sivakumaran A (2001) Letter to the editor. *Wall Street Journal* 25 May
Srinivas M N (ed) (1955) *India's Villages.* Bombay: Asia Printing House
Srinivas M N (1976) *The Remembered Village.* Berkeley: University of California Press
Tharoor S (2001) Comedies of suffering. *THE HINDU* 8 July:Sunday Magazine section, III
Varadarajan T (2001a) In Madras once, a writer pauses, visitors bear gifts. *Wall Street Journal* 18 May: Weekend Journal, Taste page
Varadarajan T (2001b) In Chennai once, a sweet talk with Narayan. *The Indian Express* 19 May
Wiser W H and Wiser C V (1963) *Behind Mud Walls, 1930–1960.* Berkeley: University of California Press
Wong S L (1995) Denationalization reconsidered: Asian-American cultural criticism at a theoretical crossroads. *Amerasia Journal* 21:1–2

Part 3

Modern Migrants/Flexible Citizens: Cultural Constructions of Belonging and Alienation

Chapter 7
Valuing Childcare:
Troubles in Suburbia

Geraldine Pratt

According to a 1998 US government study, average wages for early education and care staff ranked 757 among the 774 occupations surveyed (quoted in Nelson 2001). Americans pay more to those who attend their parked cars than to those who attend their children. Numerous feminists (Jenson and Sineau 2001; Luxton 1997) note that *now* is a key moment to challenge this undervaluing of the work of social reproduction; with the withdrawal of the welfare state within frameworks of neoliberalism, they worry about further devaluation of care work in the absence of timely, clear and concerted counter-arguments. As Fraser (2000) also notes, if this moment carries certain dangers, it also offers opportunities for feminists to articulate an emancipatory vision of a renewed welfare state.

Effective counterarguments will need to grapple with the complex weave of ideas and practices that cheapen paid domestic labour and the costs of social reproduction, ideas and practices lived by men and women alike. As a way of introducing some of these complexities, let me tell two stories, developed from interviews with two middle-class Vancouver women conducted in the summer of 1995. The first involves a lawyer living with her husband—also a lawyer—and their three children. When the children were infants, the parents hired a live-in nanny, a woman who came to Canada from Scotland through the Live-in Caregiver Program (LCP). By the end of her seven-year tenure with this family—the longest of any employer interviewed—the nanny was a Canadian citizen, lived away from her employers' home, and earned Can$28,000 a year (the highest wage paid by any employer interviewed—by a long shot). The employer knew that she was paying a relatively high wage but reasoned that,

> When you think about it, it's not a huge amount of money for some-body who's living on her own. Actually, she was sharing an apartment, but I don't think that she could have done it if she was earning less. I really think that daycare is undervalued.

This woman went on—in the next sentence—to tell me of a petition that a friend had sent to her to protest the pending changes to the British Columbia (BC) Employment Standards Act, changes that would enforce a minimum hourly wage and overtime provisions for domestic workers. Herself paying over twice the minimum wage—that is, over twice what the new regulations would require—this woman signed the petition, reasoning that the proposed changes would make it "impossible for some women to work."

On another day I interviewed a woman who was on the other side of this struggle over wages for domestic work. She had, in fact, collaborated with a domestic workers' organisation to lobby for the changes to the BC Employment Standards Act resisted by the employer discussed above. She worked for a union and was also married to a lawyer, albeit a radical one. In her home office hangs a poster that reads: "Class struggle is knowing which side you're on." In her view,

> People [don't] value domestic workers, and I think that's what is at the fundamental heart of this. I think that the wage is really a rating of what the work involves and what it's worth.

She had indeed paid a part-time, live-out Filipina nanny $13 an hour for childcare, twice the minimum wage. But her job had just gone full-time, and she had recently hired a live-in Filipina nanny at $8 an hour —a wage that still exceeded the minimum wage (which was soon to be raised to $7 an hour) … but not by much. She registered her discomfort around the wage by indicating that the nanny would have paid time off and that she might adjust the wage in the future, but (she qualified) "[I]t really depends on how my business does."

These women's stories captivate me, because their shared feminist ideals of valuing domestic work run up against some other shared assumptions and hard material realities. I want to explore these assumptions and realities more fully as a means toward articulating counter-arguments, but also to envision a way of redrawing political lines and putting these two women on the same side of the collective political struggle to increase wages for paid domestic work. One tool that I draw upon is that of geographical difference. Much feminist scholarship assumes a relentless uniformity to the devaluation of domestic labour. This is stated no more explicitly than by Leonard (2001), who conceives of changes in women's work practices to be little more than "old wine in new bottles." She (2001:67) stresses that "[D]espite regional and national variations in women's incorporation into paid employment (both formal and informal), wherever they live women continue to be primarily responsible for domestic duties and childcare." While there is general truth to this statement, I wish to pursue some of the geographical specificities in the ways these responsibilities for social reproduction are managed—in particular, through a suburban/urban distinction that existed in Vancouver in the mid-1990s. I pursue this geographical specificity because it seems to offer opportunities for articulating differently situated women within a broader, reinvigorated feminist politics.

Rationalising Low Wages

The occasion to listen to the complex beliefs that eventuate in low wages for seemingly the most prized of domestic labour—childcare—was provided by a series of interviews that I did with parents advertising for at-home childcare in Vancouver. I describe the experiences of those who pay for home daycare and not for care at a daycare centre. With only 13 infant daycare spaces (for children from 3–18 months of age) in the city of Vancouver in 1998, this describes the experiences of the majority of families with infants who require childcare (Bester 1999).[1] I found the employers that I interviewed through advertisements for nannies in local newspapers, one from the affluent west side of Vancouver and two from outer eastern suburbs.[2] Both are middle-class areas of mostly single-family housing. As Figure 1 indicates, the city study area tends to be somewhat more affluent. Considering the occupations of the women interviewed, there is substantial variability in each area, but there is a slightly larger number of "professionals" and health-care workers in the city subsample. An astonishing 90 percent of those I contacted agreed to an interview, a striking measure of how eager these parents were to talk about their experiences.

Although all had advertised for a nanny to come to their house to care for their child/ren, by the time of the interview, they had settled

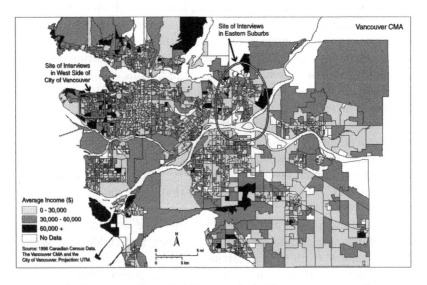

Figure 1: Study areas and household incomes in the Vancouver metropolitan area

on a range of solutions. These solutions included: live-in nanny; live-out nanny (full-time or part-time); and care outside the home, mostly in unlicensed family childcare.[3] The variety of solutions offered an interesting opportunity to assess costs, wages and experiences across a variety of childcare options. I first focus on common discourses—shared by parents who lived in different parts of Vancouver and who chose different childcare options—that work together to cheapen the costs of childcare.

The Gendered Loop

Feminists have identified a "gendered loop," in which women with paid employment hire other women to supply the labour of social reproduction they would otherwise provide for "free" (Gregson and Lowe 1994; Leonard 2001; McKie, Bowlby and Gregory 2001). The women I interviewed were operating within this loop, and generally it was taken for granted that women—even in dual-income households[4] —were responsible for paying for the domestic labour they did not perform themselves. An interview with a university professor living on the west side of Vancouver exemplifies this assumption:

Employer 13:   Well, I mean in the days when I was a post-doc it was, you know, probably over 90% that I was paying out, because I basically had nothing left. My husband paid all the [other] bills. I paid the nanny.

G P: It's interesting that you would pay the nanny.

13:            Well, I guess it was just my choice. I could have chosen to stay home and he could have chosen to pay the bills. But I didn't choose to do that. Not because I earned enough money but because I'd chosen to have an academic career.

The language of choice is persistent: the woman could choose a career or not. The interviews were replete with this kind of statement: women are responsible for childcare expenses and husbands' salaries enter in a compensatory way when the woman chooses not to work outside of the home. Another example comes from the transcript of an interview with a female television editor living in a suburban location:

Employer 27: That was one of the things we had to say right after that [when interviewing for a nanny], you know: "This is the wage: $6 an hour." Although I have to admit that wage seemed absolutely ludicrous. I pay people more than that to clean my house. But I only have to pay [for cleaning] like twice a month. But it just seems crazy to pay people more to clean your house than to look after your [3] kids. But I can't afford $12 [an hour] to look after my children. I would stay home ... there would be no point in my working if I had to pay more than [$6 an hour] ... And I thought about that too, you know, comparing what I need to what I could afford to pay out ... But for me, I wanted to go back to work [after the birth of each of her three children] because I need to work. I can't stay home full time.

Her husband, a film producer, remained quite shadowy in her ruminations about finances, although she did mention that he had asked her whether she would like to stop working, a decision he supported.

These are remarkable instances of individualized economic rationality, as each woman calculates the "opportunity costs" of her paid employment. Employer 27 begins to complicate this when she notes that she "needs to work," but she stops short of developing this analysis, and in neither case do the women make the calculations over the span of a career. This is unfortunate, because there is considerable evidence that a "break" from the labour market has long-term effects on occupational status and lifetime wages, especially for women residing in higher-status neighbourhoods (Mattingly, Hanson and Pratt 1997–1998).

The ways in which these short-term calculations (ie current wages against current childcare expenses) are structured have two effects. First, as long as payment for childcare comes out of a single wage—often the lowest in the household—there will be a low wage ceiling for childcare in all but the wealthiest private homes. Nelson (2001:11) describes the tendency to judge the affordability of childcare on the basis of a woman's salary alone as "a brick wall—a hard limit on the amount that *can* be paid for early education and care." Beyond this, gendered assumptions about responsibilities for childcare expenses force middle-class women to continually scrutinise, reassess and question their own commitment to the labour force.[5] In this sense, the "gendered loop" marginalises the paid employment of both groups of women, albeit in different ways.

Invisibility of and Ambivalence Toward Skills

Another factor that depresses wages for childcare is a strange blankness and ambivalence that exists around the requirements of the job, the skills required to do them and evidence of a job well done. Employer 40 exemplifies this ambivalence. On the one hand, she spoke of necessary skills, particularly driving and disciplinary ones. She appreciated the different skills that various nannies had brought to the care of her (now) 5-year-old son:

My Swiss nanny, for instance, was a professional artist, and so they did a lot of arts and crafts things. And my current nanny is a keen Rollerblader and likes mountain, rock-climbing.

She required her nanny to keep a daily journal, in which the nanny recorded the three meals provided to her son and a few sentences about the activities of the day. But a discussion of the wages paid to the nanny led her to comment:

> You have your transportation costs of going into work, the costs associated with eating lunch out part of the time, the costs associated with dressing for the job. You are falling behind in no time. And as well, your nanny gets to spend time with your children, and live in the house that you are paying an outrageous mortgage on, while you are never there for 11 hours a day.

Thus, while the nanny's skills were acknowledged and valued, the employer simultaneously cast the job as recreation. The ambivalence about whether domestic activities are properly classified as work or leisure—a familiar one (VanEvery 1997)—was further complicated in this case by a set of resentments of the nanny's opportunity to enjoy the employer's house and backyard pool in the company of her son.

More generally, employers spoke with a good deal of emotion, not just about the difficulty of leaving their infant, but also about their lack of confidence in their ability to assess job applicants. Part of the challenge is that they were trying to assess character as much as skills and experience. They wanted someone who was reliable, warm and firm about discipline, had good judgement about safety, was active and stimulating and would not abuse their child physically, sexually or emotionally. It was not at all clear to them how these qualities connected to skills or experience.

In some ways, a devaluation of childcare providers' skills is a specific case of a more general tendency to undervalue traditionally feminised skills, especially those associated with nurturance (England 1993). So, too, the home—particularly the more feminised spaces within it—tends to be a place in which labour is undervalued. Researchers have found that women tend to underestimate the time that domestic tasks require of them (Luxton 1997), and both men and women even trivialise the technology built into female-identified domestic objects, such as microwaves (Cockburn 1997).

But there are further peculiarities associated with paid domestic labour. In particular, this is a job for which employers are absent from the workplace and thus have few opportunities to supervise work quality. For those interviewed, there was often a striking insubstantiality to the criteria set out for a good nanny, at least until a problem developed. Employers agreed that they wanted someone who was stimulating, but what counts as stimulation? One example of an employer working through what this might mean comes from a judge who had hired a Filipina nanny with a BSc in Education and five and a half years of experience as a nanny to care for her infant. (This employer is an exception in knowing her nanny's educational qualifications and work experience.) After three and a half years, the employer's child was diagnosed at preschool as "speech-delayed," a crisis that provoked this parent to reassess what qualifies as stimulation. I quote her observations at length to convey a sense of her struggle to determine what constitutes quality care, and her effort to weigh this against concerns about labour control.

> Employer 19: What he used to do in the morning, because we had this real thing about wanting him to be out … In order to make sure that he wasn't just sitting around the house with her, while she sort of read the paper, I decided I would have him out every morning in an activity: one morning to the gym, one to music … What happened was she would get him up, and bathe him and dress him, and baby him essentially. She'd take him at 10:30 to his appointed activity for 45 minutes. At this point the kids are just tearing around, all parallel play. And then she would bring him home, get him all quiet, prepare lunch and then she'd take him off to preschool at one o'clock and pick him up at 4.

After the speech delay was identified, the employer rethought what stimulation might mean:

> So I cancelled every single class he was involved in. Cut everything out, every single activity and got out the list of kids in the class and all their phone numbers, and spent probably two days on the phone finding out who lived nearby, and I told [the nanny], "This is it. I don't care if you drive him 10 miles a day, or whether somebody else brings their kids over here, but every day there's got to be a minimum of one or two kids here, or he goes somewhere else." So that was it. Or he would spend like two hours every morning, and usually—partly to accommodate her—there would be a Filipina nanny involved. But what happened was within about seven school days, the school phoned and wondered what was happening—he's totally changed. He was interacting with kids in his class … He was talking.

There is a real tension in this woman's account between her efforts as an employer to supervise and police her nanny's movements through scheduling activities for her son and her concerns as a parent. One senses continuing discomfort about the time her nanny spent reading the newspaper and interacting with other Filipina nannies.

Other employers made fascinating observations about their efforts to stop themselves from complementing their nannies on the neatness of the house when childcare was their top priority. It was simply that the cleanliness of the house is more visible[6] than, even if it may have been somewhat at odds with, high-quality childcare. For example, Employer 5 observed:

> I've hired this lady to look after my children. I've said to her that they are her primary responsibility. That's what I want her to do well … But then I come home and the house is tidy and the laundry's done.

I don't say to her, "Thank you very much for looking after the children." I say, "Thank you for doing the laundry." So kind of, although your priorities are straight in your head, what you really react to is quite different. So I've made a real conscious effort to say, "Thanks for looking after the children. Oh, you've done the laundry, thank you very much for that too."

This quote highlights the fact that employers typically expect and actively produce the invisibility of childcare. Despite this employer's genuinely expressed sense of priorities, I think it is also true that few employers—including this one—would be pleased to arrive home to a house that displayed the chaos of a day of creative play.

The service that employers are buying, then, is very difficult to assess, in part because employers actively produce its invisibility. Many women employers have absorbed gendered constructions and persist in viewing the home as a site of leisure, rather than of work. They recognise good childcare as a natural attribute, rather than a learned skill. The work seems invisible to them. Employers diminish domestic work not only because of class or racialised difference; they do so because they hold some deeply sexist assumptions about domestic work, and possibly because they hold a conflicting set of child-centred and adult-centred priorities.

Dead-End Jobs

A further factor that depresses wages is that, with the exception of four households, employers made no plans to increase their nannies' wages over time. As an example, Employer 42 explained that "[T]here hasn't been a pay issue [with any of their childcare providers]; it has never been an issue." The interviewer ventured, "Because you haven't had a nanny long enough to give a raise to [her]?," to which the employer replied, "Yah, that's right." Granted, the interviewee was led in his response; still, it is worth noting that this household had employed one live-in Filipina, a 35-year-old woman, for a two-year period. She had worked as a live-in domestic worker in Vancouver one year previous to this. And yet, this employer also stated:

We've never looked at professional nannies, somebody who wants to do it as a career. They seem to [cost] a lot more.

Explicitly "deprofessionalising" long-term childcare workers affords employers one rationale for sidestepping the issue of wage increases. Added to this is a profound ambivalence about the benefits of a long-term employment relationship with any one employee. While frequent turnover is stressful for both parents and children, a long relationship can be equally problematic. As Employer 18 put it:

I think the truth of the matter is that for most people, being a nanny for two years is a year too long. I mean, it's not a great job, looking after kids and cleaning the house every day.

When asked whether this observation influenced their strategy as employers, the husband answered that he thought it best to change caregivers "not every year … 18 months to two years probably."

The strongest statement against long-term employment relationships came from an employer of a live-out nanny. Of all of the employers interviewed, she had sustained the longest relationship with a nanny (seven years). This employer had raised the caregiver's wages on an annual basis, to a salary of almost $28,000 annually. However, this employer described an extremely painful series of experiences when the caregiver appeared to become too attached to her children and resent the mother's presence, even at her children's birthday parties. This employer ventured the following observation:

> I would say to somebody that, no matter how well it's going, you should keep adjusting it, and think about changing every two years. But someone [actually did say that to me] and I thought at the time, "Well, that's interesting, but it's kind of cruel to the kids." But maybe [it's] not.

With a two-year employment relationship seen as ideal, there is little reason to plan for wage increases,[7] and the job is essentially constructed as a perpetually dead-end job.

Childcare Workers as Workers with Reduced Social-Reproduction Costs

There is a further characteristic of paid domestic labour that both allows and legitimates low wages: domestic workers are both seen and forced by circumstance to have low social-reproduction costs of their own. The ways in which social-reproduction costs are reduced vary for different groups of women. Uncovering this variation brings to light a geographical difference between city and outer suburbs in the labour supply of domestic workers.

The most studied of domestic workers in Canada are migrant domestic workers who come to Canada through the LCP.[8] Attention has been given to the ways in which the live-in requirement reduces the costs both of domestic workers' social reproduction and of childcare. Additionally, migrant domestic workers—many of whom come from the Philippines—are trained in their home countries and often leave their own children there in the care of an extended family. Thus, many of the costs of their own and their children's social reproduction are borne in their home country.[9] As Katz (2001:710) notes,

> [T]he social reproduction of a migrant workforce is carried out in its members' countries of origin. When they are employed elsewhere, this represents a direct transfer of wealth from generally poorer to richer countries. Variable capital produced in one site and tapped in another is no less a capital transfer than the extraction of raw materials, debt servicing, and the like.

A surprising pattern that emerged through the interviews with employers in 1995, however, was the relative paucity of migrant domestic workers and the prevalence of white Canadian women providing in-home, privatised childcare in suburban areas. Table 1 indicates this tendency, although it should be noted that census data tell us about the residential location, rather than the work location, of childcare workers[10] and that the occupational category is broad enough to include live-in caregivers and employees of daycare centres. In the city of Vancouver, employers reported that advertisements for childcare solicited about 30 calls, and they judged them to be mostly Filipina from their accented English. In the outer suburban areas, there was greater fluctuation in the labour supply. Suburban employers reported instances when they received only a handful of calls in response to a newspaper advertisement (an experience reported by none of the Vancouver employers) and other times when 20–30 applicants called. Fewer Filipina women able to do live-out childcare called, and there were more calls from young and elderly Canadian women. Employer 29 from Surrey described the response to her advertisement placed in late spring of 1995 in the following way:

> Employer 29: I would guess [I got] about 20 calls and the first 10 I interviewed. And it's not a real high quality group. It's not bad people. Most people I find definitely need the money. Or they're young girls. Again, the work just isn't for them like it was before.

Table 1: Residential Locations of Women Classified as Housekeepers and Childcare Workers[a] in the 1991 Census, Classified by "Filipino" or "British" Ethnic Origin[b]

Residential Location	% Filipina	% British	Total # (All Ethnicities)
City of Vancouver	35	17	4705
Suburban locations			
• Burnaby	16	30	1680
• Delta	11	37	930
• Langley	2	37	730
• Northeast Metro (Coquitlam, Port Coquitlam and Port Moody)	10	34	2370
• North Shore (North and West Vancouver)	22	32	1925
• Richmond	21	28	1160
• Surrey	14	32	2320

Source: Census of Canada, 1991, Special Tabulations, Table #G093.
[a] The imprecision of the occupational category should be noted. It includes a wide range of caregivers, from live-in domestic workers to those employed at daycare centers.
[b] These two ethnic categories are not exhaustive, but they do represent two large groups and demonstrate the relative paucity of Filipino caregivers in outer suburban areas.

So this is the only job they're going to get ... I found a lot of the girls applying were about 23, still living at home, couldn't find a job that they could afford an apartment and stuff like that, and this was just an alternative ... I would say most of them were single girls. [The women she hired] was the only one with a child. And I had three older women, all who had kids who were grown type of thing, looking for a job as supplementary income. With the three older women, they didn't drive ... They didn't have cars and they wanted to be on some sort of a bus route, so that sort of disqualified them there. A bunch of young girls, kinda airheady for the most part, and then I had one woman with a child.

I will return to consider the quality of childcare available in these outer suburban areas. For the present, I note the ways in which a different constellation of factors effectively cheapen the social-reproduction costs of this suburban labour supply, factors that turn in different ways around conceptualising these women within various familial scenarios: the young girl at home, the mother and the older married woman. In a variety of ways, suburban employers deployed a discourse of pin money to justify low wages. For many women doing domestic work in suburban areas, their paid employment is perceived by employers as supplemental: supplemental to a disability pension, to an old-age pension, to another job or to mothering their own children. Another geography thus overlaps the city/suburb distinction, one of an international as opposed to local labour supply. Although women in each are embedded within different family scenarios, these variable narratives provide storylines that legitimate low wages in different ways.

Suburban Stories

I focus attention on suburban stories in part because wages for childcare were lower in the outer suburban areas (Table 2)[11]. There is considerable wage variation across types of care, with the highest wages paid to live-in domestic workers. A median net wage of $900 a month amounts to about $7.80 an hour once the relevant deductions are added back in. The wages of live-in domestic workers are somewhat lower in suburban areas, but still at minimum wage.[12] In some ways, this finding is unremarkable, because the LCP is more closely monitored than the other childcare under consideration. Live-in caregivers are well organised; there are three activist groups in Vancouver alone. Nevertheless this wage gradient is somewhat surprising, because it runs against preconceptions about racialised labour segmentation. The women who earn the lowest wages for childcare are white women living and working in suburban areas,[13] and, in contrast to live-in domestic workers, their social reproduction costs are not so directly cheapened by living in their employers' homes.

Table 2: Geographies of Wages for Different Types of Childcare

	Vancouver City				Suburbs			
	Hourly Wage ($)	Range (Monthly Net)	N	N under Minimum Wage	Hourly Wage ($)	Range (Monthly Net)	N	N under Minimum Wage
Live-in	7.8	$800–$1800	11	0	7.0	$650–$1600	9	0
Live-out								
• Full-time	7.5		8	1	5.9		6	3
• Part-time	6.8		7	3	7.0		4	0
Family care (outside child's own home)	5.6		1	1	4.5		7	5

Note: The wage estimates are based on the wages of the most recent employee. In the case of a recent change of employee, the wages of both recent employees were recorded. Hence, the total numbers in this table exceed the total number interviewed.

A second reason for attending to the situation in the outer suburbs is that it more accurately represents the stresses within the national childcare system. Many of these stresses are veiled in the city of Vancouver by the supply of migrant labour generated by the LCP.[14] The suburban situation allows a type of thought experiment: what does the Canadian care situation look like in the absence of a federal program (the LCP) that exploits global uneven development and economic misery elsewhere? England (1993) has rightly criticised a type of feminist narrative that portrays suburban women as hapless victims of their spatial circumstances.[15] I do not want to do this. But it is also the case that the relative absence of migrant domestic labourers exacerbates a care crisis for suburban women. Folbre (2001:1) has argued that economists have assumed that "God, nature, the family and 'Super Mom'—or some combination thereof—would automatically provide whatever care was needed … This assumption is wrong. Both the quantity and quality of care for other people are coming under increasing economic pressure." This pressure is clearer in outer suburban Vancouver than it is in the city.

Certainly there were stories of difficult situations with nannies in Vancouver—for example, a nanny who got clinically depressed in her second year of employment. Another Vancouver employer told of hiring an older Canadian woman as a live-in nanny. The employer found the woman odd: wearing her transparent "negligee" to the breakfast table was only one example. But she fired this employee within a week and hired a Filipino nanny who stayed for four and a half years. Another Vancouver employer described an acrimonious relation with a Filipino nanny who worked for her for a year. She resented that she was, in her words, "being held responsible for the economy of the Third World by this [Filipino] community [of which her nanny was a part]." Of her nanny, she said,

> She was a smart woman. In fact she was probably too smart. She was an accountant.

But these stories of problems between employers and domestic workers are of an entirely different nature than the ones told in suburban areas, many of which were stories of chronic and irresolvable stress—or at least not always resolvable in a way that allowed the female employer to remain in the paid labour force.[16] Employer 29, a banker who lived in an outer suburb, described herself as the "only woman with 100 nannies." Unfortunately, this was not the case. I describe just two women's experiences to give a sense of the situation.

Employer 20 lived in Coquitlam with her husband and two children, one four years old and the other 19 months. She returned to her job as an insurance adjuster on a part-time basis after maternity leave. She advertised in the local newspaper, interviewed six women and found a "wonderful lady" in her forties. This woman had a slight disability that prevented her from lifting heavy objects (but not from performing the work of infant care), and she agreed to a wage of $4.50 an hour, an instance of the way in which below-minimum wages are constructed by and for childcare workers. This arrangement continued until the second child was born. After the second maternity leave, she again advertised for part-time childcare. No suitable candidates were found, so she went to a suburban-based agency called Grannies and Nannies. She agreed to a wage of $7.50 an hour. The first older woman sent to her lasted three weeks; this is because the employer had the impression that the nanny and the employer's daughter sat in front of the television much of the day. A second, younger woman supplied by the agency was studying to be an art teacher through correspondence courses. She was good, but after two weeks she hurt her back and was gone. The first woman was rehired temporarily. Then a woman in her thirties who had previously worked as an office manager was supplied by the agency. She was efficient, but soon quit because her boyfriend's job led them to relocate their housing farther away and, without a car, she found it difficult to get to work. Next was an older woman who had raised seven children on her own. She was fired after it was discovered that she had allowed the 4-year-old to play on the front street unsupervised. The next caregiver was a 22-year-old woman who worked part-time at an animation job at night. Five caregivers had been hired within the space of ten months. At the time of the interview, Employer 20 had resigned from her job and planned to provide unlicensed daycare in her home. Although she had paid $7.50 an hour for care, she had agreed to sell her labour for $4.50 an hour.

Employer 25 also lives in Coquitlam and worked as a legal assistant, earning $40,000 a year. When interviewed, her oldest child was three and a half and her baby fourteen months old. After maternity leave, she put her first child in the home daycare of an older retired woman. This lasted for four months, and ended because of disagreements about what and how her baby should be fed. Next, they tried the next-door neighbour's unlicensed daycare, for which they paid just $450 a month. This lasted 16 months but it was not a happy arrangement; there was inadequate equipment and poor care. Now with two children, Employer 25 advertised for a caregiver to come to her home. Paying $1100 a month for full-time childcare, they hired a 19-year-old woman. This woman was chronically late or absent and in any case lasted just four months before taking a job cleaning instruments at a dental office. Another advertisement was placed in the newspaper. This time there were 25 responses and two looked good: a 20-year-old from down the street and a mother living in a nearby suburb. They chose the former because of her proximity to their home. By this time Employer 25 explains that she and her husband were quite undemanding: "[W]e just went: 'If you can drive, if you can speak English, if you're normal, and you don't look like you're doing drugs and you've got experience [babysitting], that will do.'" So they hired the 20-year-old, who lasted three days; the young woman now works as a retail clerk at the local shopping mall. Employer 25 returned to her list of responses to her recent advertisement and hired a 39-year-old mother of four children, the youngest of whom was 13. The woman had apparently been work-ing as a nanny for five years, which demonstrated some commitment to the job. At the time of the interview, she had been in the employ of Employer 25 for four months. I will let Employer 25 tell you how well it was going.

> The first thing was she got sick, then her mother had heart prob-lems ... [Then she] missed a day because her oldest daughter had a baby ... Then the really good one is that back in May there was an automobile accident in Maple Ridge, where a 13-year-old stole a car and went joyriding ... Well, it was her 13-year-old!"

At the time of the interview, Employer 25 was about to take her vacation and then return to work to give her notice. About her job, she said,

> I very much enjoy it. I get very high job satisfaction out of it. It's funny because my girlfriends say to me that my priorities are chang-ing [with her decision to stay home with her children]. My priorities would not have changed that much if I had not being going through this much stress. [My priorities have] changed to this point because we have not been able to find anybody that would have worked out.

Doucet (1995) notes a tendency within feminist accounts of domestic labour to trivialise commitments to maternal care, especially when they lead women to leave paid employment. This has the effect of further devaluing domestic work. This is certainly not my intent. By quoting Employer 25 so fully, I hope to give voice to her frustration about her childcare options, the poverty of which prevented her from combining paid and domestic labour in the way in which she wished and forced her to reprioritise her commitments to the two forms of labour.

The suburban employers describe an acute shortage of qualified, committed childcare providers in their suburban location. A comparison of the training and circumstances of care providers not enrolled in the LCP (Table 3) demonstrates that there is a larger number of caregivers with dedicated training in childcare in the city than in suburban areas. While one could argue that the mothers and retired, older women who provide considerable amounts of market childcare in suburban areas hold amongst them vast knowledge and experience, numerous employers reported that their care was of variable quality. The extremely low wages paid to these women likely contribute to high rates of turnover and variable commitments to the job. Indeed, studies have found that salary paid to the childcare provider is the best indicator of the quality of care delivered—a clearer indicator than this person's education or training (Doherty 2001:133).

Conclusions

Although I have located concerns about the quality of informal, home-based childcare in the suburbs, they certainly reach beyond this location. Childcare advocates estimate that 69 percent of Canadian

Table 3: Circumstances/Training of Live-out Domestic Workers

	Vancouver City	Suburbs
Education in childcare	4	1
Landed live-in caregiver	3	0
Break from university degree	4	1
Travelling, working illegally	2	1
Recent immigrant/not working in area of training	1	0
Young mother bringing infant to employers' home	1	2
Mother with older children in school	0	2
Young Canadian woman, not otherwise employed	0	2
Young underemployed Canadian woman supplementing income	0	1
Disability	1	2
Elderly/retired	2	7

Note: Information from recent previous employees included. Hence, the total numbers in this table exceed the total number interviewed.

children under six in family childcare are in unregulated situations that do not meet basic health and safety requirements (Doherty 2001:133), and "the vast majority" of Canadian children are now cared for in informal arrangements that are purely custodial and are not "by [any] stretch of the imagination 'early childhood education'" (Friendly 2001:26). National polls indicate that the majority of Canadians wish to improve this situation and explicitly favour more government support for a national childcare programme. For example, a poll sponsored by Human Resources Development Canada in 1998 found that 88 percent of those polled strongly agreed with such expanded government support (cited in Friendly 2001:51). I have tried to show, however, that through everyday practices that render childcare as gendered, invisible and low-skilled, middle-class Canadian employers reproduce childcare as undervalued and low-paid labour.

Feminists have a long history of tracing and retracing (and retracing) the connections between valuing childcare and attaining the quality childcare that so many Canadians desire. I would be pleased if my analysis brought the two women with whom I began this essay to align themselves on the same side of a political struggle for higher wages for domestic workers. One way that I have attempted to do so is by arguing that middle-class Canadian women's childcare needs are not achievable as long as wages for childcare are low. Beyond this, all of the interviewed women's lives were affected by gendered assumptions about childcare responsibilities and their worth. The 20-year-old suburban childcare provider who still lives with her parents because her wages are low inhabits the same discursive world as the stressed middle-class legal assistant who quit her job because the $1100 she paid monthly for childcare was insufficient to purchase adequate care. By her calculation, this left only $700 in her pocket at the end of the month—a sum that presumes that childcare expenses come out of her pocket alone. We need to trace these connections to build more effective organising around domestic labour. We also have to pay attention to the blurring of and mobility around some of the lines of difference (eg class, race, nationality) that have preoccupied feminists over the last decade—as, for example, when a middle-class employer paying $7.50 an hour for childcare repositions herself as childcare provider who receives only $4.50 an hour. There is an affinity between her fluid movement between professional and domestic labour and the experiences of Filipino live-in caregivers who leave professional jobs in the Philippines (often as nurses) to take up domestic work in Canada. Profoundly sexist assumptions naturalise both of these transitions in employment situation; these assumptions do the violence of rendering both as unremarkable. These blurred moments provide important opportunities for political identification among women, identification that builds from documenting the concrete, specific, material points of connection between women situated differently in terms of other social relations.

Social exclusion resulting from the devaluation of domestic work thus remains an important pivot around which to organize across various groups of women. If Friendly (2001) is right that childcare has only deteriorated in Canada through the 1990s, forging these identifications is critically important for building a political will to achieve high-quality and affordable childcare that pays a fair, living wage to those who provide it. This requires a domestic revolution, one that transforms our thinking about the entire economy. As Folbre (2001:79) argues, "We can't continue to visualize the economy as a man's world of cars and trucks and steel, things that can be easily counted and weighed ... We need to improve our measure of the kinds of success we care about. Otherwise, we will not be able to reward the kinds of behavior we most value."

Rethinking the economy is especially pressing given existing pressures on the welfare state. The prevalence of elderly suburban women supplementing their pensions with below-minimum wages, for instance, calls up an even wider set of articulations across women and other categories of social exclusion. The direction that this revolution in thinking and practice should take is open for discussion, and will usefully include childcare options that both exceed the market (Wheelock and Jones 2002) and address desires that some parents may have to provide more care for their children over extended periods of time (Folbre 2001). That so many Vancouver parents were so eager to discuss their current troubles can only be a good thing.

Acknowledgments

I thank Richard Dennis for his invitation to participate in the Gender and Work in Canada, London Conference for Canadian Studies in November 2000, where this essay was first presented, Itesh Sachdev for his editorial work, Dan Hiebert, Greg Cunningham and Eric Leinberger for assistance with Table 1 and Figure 1, and Trina Bester for her assistance conducting interviews. Thanks to Cindi Katz, Sallie Marston and Katharyne Mitchell for their editorial and organizational work, and Liz Bondi, Ruth Fincher and an anonymous referee for their helpful comments. The research was funded by the Social Sciences and Humanities Research Council of Canada.

Endnotes

[1] A national study indicated that in 1994, only 20% of 0–5-year-olds were cared for in daycare centres, while 48% were cared for in unregulated care outside the home. Middle-class parents, in particular, were less likely to use daycare centres: low-income parents, lone parents, very young and old mothers, and mothers with less than secondary-school diplomas were most likely to place their children in daycare centres (Norris, Brink and Mosher 1999).

[2] One, *The Courier*, is distributed free of charge to households living in the more affluent west side of Vancouver and is known as "the" place to advertise for nannies. Another is delivered to the outer suburbs of Coquitlam, Port Coquitlam and Port Moody, and a third is circulated to Surrey households. I drew a random sample of advertisements placed between June 1994 and July 1995. Five employers who advertised in *The Courier* lived in the less affluent area of East Vancouver; their advertisements in their local newspaper, *The Echo*, were also published in *The Courier*. I did not persist with this subsample once the contrast with the outer suburban households became so compelling. This strategy follows Glaser and Strauss's (1967) notion of sampling to develop grounded theory. In the tables accompanying this essay, data from different areas in the city of Vancouver are combined, because profiles in terms of employer occupations, wages paid and labour supply were fairly similar. I would like to thank Trina Bester for her research assistance. I conducted 35 of the interviews and Trina conducted a further 15. The interviews were unstructured and in-depth, typically lasting for over an hour.

[3] The British Columbia government allows two types of family childcare situations (ie care that is not centre-based): license-not-required family childcare, in which childcare is provided for no more than two children unrelated to the caregiver, and licensed family childcare, for which there is typically a limit of seven children (Unit for Childcare Research 1998).

[4] With the exception of one single-parent household and two Vancouver households in which the female parent was only marginally engaged in paid employment, all of the households interviewed were dual-income ones.

[5] None of the employers interviewed mentioned the effects of the Child Care Expenses tax deduction in their calculations. Since 1972, families with childcare expenses related to work have been allowed to deduct expenses up to Can$7000 per child under seven years of age and $5000 for each child between seven and sixteen. Currently, this tax deduction must be claimed by the parent who has the lowest income, usually the woman. This has the effect of both lowering the amount of the deduction and implicitly linking the costs of childcare to the woman's wage. This is an instance, then, in which state policy reflects and reproduces existing gender ideology. The deduction is unlikely to cover the actual costs of childcare, and Cleveland and Krashinsky (2001:6) argue that it is misleading to claim that the deduction even reduces those costs. They argue that it should be seen as part of the process of defining taxable income. The fact that this tax deduction does not seem to enter into interviewed women's calculations of their direct childcare expenses tends to support this interpretation.

[6] Because the connection of quality childcare to experience and skills and the meaning of desirable employee characteristics (such as what it means to be stimulating) are loosely and contingently formulated, employers often rely on seemingly odd concrete markers for evidence of work done. Aside from focusing on housework rather than childcare, a number of employers read nannies' bodies for evidence of energy exerted, and they made harsh comments about overweight nannies: eg Employer 41 refers to her Canadian ex-live-out nanny as "the fucking fat pig"; Employer 35 refers to her Quebecois ex-live-in nanny, who "was kind of large [and] getting larger," as a "sloth"; employer 29 also complained about the weight of her Ex-live-in nanny from New Zealand ("It wasn't that she was unattractive or anything but she must have been … well, when my husband picked her up at the airport, he was really caught off guard, because I would say she was close to 300 lbs"); Employer 18's husband did not like their current live-out Canadian nanny, and her weight and wandering eye seem to figure into his discomfort with her. One way of understanding these comments about weight is that employers may assess level of activity—something they cannot actually observe during the day—by what they can observe: the physical body of the nanny. As Liz Bondi, referee of this essay, notes, this also points to the sexualised

performances demanded by caregivers. It is noteworthy that this was one of the key areas where husbands' comments were brought into women's assessments of their nannies.

[7] I do not wish to dispute the accuracy of parents' assessment about the ideal length of time to sustain a relationship with any one nanny, but simply to point out one of the consequences of it for nannies' wages.

[8] There is now a voluminous literature on overseas contract domestic workers. Considering Canada alone, see Arat-Koc (1989, 1990, 1992), Bakan and Stasiulis (1994, 1995, 1997), Daenzer (1993), Macklin (1992), Pratt (1997, 1999), Schecter (1998), and Stiell and England (1997). For an international overview, see the volume edited by Momsen (1999).

[9] There are certainly costs to mothering at a distance. Parrenas (2002) reports on Filipina overseas domestic workers who function as good mothers by calling home to speak with their children on a daily basis.

[10] These two locations—residence of domestic worker and residence of employer—do, however, bear a close relationship because of the extremely local searches conducted by employers. A number of employers noted their preference for advertising in local community-based newspapers, because the respondents were more likely to live close to their homes.

[11] It is no easy matter to figure out the equivalencies between the wages paid across these different categories of childcare because they are calculated in different ways. It is arguable that the manner of calculating costs of at least some forms of childcare dampens wages, albeit in different ways. For example, live-in nannies and their employers speak about net monthly wages (minus deductions for room and board, taxes and other deductions). This has the effect of directing attention away from hourly wage and close accounting of number of hours worked daily. Full-time live-out nannies speak in terms of gross monthly wages. Part-time liveout nannies receive hourly wages. Care outside the home is paid as a daily, biweekly, or monthly fee. These differences are themselves important and embedded in historical circumstances. It is only since 1995, for instance, that live-in caregivers have been regulated by minimum hourly wage and overtime regulations in British Columbia. So it is only since this time that it makes sense to calculate hourly wages. Nevertheless I have translated the information that employers gave me into hourly wages. The minimum wage was $6.50 at the time of interview, soon to be raised to $7 an hour. In the case of family home care, the hourly wage was calculated from information that I obtained on the number of children cared for and the fee charged for each child.

[12] This is as long as domestic workers are able to enforce the 40-hour work week—an ever-present struggle for a domestic worker who lives in her employers' house (Pratt in collaboration with the Philippine Women Centre 1999).

[13] The extremely low wages for family childcare are well documented. A national study indicated that, on average, regulated caregivers earn an annual income of $8400 before taxes, and caregivers in the unregulated sector earn $6400 annually before taxes (Gilroy 1998:28–31). The more specific geographical pattern of city/suburban differences was also found in a large 1997 survey of license-not-required family childcare in BC (Unit For Child Care Research 1998). The mean daily fee for preschool (3–5) children was $24.09 in Surrey, for example, and $27.97 in Vancouver. Given that the average number of hours worked daily was 10.5 (and assuming that the caregiver cared for the maximum number of children allowed for nonlicensed family childcare), the hourly wage was $4.58 in Surrey and $5.33 in Vancouver.

[14] A satisfying explanation for why LCP registrants were less evident in the outer suburbs is beyond the reach of this article, and even the scope of the research project, given that specific geographies of childcare supply only emerged as the research progressed and did not frame the research question. There are probably a number of factors involved. Filipina live-in domestic workers with whom I have collaborated are

less enthusiastic about employment in outer suburbs, located far from the Filipino community in Vancouver, especially given the common practice of sharing rental accommodation with other Filipino caregivers on weekends. The few employers who made negative comments about Filipinos' accented English were suburban ones, possibly an indication of cultural intolerance. Further, live-in caregivers commanded the highest wages among those providing privatised childcare, and incomes tended to be somewhat lower in these suburban areas (Figure 1).

[15] See also Dyck (1990) for this argument in direct reference to the suburb considered here.

[16] The point about the different nature of the stories is important to underline given the sampling frame, which would seem to select for employers who were having difficulties with their childcare providers.

References

Arat-Koc S (1989) In the privacy of our own home: Foreign domestic workers as solution to the crisis in the domestic sphere in Canada. *Studies in Political Economy* 28:33–58

Arat-Koc S (1990) Importing housewives: Non-citizen domestic workers and the crisis of the domestic sphere in Canada. In S Arat-Koc, M Luxton and H Rosenberg (eds) *Through the Kitchen Window: The Politics of Home and Family* (pp 81–103). Toronto: Garamond

Arat-Koc S (1992) Immigration policies, migrant domestic workers and definition of citizenship in Canada. In V Satzewichg (ed) *Deconstructing a Nation: Immigration, Multiculturalism and Racism in '90s Canada* (pp 229–242). Halifax, Nova Scotia: Fernwood

Bakan A and Stasiulis D (1994) Foreign domestic worker policy in Canada and the social boundaries of modern citizenship. *Science and Society* 58:7–33

Bakan A and Stasiulis D (1995) Making the match: Domestic placement agencies and the racialization of women's household work. *Signs: Journal of Women in Culture and Society* 20:303–335

Bakan A and Stasiulis D (eds) (1997) *Not One of the Family: Foreign Domestic Workers in Canada.* Toronto: University of Toronto Press

Bester T (1999) "Negotiating Parenting and Places of Care in Vancouver, BC." Masters thesis, Department of Geography, University of British Columbia

Census of Canada (1991) *Special Tabulations, Table #G093*

Cleveland G and Krashinsky M (eds) (2001) *Our Children's Future: Child Care Policy in Canada.* Toronto: University of Toronto Press

Cockburn C (1997) Domestic technologies: Cinderella and the engineers. *Women's Studies International Forum* 20:361–371

Daenzer P (1993) *Regulating Class Privilege: Immigrant Servants in Canada, 1940s–1990s.* Toronto: Canadian Scholar's Press

Doherty G (2001) Moving towards achieving quality child care. In G Cleveland and M Krashinsky (eds) *Our Children's Future: Child Care Policy in Canada* (pp 126–141). Toronto: University of Toronto Press

Doucet A (1995) Gender equality and gender differences in household work and parenting. *Women's Studies International Forum* 18:271–284

Dyck I (1990) Space, time and renegotiating motherhood: An exploration of a domestic workplace. *Environment and Planning D: Society and Space* 8:459–483

England K (1993) Changing suburbs, changing women: Geographic perspectives on suburban women and suburbanization. *Frontiers* 14:24–43

Folbre N (2001) *The Invisible Heart: Economics and Family Values.* New York: The New Press

Fraser N (2000) After the family wage: A postindustrial thought experiment. In E Hobson (ed) *Gender and Citizenship in Transition* (pp 1–32). London: Macmillan Press

Friendly M (2001) Child care and Canadian federalism in the 1990s: Canary in a coal mine. In G Cleveland and M Krashinsky (eds) *Our Children's Future: Child Care Policy in Canada* (pp 25–61). Toronto: University of Toronto Press

Gilroy G (1998) *Providing Home Child Care for a Living: A Survey of Providers Working in the Regulated Sector.* Ottawa: Canadian Child Care Federation

Glaser B and Strauss A L (1967) *The Discovery of Grounded Theory.* Chicago: Aldine

Gregson N and Lowe M (1994) *Servicing the Middle Classes: Class, Gender and Waged Domestic Labour in Contemporary Britain.* New York: Routledge

Jenson J and Sineau M (eds) (2001) *Who Cares? Women's Work, Childcare and Welfare State Restructuring.* Toronto: University of Toronto Press

Katz C (2001) Vagabond capitalism and the necessity of social reproduction. *Antipode* 33(4):709–728

Leonard M (2001) Old wine in new bottles? Women working inside and outside the household. *Women's Studies International Forum* 24:67–78

Luxton M (1997) The UN, women and household labour: Measuring and valuing unpaid work. *Women's Studies International Forum* 20:431–439

Macklin A (1992) Foreign domestic worker: Surrogate housewife or mail-order servant? *McGill Law Journal* 37:681–760

Mattingly D, Hanson S and Pratt G (1997–1998) Women's lives, local geographies and the effects of maternal breaks on women's employment. *Michigan Feminist Studies* 12:1–25

McKie L, Bowlby S and Gregory S (2001) Gender, caring and employment in Britain. *Journal of Social Policy* 2:233–258

Momsen J H (ed) (1999) *Gender, Migration and Domestic Service.* London: Routledge

Nelson J (2001) *Why Are Early Education and Care Wages So Low? A Critical Guide to Common Explanations.* Foundation for Child Development Working Paper Series. http:// http://www.ffcd.org/pdfs/nelson.pdf (last accessed 20 February 2003)

Norris C, Brink S and Mosher P (1999) *Measuring Non-Parental Care in the NLSCY: Content and Process Issues.* Technical Document, Applied Research Branch, Human Resources Development Canada T–00–1E

Parrenas R (2002) "The Care Crisis in the Philippines: Children and Transnational Families in a New Global Economy." Paper presented at Sex, Race and Globalization Conference, University of Arizona, Tucson, 5 April

Pratt G (1997) Stereotypes and ambivalence: Nanny agents' stereotypes of domestic workers in Vancouver, BC. *Gender, Place and Culture* 4:159–177

Pratt G (1999) From registered nurse to registered nanny: Discursive geographies of Filipina domestic workers in Vancouver, BC. *Economic Geography* 75:215–236

Pratt G in collaboration with the Philippine Women Centre (1999) Is this really Canada? Domestic workers' experiences in Vancouver, BC. In J Momsen (ed) *Gender, Migration and Domestic Service* (pp 23–42). New York: Routledge

Schecter T (1998) *Race, Class, Women and the State: The Case of Domestic Labour.* Montreal: Black Rose

Stiell B and England K (1997) Domestic distinctions: Constructing difference among paid domestic workers in Toronto. *Gender, Place and Culture* 4:339–359

Unit for Child Care Research (1998) *1997 Provincial Child Care Survey.* Prepared for the British Columbia Ministry for Children and Families Child Care Team. Victoria: School of Child and Youth Care, University of Victoria

VanEvery J (1997) Understanding gendered inequality: Reconceptualizing housework. *Women's Studies International Forum* 20:411–420

Wheelock J and Jones K (2002) Grandparents are the next best thing: Informal childcare for working parents in urban Britain. *Journal of Social Policy* 31:441–463

Chapter 8
Toque una Ranchera, Por Favor[1]

Altha J Cravey

On a Sunday morning a few weeks ago, some Mexican friends invited me to go along when they were buying *carnitas* (cooked pork). We headed down a residential street only a few blocks from my place and pulled up in front of a small house. There were no visible signs of any commerce, although I started to smell the *carnitas* as we went toward the back porch to select our purchase. Chunks of meat were swimming in vats of hot lard and—along with several other customers— we waited until this batch was ready. Once we had our meat, my friends wanted to stop at Johnny's store, a tiny fishing supply place only a block from my house. While I'd been to Johnny's store a few times, I had always entered from the front and had frequently wondered how the good-ol'-boy owners stayed in business selling worms, crickets, minnows, and Coca-Cola. I hadn't realized until this particular Sunday that there is a Mexican *tienda* with an entrance at the backside of the same tiny building. My friends bought some *bolillos* (white buns) in the *tienda* (store) and we set out for a tasty picnic.

I begin with this anecdote because I have some expertise in Mexican labor markets and Mexican experience in the US South. And in the last few months, as part of a research project, I have been immersed in Mexican activities in North Carolina, or *Carolina del Norte,* as my friend Elva says of her own leisure-time destinations: "When I'm not at work, I head out to *Carolina del Norte.*" So how can it be that I keep finding new "Mexican" places right under my nose?

The literal spaces of transnational social reproduction for Latinos and Latinas in central North Carolina constitute a parallel universe, a world that is largely invisible to long-term residents (Davis 2000; Smith 2001). As soon as one steps through the right parallel door, however, one encounters a whirlwind of activities that provide cultural, social, political, and economic sustenance to migrant communities. Places such as the *carnitas* vendor and the nearby *tienda* are connected through dense social ties with places such as the *pulga* (the rural

Mexican flea market), the work exchange organized at a local strip mall at Chilango's corner, apartments and apartment complexes where one can get one's hair cut by a professional from El Salvador, soccer leagues, bars, pool halls, and dance clubs. These local social networks are also closely linked to faraway locations through family and community connections. This translocal way of life involves living intimately in two or more disparate places at once and is often a creative response on the part of migrants as they adjust to—and, in turn, influence— changing opportunities and constraints in disparate places (Burawoy 2000; Davis 2000; Smith 2001). The intimate and distant social connections that constitute this translocal way of living help to facilitate the very same globalizing labor markets that entice and propel migrants to seek "greener pastures" in the US South.

In this paper, I argue that examining these spaces and circuits of social reproduction can enhance our understanding of globalization by making globalization processes at once less abstract and less indisputable. Others have argued that analyzing social reproduction provides insight on globalization, yet this idea is not necessarily widely accepted (Cravey 1999; Katz 2001; Marston 2000). Economic production is so central to both proponents and critics of globalization that, by and large, social reproduction gets ignored. Yet, by bringing in the gender dynamics of social life and by focusing on the smaller scale processes of social reproduction, it is possible to recover some of the complex sociospatial elements that facilitate contemporary, neoliberal forms of globalization. More importantly, shifting our perspective to the microgeographies of social reproduction gives us the tools with which to imagine alternative models of globalization that might spring from more egalitarian social relationships, from social and economic justice ideals, or directly from creative translocal ways of living and self-expression. That is, in pursuing his goals and his freedom to do so, the unauthorized migrant "lives his life more as a citizen of a non-bounded society (one shaped by extraterritorial social, economic, and cultural forces) than as a citizen of a bounded territorial state" (Nevins 2002:180). For these reasons, I believe attention to social reproduction is important for understanding and theorizing globalization and, more significantly, for imagining and constructing alternative forms of globalization.

I want to examine some spaces of social reproduction that involve translocal lives and transnational identities for Latinos in central North Carolina. Transnational identities—as feminist theorists have shown—are worked out simultaneously at many geographical scales, from the scale of the body to the scale of the globe (Marston 2000). Transnational spaces and identities are particularly interesting for this reason, because microscale processes so clearly intersect and shape macro ones, and vice versa. Furthermore, if we accept the idea that many Latinos in the US are living at two or more places at once, then we can explore the direct causal relationship between the most microscale processes and global ones. For instance, social exchanges between places such as Carrboro, North Carolina[2] and Guanajuato, Mexico are so intense that people are on the phone enough, and back and forth enough, and sending cash remittances to the extent that they are literally keeping up with who stopped by for a chat that afternoon, how much rain fell, and who is dating whom in both places.

In this paper, I seek to contribute to our understandings of the links between the construction of translocal identities and the spaces of social reproduction through which these constructions are translated. Immigrants create and appropriate new social spaces that are highly contested, intensely expressive, and densely networked with other immigrant circuits. Specifically, I argue that certain forms of social reproduction practices facilitate and sustain transnational migration flows. In turn, gender relations, sexual expression, and desire are all altered by the need to substitute new spaces of social reproduction for family and household forms not available in North Carolina. That is, when they migrate to the US South, Latinos and Latinas creatively adapt to and substitute for the loss of two important sites of social reproduction in their daily lives: household/family systems of support and state-funded channels of social provision. In this way, transnational migrants provide a vast subsidy to the regional economy and to employers. At the same time, migrant flows are fueled by a desire for certain personal freedoms that are not available in Mexico. Thus, the pursuit of adequate wages is entwined with cultural ferment in everyday locations and a quest for human freedom.

I begin by describing the general situation of Latinos and Latinas in the US South and, more specifically, in North Carolina. These recent migration flows are directly tied to contemporary production changes and are distinct from earlier migration flows to the US in several ways. From this contextual background, I turn to an examination of some specific places that extend and substitute for household and family relationships. I focus on dance halls, bars, and clubs to illuminate some of the everyday ways in which transnational identities and social relationships are sustained and reproduced in order to shift the angle of view to the scale of daily life. Mainstream corporate, government, and academic representations of globalization tend to neglect this scale. To take that same stance as a critic of neoliberal globalization models is to reify this one understanding of globalization. On the other hand, a shift in scale can reveal crucial dynamics that, when examined closely, suggest an alternative version of globalization, one based less on governmental and economic understandings and more on the personal, day-to-day lives of individuals swept up in globalization processes. The social sites examined are places where immigrants relax, drink, meet and make friends, dance, date, and often make temporary and long-term household arrangements. Through music and dancing, migrants —who are predominantly men—appropriate certain spaces as Mexican, find an outlet for sexuality, desire, and anger, and distract themselves from the difficulties of living far from home.

This work is part of a larger research project—partly collaborative and partly my own—that examines Latino migration in the US South. The discussion draws upon in-depth interviews, as well as nine months of participant observation research in 2001 and 2002 with the Latino community in central North Carolina. Because immigrant households are stretched across vast geographical distances, I have made an effort to spend time in those places that seem to compensate—at least in part—for the household relationships and activities that migration displaces and alters.

Context: North Carolina and US South
The interplay of regional commodity histories, place-based social histories, and regional racial dynamics has shaped particular federal policies and practices designed to assist powerful growers and grower organizations and to sustain and increase US farm production and profits. In the US South, the legacy of slavery, sharecropping, and reconstruction produced a highly distinct, agrarian social history that relied upon a reserve army of African Americans and poor whites as seasonal migrant and nonmigrant agricultural labor. The confluence of a number of macro- and microscale processes facilitated the rapid globalization of labor markets in the US South.

In the last two decades, the US South has been transformed by the rapid influx of foreign immigrants, the majority of whom are Latinos. Of the Latinos, a large proportion—about 75% in North Carolina—are Mexican, predominantly from the working class. Of course, the movement of Mexicans to the US South is part of a long and cyclical history of Mexican migration to the US.[3] The specific racial dynamics of the US South, and the racialized division of labor in agriculture in particular, made the South the last region of the United States to be attractive and hospitable to Mexican migrants. A relatively strong regional economy and state intervention in a guest-worker program (H2A), however, help to explain many contemporary changes in spatial divisions of labor and a corresponding "Latinization" of the region. The very rapid pace of change has created hardships for Latino immigrants and for certain communities that are caught up in these changes.

Racialized regional patterns of temporary labor supply in US agri-culture remained in place for decades, only beginning to shift in the 1980s and 1990s. The structured coherence of agricultural production in the South (with the exception of Florida) is particularly notable: regional stability rested on a continued marginalization of black workers and poor whites, such that a large racialized reserve army of labor could be mobilized as needed (Harvey 1989).[4] At the same time, white southern farmers also historically fought for and depended on the exclusion of foreign labor. Thus, while the geographical pattern of un-evenness in the use of seasonal immigrant labor has been partially an ad hoc policy, federal intervention—and the varied responses to it— produced a pattern of labor supply that connected specific US regions to certain racialized labor groups for much of the last century. For in-stance, immigration policy was used to channel *nearby* sources of labor to specific limited areas of the country: Mexican immigrants worked in the Southwest, West Indians went to the east coast of Florida, and Canadians helped bring in the harvest in Maine, while the rest of the nation's farmers had to rely on domestic sources of labor (Hahamovich 1997:96). Thus, in spite of a surge in Mexican immigration into the United States during World War I, the demographic impact was extremely uneven geographically.

The binational Bracero program mobilized and funneled similarly patterned flows of Mexican migration during World War II. Between 1942 and 1964, agribusiness played a decisive role in the administration of the Bracero program, which supplied Mexican workers to southwest-ern states, as well as to some growers in the Northwest and Midwest. While the Bracero program supplied Mexican labor, the H2 program, administered by the Immigration and Naturalization Service, has been used since 1943 to secure contract labor from the West Indies and Jamaica to work the sugar harvest in Florida and other specific crops up the East Coast. Even so, these immigrants had little opportunity to work in former plantation districts of the US South. In this way, dis-tinct national groups were channeled into separate migratory streams in the western, central, or eastern parts of the country.

Regional patterns in agricultural labor have shifted dramatically in the last two decades. As part of the 1986 Immigration Reform and Control Act, the H2 program became the H2A program. During this same period, mechanization reduced the demand for Jamaican sugar workers, and the Mexican agricultural work force simul-taneously expanded to become the largest group of H2A participants. In particular, the federal H2A program expanded rapidly in North Carolina in the 1990s, bringing seasonal contract workers ("guest workers") to a transport hub in Vass, North Carolina,[5] where they could be matched with specific employers in North Carolina and eleven neighboring states. Under the program—aggressively promoted by Stan Eury, a former North Carolina Labor Department official—each farmer specifies the number of workers and length of time necessary for harvesting their crops. Farmers and workers each pay a fee up front in order to enter into a contract. By the tenth year of operation, some 40% of all H2A workers in the United States were disembarking in Vass (Smith-Nonini 2002). In Eury's small warehouse, workers are regularly asked to throw away pamphlets describing their legal rights before receiving their work assignments and contracts (Hicks 2002; Human Rights Watch 2000; Smith-Nonini 2002). The rapid expansion of formal regulated labor markets (through H2A) has encouraged informal flows, so that in the last decade such industries as poultry-processing, Christmas-tree and wreath production, and other related agricultural activities, service industries such as entry-level hotel and restaurant work, and heavier jobs in construction and landscaping have quickly become reliant on Latino workers, whether Mexican, Guatemalan, or Honduran (Cravey 1997; Johnson-Webb 2000).

Social Reproduction in North Carolina

Analyzing social reproductive practices provides some insight into how and why these economic transformations driven by contemporary globalization processes proceeded so rapidly in the region. For instance, if we simply consider the social and economic cost of producing and raising children (who are ultimately destined to become laborers), we can see how guest workers provide a substantial subsidy to US employers *outside* the United States. No one has expressed this more clearly than Cindi Katz:

> [T]he social reproduction of a migrant workforce is carried out in its members' countries of origin. When they are employed elsewhere, this represents a direct transfer of wealth from generally poorer to richer countries. Variable capital produced in one site and tapped in another is no less a capital transfer than the extraction of raw materials, debt servicing, and the like." (Katz 2001:710)

In this way—via this direct transfer—massive flows of both formal and informal migration lower the cost of labor in the US South. In both cases, migrants find themselves stretching their household and family relationships across vast geographical distances. Social reproduction occurs mostly (though not entirely) at the sending end of stretched community and household relationships, while more formal economic production occurs mostly at the receiving end. Quite literally living in two or more places at once, migrants find creative ways over time to sustain themselves and their families.

> Ranulfo's confident hands carefully and quickly pick through a mountain of fresh green jalapeño chiles while he fills a shopping bag at the rural flea market near the Buckhorn Jockey exit of Interstate 85. Without pausing, he moves along in the early morning light to gather nopales and select sugar cane from the bountiful displays at

the weekend *pulga*. The hum of low voices and the straining of wooden crates being unloaded signal the steady flow of commerce. Ranulfo's gaze leads him forward in a deliberate fashion as he searches for the best produce for Chilango's clientele.

Heaps of tortillas and *limones* are displayed for those who come for serious shopping; others come to stroll with their families, or to show off their newly painted ride with the image of the Virgen de Guadalupe on the van's wheel cover. Everyone is on the move this crisp market morning.

Back in the city, the procession at the church is moving along too, yet at a slower pace. Individual voices fade in and out of range as they pass by with reverential expressions. Priests, lay workers, altar boys, mariachis, and finally the members of the flock wind their way along the path. The faithful sing *"Adiós la alegría, adios hermana mía, adiós, adiós, adiós"* and carry candles. Two men lead the way out of doors into the crisp December air carrying a six-foot tall image of the Virgen de Guadalupe in an ornate gilt frame. Later on, back inside the warmth of the church, a peasant's vision of the Virgen is re-enacted as participatory theater. The virgin reappears on a very large cloth that is folded out from one man's clothing as others crowd around him and proclaim *"[L]a santísima virgen—que buena es la santísima virgen … "*[6]

In some ways, stretched relationships of Mexican communities and households compensate—or temporarily compensate—for the spatial disconnect between globalized labor markets and less-globalized networks of social reproduction. In other ways, Latino migrants creatively find and appropriate new spaces of social reproduction in North Carolina and other southern states. As the vast majority of these migrants are men, it is interesting to see the ways in which gender shapes these processes. The evolution of a fairly new Mexican neighborhood illuminates how some of these gendered and national identity dynamics play out.

On the edge of Carrboro, large numbers of Mexican men have moved into a cluster of apartment complexes. A traffic intersection with a mini-market, laundromat, and restaurant/bar serves as the hub of the community. In particular, the restaurant/bar—Chilango's—has been appropriated as Mexican space and becomes more intensely Mexican on certain nights, and even from moment to moment, with specific types of music or a certain mix of clients. The owner of Chilango's[7] wanted to serve good Mexican food when he first established the restaurant in this relatively low-rent area. At the same time, he made an effort to provide a space for cultural exchange and talked of forming a nonprofit community-center organization.[8] He set up work-notification bulletin boards near the front entrance of the building and offered regularly scheduled language classes in both English and Spanish, as well as Latin dance lessons and music. To promote other types of

cultural exchange with non-Latinos, he devotes one night each week
to live, "old-timey" fiddle and banjo music.

> Bright red and black splashes of movement are perfectly synchron-
> ized with each other and with a challenging rhythm. The woman's
> faultless body is encased in a sexy, red-fringed sparkling miniskirt and
> red bra, while the man is all in black. The drama of their movement
> is heightened by the completely still moments that punctuate their
> dancing as they reverse directions and spin and gyrate in precise
> harmony. The spiky gold lamé heels accentuate the woman's shapely
> legs and draw admiring stares from the hundreds crowded inside
> the high school auditorium for Fiesta del Pueblo. At the outdoor
> stage a few paces from the auditorium, the music blares: "*Suave, suave,
> suavement … un beso es lo que quiero … ,*" while many more couples of
> all ages dance. Baseball caps shade a few brown faces of various
> tones, and one man has a big gold cross around his neck. Other dancers
> have extremely light and very dark complexions. Anglo bodies are
> sprinkled among the mostly Latino crowd. The tiniest of children are
> dancing with intricate steps and keeping up with the music.
>
> La Fiesta has something for everyone, and those who want to bring
> along something different just do so. Guys who like cars are checking
> out each other's hydraulic systems, which lift a car several additional
> inches off the road. One car that is going up and down and up and
> down and up and down is bright yellow. The entire hood has been
> painted with a big design that says "*Que bonita es mi raza.*" Another
> car has a Mexican flag, while yet another car is opening up to show
> the levers and the hydraulic containers that make these movements
> possible. Two guys watching the demonstration have identical t-shirts
> that say "Delinquentz Car Club" across the back.

A great proportion of Chilango's clientele are Mexican men who
work at low-paying menial jobs. Many live in one of the large apartment complexes at the same intersection or just down the road. Most
live in crowded apartments with other men. Entering a typical apartment, one immediately sees photos from home tacked onto the wall,
next to a list of domestic tasks such as "Thursday, Jose'[s day for]
cleaning the floor in the bathroom, kitchen, bedroom, and living room,
Alonso's day for cooking. Cable must be paid on the 15th." The arrangements tend to be fluid and variable, and many migrants suggest that
they have learned to adapt to roommate situations that are constantly
in flux. Profound changes in the gender division of domestic labor,
however, are typical, because of the shortage of women to do tasks that
are considered "women's work." It is also not uncommon for some
men to become adept at "owning" apartments and renting out space to
others. In another apartment that I have visited many times, Guadalupe
has been renting out space for four years in a "two-bedroom apartment"
(really one bedroom and a living room). He himself has very stable

employment and good English-language skills, and is able to profit by skillfully managing many details that newcomers find perplexing. For most of the past year, he has had five or six men living in his apartment.

While such makeshift households replace some of the functions of Mexican households, and other functions are stretched through regular remittances, frequent phone calls, and circulation patterns, still other activities spill into the public areas of apartment complexes, cultural centers, and such convenient public places as Chilango's. These new spaces become the sites of creative expression, interchange, and identity formation. Drinking and dancing at Chilango's, for example, is of major importance to many nearby residents. According to Rafael, "I think about the music and dancing everyday at work and it helps me get through the week" (interview, 2001). Because the clientele is largely Mexican, the restaurant always feels very Mexican, although on certain nights, because the mix of people and types of music played varies considerably from night to night, it can become more or less so. Even in the course of a single night, with music such as *ranchera* music, it can become more intensely Mexican, with men racing around the room to compete for the limited number of female dance partners and with Valentine and other regular Chilango clients accompanying the music with loud *gritos*, or shouts.

Chilango's is part of an expanding dance/music scene in central North Carolina. Migrants who have transportation might begin the weekend at Chilango's and go to another club later in the evening. As Jose says: "If nobody shows up or if the Hondurans show up [meaning too many Hondurans], we can always go somewhere else" (interview, 2002). While a mix of nationalities shows up at almost all of the many dance places in the region, audiences range from nearly exclusively Mexican to one near the Research Triangle Park that is very Latino yet, at the same time, decidedly non-Mexican (and quite middle class). The gender balance is much more equal at such "non-Mexican," more international clubs. Based on my observations, Mexican migrants are relentlessly creative in claiming and policing Mexican spaces. While this may sound to some like an innocent few hours on the dance floor, I suggest that in these moments of leisure, national identities are intensely challenged, contested, affirmed, reinscribed. At the same time, race, gender, and class aspects of identity are negotiated in the subtle and not-so-subtle rituals of dancing, drinking, fighting, and courtship. Gender dynamics seem particularly fluid in a situation in which a shortage of Spanish-speaking women is reinforced through state practices and polices. In this vacuum, various groups of women emerge and are recruited to each dance hall, bar, and club, creating situations similar, in some ways, to wartime dating rituals (Cooper 1996; Howard 2001; Rose 1997).

At El Toro's, for instance, a bar with live music in nearby Durham, there is a persistent shortage of women. This is true even on Fridays, when women are admitted free. The clientele is mostly Mexican men in their 20s and 30s. The majority of women are Anglo women from Durham's eastside working-class neighborhoods. The scene is one of extremes: some women are exceptionally overweight, while others are 15–20 years older than their dancing partners. A few Mexican women and a few Black women are usually there. In addition, some gay men and transvestites attend. Thus, while Mexican men at El Toro are faced with a shortage of Mexican dance partners, they have a wide range of others to choose from. The dance floor is the site of transnational romance, as well as the site of frequent conflict. Insults and shoving quickly escalate to violent displays. Such fights tend to be quickly contained by police and security guards, although one night I witnessed a brawl that swept up much of the crowd and continued for several minutes. At the height of the mêlée, the bartender whacked the surface of the bar with a large baseball bat, but no one really paid much attention to her. Likewise, it seems few patrons are concerned about rule number 4 on El Toro's list of rules[9]:

1. No spitting on the floor.
2. Neat dress.
3. Put trash in wastebasket.
4. No fussing and fighting:
First offense: 30-day suspension. Second offense: 60 days. Third offense: permanent suspension.

During the daytime—especially the early morning hours—the space in front of Chilango's becomes a bustling informal labor market where Mexican men gather and wait for trucks to arrive with offers of both skilled and unskilled work. Many *patrones* or *patronas*—usually English-speaking—pull up near the densely packed clusters of men and announce that they need a certain number of workers for a certain amount of hours. Sometimes the boss will specify a skill, such as drywall finishing. The motivating element for the men seeking work, however, is the wage. A boss who offers US$8 will be able to hire workers quickly, whereas another who offers only $7 may have to stand and haggle for a while before finding someone who is willing to get in the truck and go wherever the job may be.

Lalo Quintero, a recent, undocumented migrant worker from Morelos, Mexico, told me that he was able to get work at the Chilango intersection the very first weekday he was in North Carolina. He added that he was careful to separate himself a bit from the crowd so that he could approach vehicles as they stopped and ensure that he had a good chance to be selected for employment. "When I stand at some distance from the crowd, I can move quickly" (interview, 2002). Another strategy that worked for Lalo was to arrive very early, around 6:30 am, so that he would not miss any opportunities. In fact on some occasions, Lalo returned from one job in time to get a second one. When I suggested to Lalo that he was hard-working, he confided that he was anxious to pay off the costs of his illegal international passage so that he could begin earning his own money. A month before, he had been deported from South Texas and forced to forfeit his savings in the process of trying to cross into the United States. Stranded at the international border with no possessions and little cash, he desperately placed calls to family members and close personal friends to see if he could salvage his plans. As it turned out, two former employees of Lalo's (who also happened to be brother and sister) offered to fix him up with a trusted coyote[10] and pay $1500 for his passage to North Carolina. To make this connection, Lalo had to travel west along much of the 2000-mile-long US-Mexico border. From his new location, he proceeded with a group that walked for three days and nights in the dangerously rugged desert area of western Arizona.[11]

Rosario, one of Lalo's North Carolina sponsors, said that she wanted to help Lalo because he had been a good friend to her and to her family in her hometown in Morelos. "I was working for Lalo when I first decided to go and harvest crops in California—he bought me a pair of shoes for the trip." After reflecting a couple minutes, Rosario added, "We've known Lalo since we were little kids" (interview, 2002). She explained that lending a helping hand involved a lot of late-night calls to arrange the details, trips across town to wire money to Lalo and to the coyote, and some anxious nights awaiting the delayed arrival of the "freight-handlers" in Carrboro. Rosario and her brother made the final payment to the coyote when he delivered Lalo to a shopping plaza a few blocks from Chilango's. Rosario, her brother, and a few friends celebrated Lalo's safe arrival with a case of Bud Light and tales of the North Carolina work scene. As a visitor at Rosario's place that evening, I enjoyed a very special festive atmosphere that had been created by the combination of relief over Lalo's safe arrival and the joy of being with a friend from home. Everyone was talking at once and keen to give Lalo advice about the local labor market. A common sentiment—expressed in a variety of ways—was that Lalo should say that he had whatever skills the boss needed. Rosario thought Lalo's best opportunities would be in restaurants or grocery stores, while her brother, who had also helped to sponsor Lalo, insisted that the wages were much higher at the informal labor exchange at the Chilango's corner.

Lalo is an example of someone who has temporarily given up a successful career in Mexico to work in "whatever comes along." He managed a small fresh vegetable and fruit stand for 19 years in Morelos.

Many factors will influence Lalo's ability to stay in the United States as an undocumented worker for an extended period of time but—at least at this moment in time—stay is exactly what he intends to do. He wants to provide a good living for two children who are still in school and to save enough to bring his girlfriend across the international line. While his own parents had no previous experience in the United States. Lalo knew that Rosario's father (also a close friend and neighbor of Lalo's) earned a considerable amount of money picking cotton as a *bracero*[12] in Pecos, Texas in the early 1950s. He had seen first-hand that this income had helped Rosario's father improve his land and harvest in Morelos. In more recent years, Lalo had gotten regular reports from Rosario's family of the success that she and her brothers were enjoying. "I had some other friends from home who are working in California and Nevada," he says "but I'm glad things worked out so that I could come to North Carolina" (interview, 2002). Many immigrants use social networks and personal knowledge of the previous generation to guide their decisions about whether and where to migrate. Thus, while communities in Mexico lower the socially necessary labor time—and thus the cost—of future migrant workers, the experience of an older generation inspires some to travel north and work in the United States.

The space in front of Chilango's is also a site of much commerce. Available goods include steaming fresh tamales at the bus stop, a selection of international telephone calling cards at Teresa's apartment door, and haircuts at Margarita's. On the street itself, one can ask for and purchase illicit drugs, stolen jewelry, and stolen brand-name clothing at most times of the day or night. Every now and then, a prostitute or group of prostitutes seeks clients by strolling along in front of the gas station and convenience store. One of the most popular sites of commerce is a makeshift weekend restaurant in a two-bedroom apartment near the bus stop. While there are usually only two or three items available at any given time, the food is so good and so reasonable that people line up to sit at the single table available or on couches in the living room of the apartment. Of course, some clients ask for a carryout and take their food home. Sunday mornings are especially competitive, because the mother and daughter who run this business always prepare *pancita* (a tripe stew, also known as *menudo*) and it goes quickly. Marta, the mother, told me that this business is thriving because they always use fresh ingredients and cook as if they were cooking for themselves. "We enjoy getting the kitchen organized so that we can feed a lot of people each week" (interview, 2002). In the course of two years, Marta has been able to finance the expense of bringing much of her extended family to North Carolina. "When we combine our earnings [from the restaurant] with my husband's and my son's salary, we can save quite a bit each week" (interview, 2002). They continue to live in the same apartment that they use as a restaurant, but in the past year, as the family has expanded to include five more individuals, they have rented a second apartment that faces their own. Marta's grandchildren circulate between the two apartments during business hours.

Blond hair spins around the dancer in the skin-tight snakeskin blue blouse, while the black man who is her partner reveals a perfectly sculpted chest underneath his cut-away t-shirt. They have the full attention of La Fiesta's audience. One guy brought his lizard and carries him along on his shoulder. Couples are crowded onto the makeshift dancing area of the high school parking lot.

The *cumbia* contest at La Marakas draws a slightly more homogenous crowd. Most of the couples are young Latinos. Those who want to compete have numbers taped to their backs. They spin around under the disco lights while the crowd sips beer at one of many bar tables encircling the generous dance floor. When a few couples advance to the final round of the competition, some—including one woman in black boots and a black miniskirt—appear tired from the strenuous dancing.

The DJ at El Chilango's announces that he wants to play something special for those from Mexico this evening. He flips through his massive collection of CDs to pull out a *ranchera*, and people spring to their feet and head toward the cozy dance floor. After the dance, the DJ announces that a live group will be playing tomorrow. The band is free, he insists, and the *cervezas* will be *bien frías*.

As couples dance to *rancheras*, *cumbias*, *bachatas*, Guatemalan animal masks stare down from the walls at the densely packed crowd. Many regular customers live nearby and know most of the others who are here. The hairnet gang guy has earrings and a snake tattoo on the back of his neck, yet he sits calmly with some very young friends who are intently watching the dancers. A Ricky Martin look-alike is dancing with a heavy-set Anglo schoolteacher who wears glasses. Another Mexican man with a "Tar Heels" T-shirt dances with a woman in a cutaway red blouse. The music throbs relentlessly and bodies twist and turn on the small dance floor. People's relaxed expressions burst into hilarity from time to time.

The ancient masks on the wall compete with bright neon beer signs: the yellow Corona bottle stands beside a green palm tree and a blue ocean wave, while the Dos Equis symbol is a bright red double XX. TECATE is displayed in capital letters on a white neon map of Mexico.

One of the men drinking in the bar has the Virgen de Guadalupe on the back of his T-shirt. This Virgen has the Mexican flag on one side and the US flag on the other. Many Latino men are dancing with Anglo women. Several guys don't even bother to come in—they stand in the parking lot outside and watch the festivities from the front window. Quite a few women are taller than their partners, some are noticeable older, while yet a few others are rather heavy, or have features that might cause them to be considered unattractive in other contexts.

Translocal Lives, Transnational Ways of Living

Latino migrants in the South typically maintain familial ties through techniques such as remittances, frequent phone calls, and return visits. For many migrants and migrant communities, these techniques become a way of living in more than one place at a time, or of living translocally. At the same time, migrants must form some kind of household arrangement in order to meet immediate daily needs. For recent migrants to the US South, these makeshift households often involve a profound transformation of gender divisions of labor in housework. While such household arrangements may be temporary for some, they can also be a source of long-term profit for others, such as Guadalupe, mentioned above.

Likewise, through transnational migration, Mexican men can improve their wages tenfold in many economic sectors. The more modest claim often heard in North Carolina is that one can make the same amount here in a single day that one can make at home in a week. Such an extreme wage gap is a powerful incentive that overrides many risks and hardships. The extent of the wage gap also fuels cultural stereotypes that newcomers are "hard-working," while the previous employees (and the domestic cultural groups with which they identify) are "lazy" (Hicks 2002; Johnson-Webb 2000; Rosenberg 2002). In these popular assessments, the ways in which Latinos hold personal costs to a minimum and the way in which immigration and labor policies lower the costs of social reproduction are ignored. The degree to which domestic employers and the US economy have come to rely on globalized flow of labor is also neglected. Tracing these transnational human pathways, with particular attention to the rate of exploitation (ie, the ratio of surplus labor to socially necessary labor time), is one way to illuminate the personal impact of these globalized jobs. Even so, such calculations miss crucially important factors such as unhealthy working conditions, the degree of control over the work situation, and the extent to which household and other undervalued forms of labor may by subsidizing wages (Cravey 1998).

Along with the stretching of household/family/community relationships, creative approaches to microscale social reproduction facilitate the globalization of labor markets. This process is quite complex, and the gender dynamics within households, workplaces, dancehalls and along immigration pathways only make it more so. Gendered divisions of labor in Carrboro's Latino households are profoundly distinct from those in most households in Mexico or North Carolina. While these households are often organized in temporary and experimental ways, this very flexibility and fluidity in gender systems and household dynamics has benefited North Carolina employers, while simultaneously propelling wider economic and cultural transformations.

Cultural change is perhaps the most disorienting angle of view on transnational migration in the South. On the one hand, state policies and practices are reinscribing race in the region through labor-importation programs and selective enforcement of immigration policies. Recruitment of foreign workers is carefully balanced with subtle and overt efforts to criminalize the same people that are recruited. In addition, difference is being actively produced in workplaces and places of leisure. The advantage of exploring cultural difference in dancehalls and public places is perhaps that the creative potential of migrants is so palpable. Various national groups of Latinos compete, date, fight, fall in love, negotiate, and dance seductively with each other and with US Anglos and Blacks. If we want to understand globalizing labor markets in North Carolina, we must learn more about processes of social reproduction on the dance floor, at the *pulga* (flea market), and in temporary and stretched households.

Conclusion

[I]n the course of this activity, i.e. labour, a definite quantity of human muscle, nerve, brain, etc. is expended, and these things have to be replaced. Since more is expended, more must be received. If the owner of labour-power works today, tomorrow he must again be able to repeat the same process in the same conditions as regards health and strength. His means of subsistence must therefore be sufficient to maintain him in his normal state as a working individual. His natural needs, such as food, clothing, fuel, and housing, vary according to the climatic and other physical peculiarities of his country. On the other hand, the number and extent of his so-called necessary requirements, as also the manner in which they are satisfied, are themselves products of history, and depend therefore to a great extent on the level of civilization attained by a county; in particular they depend on the conditions in which, and consequently on the habits and expectations with which the class of free workers has been formed. In contrast therefore, with the case of other commodities, the determination of the value of labour-power contains a historical and moral element. (Marx 1990:275)

As Marx suggests, the value of labor power—and thus, the value of the peculiar commodity that is a human worker—is highly contingent on historical and geographical context. Social reproduction of quantities of "muscle, nerve, [and] brain" occurs in discrete households and other sites where workers are fed, nurtured, and educated. Thus, examining the geography and dynamics of social reproduction provides insight into globalization processes such as transnational labor markets and transnational identity formation. When we consider the social reproduction of transnational migrants in the US South, it is clear that these migrants provide several subsidies to capital: a generational subsidy, a daily or short-term subsidy, and racialized workplace practices and wages. As Katz suggests in the quote cited above, workers produced at lower cost elsewhere provide a substantial savings to employers' contexts such as the United States. In the situation examined here, this spatial arrangement—between US employers and Mexican employees —has a long history. Lalo and Rosario followed the example of Rosario's father, who had worked in US cotton harvests. Thus, not only is Rosario's labor power subsidized by having been produced elsewhere, but also, in her family and in her community, transnational incomes are becoming increasingly necessary for survival. A strong, healthy worker's body is capable of traveling these circuits and taking these risks. Other family members—especially the infirm and the young, and oftentimes women—find that the hazards of international migration outweigh the possible benefits (Nevins 2002).

A subsidy to capital is also provided through the circuits of daily and short-term social reproduction. This happens in a variety of ways. The various creative approaches that transnational migrants have for daily survival are central to this process. For instance, the extremely crowded conditions in apartments and other households allow transnational migrants to trim expenses and live cheaply. The novel ways in which they organize labor within these households likewise allow them to cut certain costs and to hold other costs below the norm for nonmigrants living in North Carolina. More interestingly and more importantly, the very fact of transnationality lowers the cost of "socially necessary labor time," because social needs and expectations are shaped partly—in many regards, almost totally—by distinct national and local contexts and norms. Thus, when one's neighbors back in Guanajuato are surviving on one-tenth the wage, the socially necessary labor time of the transnational migrant from Guanajuato is considerably lower than for those with whom he may work in North Carolina.

Another key issue to emerge from examining these spaces of social reproduction is the creative potential of transnational identities themselves. One can glimpse new ways of living and interacting in these transnational spaces of social reproduction. Pan-American exchanges occur, while transnationality constantly calls up place identity such as nationalism and other place-based identifications in an endless swirl of unexpected encounters. New spaces that can be claimed or appropriated are essential to this way of life. Thus, as Hardt and Negri (2001:397) suggest, the pathways of transnational migrants "often cost terrible suffering, but there is also in them a desire for liberation that is not satiated except by reappropriating new spaces, around which are constructed new freedoms."

Acknowledgments

I want to thank Allen Feinberg for his encouragement and Elva Bishop for the video images of *Carolina del Norte*. I am also grateful to Michael Petit, Sallie Marston, and three anonymous reviewers for their constructive comments on an earlier draft of the paper.

Endnotes

[1] "Play a ranchera [song], please."

[2] Carrboro is a former textile town that abuts the college town of Chapel Hill, North Carolina. Both Carrboro and Chapel Hill are part of the Research Triangle metropolitan area and enjoyed the extremely low unemployment rates in the Triangle area in the 1990s.

[3] It is important to remember that Mexicans "have lived 'here' since before there was a Mexico or a United States. And they have been immigrating to this country almost from its inception. Since 1820, when the federal government began keeping immigration records, only one other country, Germany, has sent more immigrants to our shores" (Gonzalez 2000:96).

[4] While the idea of a structured coherence originated with the notion of a balance of power at the urban scale, such a conceptualization is also useful in understanding the way in which regional power dynamics remained relatively static for decades in the US South, particularly when seen from the angle of rural labor markets.

[5] Vass is in central North Carolina, approximately 50 minutes south of Carrboro.

[6] I am grateful to Elva Bishop for the video images of cultural transformation in North Carolina upon which these descriptions are based.

[7] *Chilango* denotes a person from Mexico City. In some contexts, the term is used derogatively. There is even a popular saying reflecting provincial resentment toward urban Mexicans: "*Haz patria, mata un chilango*" (Be patriotic, kill a chilango).

[8] The owner has transnational claims of his own: he is of French ancestry and has lived many years in France, Mexico, and the United States.

[9] Rules are posted in English and in Spanish in prominent locations.

[10] A person who smuggles Mexicans into the United States.

[11] Such high-risk desert crossings are increasingly common, due to heightened surveillance in urban portions of the international boundary (Nevins 2002).

[12] The bracero program brought Mexican workers to the United States, beginning during World War II and ending in 1964.

References

Brier J and Niles A (1998) *Immigrant Labor and Guest Workers in Oregon: Case Study and Policy Context for the H-2A Guestworker Program*. Salem, OR: CAUSA

Burawoy M (2000) *Global Ethnography: Forces, Connections, And Imaginations in a Postmodern World*. Berkeley: University of California Press

Calavita K (1992) *Inside the State: The Bracero Program, Immigration, and the INS*. London: Routledge

Cherry A E (1995) "Organized and Planned Patterns of Movement of Migrant Farmworkers in Selected Counties in North Carolina." MA thesis, Appalachian State University, Boone, NC

Cooper B L (1996) From "love letters" to "miss you": Popular recordings, epistolary imagery, and romance during wartime, 1941–1945. *Journal of American Culture* 19(4):15–27

Cravey A J (1997) Latino labor and poultry production in rural North Carolina. *Southeastern Geographer* 37(2):295–300

Cravey A J (1998) *Women and Work in Mexico's Maquiladoras*. Lanham, MD: Rowman and Littlefield Publishers, Inc.

Cravey A J (1999) "Toothless tigers and mouldered miracles: Geography and a global gender contract in the NICs." Unpublished manuscript

Cravey A J, Arcury T and Quandt S (2000) Mapping as a means of farmworker education and empowerment. *Journal of Geography* 99:229–237

Davis M (2000) *Magical Urbanism: Latinos Reinvent the US City*. London: Verso

Gonzalez J (2000) *Harvest of Empire: A History of Latinos in America*. New York: Viking

Hahamovitch C (1997) *The Fruits of Their Labor: Atlantic Coast Farmworkers and the Making of Migrant Poverty, 1870–1945*. Chapel Hill: University of North Carolina Press

Hardt M and Negri A (2000) *Empire*. Cambridge, MA: Harvard University Press

Harvey D (1989) *The Urban Experience*. Baltimore: The Johns Hopkins University Press

Hicks S G (2002) "Framing Justice in the Promised Land: North Carolina's Immigrant Farm and Crab Workers." Undergraduate honors thesis, University of North Carolina at Chapel Hill

Howard J (2001) The politics of dancing under Japanese-American incarceration. *History Workshop Journal* 52:122–151

Human Rights Watch (2000) *Unfair Advantage: Workers' Freedom of Association in the United States under International Human Rights Standards*. New York: Human Rights Watch

Johnson-Webb K D (2000) "Formal and Informal Hispanic Labor Recruitment: North Carolina Communities in Transition." PhD dissertation, University of North Carolina at Chapel Hill

Katz C (2001) Vagabond capitalism and the necessity of social reproduction. *Antipode* 33(4):709–728

Marston S A (2000) The social construction of scale. *Progress in Human Geography* 24(2):219–242

Marx K (1990) *Capital*. Vol 1. London: Penguin Books

Nevins J (2002) *Operation Gatekeeper: The Rise of the "Illegal Alien" and the Making of the US-Mexico Boundary*. New York: Routledge

Norton M E II and Lindner M (1996) Down and out in West Laco Texas and Washington, DC: Race-based discrimination against farmworkers under federal unemployment insurance. *University of Michigan Journal of Law Reform* 29:177–216

Rose S O (1997) Girls and GIs: Race, sex, and diplomacy in Second World War Britain. *International History Review* 19(1):146–160

Rosenberg K (2002) "The Impact of Latino Migration on the Black Community." Undergraduate honors thesis, University of North Carolina at Chapel Hill

Smith M P (2001) *Transnational Urbanism: Locating Globalization*. London: Blackwell

Smith-Nonini S (1999) Uprooting injustice. *Southern Exposure: A Journal of Politics and Culture* 27(2):40–57

Smith-Nonini S (2002) Seeing no evil: The state, the federal H2A program and private farm labor brokers. Paper delivered at workshop on Globalization and the Changing Countryside: Organizing for Land, Labor and the Right to have Rights in the US and Brazil, University of North Carolina, Chapel Hill, NC, 27 April

Interviews
Rafael Montoya. 17 November 2001.
Rosario Nuñez. 28 August 2002.
Marta Quesada. 15 July 2002.
Lalo Quintero. 19 August 2002.
José Ramírez. 22 January 2002.

Chapter 9
Human Smuggling, the Transnational Imaginary, and Everyday Geographies of the Nation-State

Alison Mountz

Introduction

In Canada, immigration has long been a strategy utilized to sustain and build a population with negative rates of "natural" growth (Ley and Hiebert 2001). Both federal and provincial governments attempt to boost the economy by recruiting highly skilled or wealthy immigrants, such as entrepreneurs from Hong Kong drawn to business immigration programs (Ley forthcoming; Mitchell 1993). Like other countries, Canada also utilizes immigration strategically to fill gaps in the labor market, recruiting, for example, nurses, high-tech workers, and domestic workers through the Live-In Caregiver Program (Pratt in collaboration with the Philippine Women's Centre 1998; Pratt 1999). In addition to landing the highest number of immigrants per capita in the world—at twice the per capita rate of the United States (*New York Times* 2002)—Canada has been, in recent decades, reputed to be among the most progressive and humanitarian of refugee-granting nation-states.[1]

While Canada has excelled in the global competition among states to strategically recruit certain groups, public opinion has not always aligned with federal goals. Discourse surrounding different migration streams reflects shifting contexts of reception over time and across space (cf Ellis and Wright 1998; Fincher 2001; Hage 1998; Nevins 2002). For instance, in the 1990s, Canadians experienced poorly performing national and provincial economies, and their faith in Canada's refugee determination process wavered. Declining confidence coincided with shifts in human smuggling and trafficking methods[2] (see Kyle and Koslowski 2001) and with growing public awareness of the phenomena. Simultaneously, internal and US pressure on Canada to step up enforcement along its borders increased. US officials maintain interest in Canadian immigration policy because of their shared border and because of the perception, heightened since the terrorist attacks on New York and Washington DC on September 11, 2001, that immigrants slip easily across Canadian borders. Such was the context within which the human smuggling incidents on which this essay is based unfolded.

During a nine-week period between July and September of 1999, the federal government intercepted four boats carrying migrants smuggled via a continuous route from Fujian, China to the west coast of Vancouver Island. After migrants from the first boat made refugee claims, many were released and quickly disappeared.[3] Following their disappearance, a second boat arrival prompted the first instance of mass detention of refugee claimants in recent Canadian history.[4] A total of 599 migrants were intercepted on four boats, 549 of whom made refugee claims (CIC 2000). Twenty-four eventually received refugee status; most were deported in 2000.

The arrivals and eventual deportations, coupled with the announcement of new immigration legislation in April 2000, marked the culmination of a decade of tightened controls over immigration, during which time, remarked Sherene Razack (1999:160), "The criminal attempting to cross our borders featured as a central figure in the discursive management of these new [federal] initiatives." The boat arrivals provoked a shrill response with political, social, racial, and economic dimensions among the Canadian public. The public outcry accompanied racialized and criminalized representations of the migrants in the mainstream media, where they were positioned as "queue jumpers," perceived to have cut to the front of an imaginary line. This heated objection paralleled trends in Australia and the European Union, where it was becoming increasingly difficult to be a "legitimate" refugee. After making refugee claims, the smuggled migrants were scripted as "bogus refugees" and as "economic" rather than (legitimate) political refugees. The boat arrivals marked a significant shift in discourse surrounding immigration to Canada more broadly (Mahtani and Mountz 2002) and highlighted the conflicting roles played by the nation-state as facilitator and enforcer.

These desires to facilitate and enforce exist in tension and are manifested everywhere in the operation of the federal department of Citizenship and Immigration Canada (CIC): in its mandate[5] and policies and in the day-to-day work of bureaucrats. In an attempt to explore the careful balancing act performed by the state, this essay contemplates the ways in which nation-states mediate transnational migration through categorization. CIC constructs the identities of transnational migrants through its immigration programs by categorizing them along a spectrum of desirability. Through such bureaucratic practices, nation-states legalize forms of belonging. In its efforts to see and place migrants in categories for the purposes of management, the state is distanced from and often misses the complex reasons for which people decide to move (cf Scott 1998).

CIC employees who regulate federal immigration policy come to see transnational migrants in different ways according to various axes of difference and location, including—not exclusively—the class, "race," ethnicity, gender, sexual identity, language capacity, work experience, religion, nationality, and regional affiliation of immigrant and refugee applicants. Employees of the state, themselves located in complex webs of social relations, also experience the world in distinct ways along these axes of difference and so relate to different immigrants in different ways. These practices materialize within the bureaucracy of CIC, in which diverse institutional subjects operationalize immigration policies in relation to the ways they construct and relate to migrants. They actively define themselves and their nation in relation to those whose entrance they facilitate or prohibit. It is important, therefore, to contemplate the social relations within which the nation-state is enacted by examining the interface between discourse and materiality (cf Painter 1995)—in this case, between the *language* of categorization and actual *access* to the nation-state (see Sharma 2001). Qualitative research offers the opportunity to pull apart the narratives of government and nongovernment employees. In interviews conducted for this essay, individuals articulated the ways in which their views on and roles in the response to human smuggling worked both symbiotically and in tension with policy. Alternative narratives of the state disrupt some of the more audible narratives about transnational migration— for example, the state as facilitator of capital flows for investment and economic growth—that have become normalized as culturally acceptable narratives.

Agent-based analysis of the response to human smuggling prompts deconstruction of the conceptual boundaries surrounding "the state" and governance in more abstract epistemological approaches. Such analysis also challenges various binaries constructed between state and nonstate institutional actors, between policy and practice, and between state and civil society more broadly, such that the state is not only constitutive of but constituted by spheres of social reproduction.

Conceptualizing Everyday Geographies of the Nation-State

Social scientists often theorize "the state" as an abstract concept. Phillip Abrams (1988:77) called this "the idea of the state," an abstraction to which Timothy Mitchell (1991:91) attributes "ghost-like" qualities. Michael Taussig also queried the ghost-like status of the state, by asking, in *The Magic of the State* (1997:3), "Could it be that with disembodiment, presence expands?" In other words, the state is something elusive, "out there" (Mitchell 1991:94), mythical by nature (Hansen and Stepputat 2001:20–21). Andrew Kirby (1997:5) argued that academics do not understand the state because they fail to "know" it through personal experience. Abrams (1988:59) noted with frustration that theorists had come to take the state for granted and had lost sight of a more nuanced dialogue: "We are variously urged to respect the state, or smash the state or study the state: but for want of clarity about the nature of the state such projects remain beset with difficulties." Indeed, attention to the state seems to move cyclically, the dialogue among theorists from various disciplines ebbing and flowing as they alternately call for the demise and the regeneration of the concept.[6]

I attribute the myth of the state with autonomous power to the tendency of some theoretical approaches to underestimate the role that people play in its enactment. The field of political geography, for example, suffers from a dearth of work on everyday approaches to the *embodied* nation-state (cf Hyndman 2001). Behind each decision are individuals acting within varied institutional and geographical contexts. Most state theories, however, do not locate geographies of the nation-state in a time or a place; rather, they assume its pervasive nature. My endeavor to research the daily operations of the federal department of CIC is, in part, a response to the *disembodiment* of theories of the state. As such, this work contributes to a growing interest in the literature on transnational migration in the powerful role that nation-states play in mediating migration by scripting the identities of trans-national subjects (eg Mountz et al 2002; Nevins 2002; Sharma 2001; Tyner 2000; Walton-Roberts 2001). The state *is* powerful, but *not* all-powerful and knowing. If the power or "ghost-like" stature of the state expands through disembodiment (Taussig 1997:3), it is through the feminist strategy of embodiment that the actual power of the state materializes in daily practice (Mountz 2002; see also Hansen and Stepputat 2001).

Social scientists also tend to construct artificial divides by theorizing the state and civil society as separate entities, both conceptually and spatially (Gupta 1995; Mitchell 1991). Some scholars, however, have questioned the distinction. Mitchell (1991:91) asked, "What is it about modern society, as a particular form of social and economic order, that has made possible the apparent autonomy of the state as a free-standing entity?" Gupta (1995:393) identified this division as a limited construction of Western political thought, or a "Western conceptual apparatus," that fails to account for variations in the ways states operate at different levels in distinct locales. Rather than an abstract, hegemonic, repressive, autonomous body that affects social relations, I conceptualize the state as an everyday social construction. This approach entails looking at the bureaucracy as a site where the nation-state is produced unevenly across time and space and where the everyday relations among those theoretically conceived of as "outside" of the state bleed into the dimensions of bureaucratic life in fascinating ways. The work of immigration officers entails daily nation-building exercises as they operationalize mechanisms to determine national identity by deciding who belongs within or outside of the nation, and it supports the idea that the state not only influences but is influenced by social contexts (Calavita 1992; Heyman 1995; Nevins 2002).

Joe Painter (1995:34) proposed a helpful "working definition" of the state, which he, like Mitchell and Abrams, identified as an ill-defined concept: "States are constituted of spatialized social practices which are to a greater or lesser extent institutionalized (in a 'state apparatus') and which involve claims to authority which are general in social scope and which secure at least partial compliance through either consent, or coercion, or both." Painter infused into the legal and territorial parameters of the state the notion that its very glue is social praxis. He located these practices in an institution or "state apparatus": the bureaucracy (cf Gramsci 1994). Painter's work (1995) suggests that reconceptualizing the discursive and material social geographies of the state may enable a reframing of political agendas.

Perhaps the spatial "othering" of the state is attributable to the difficulties of actually conducting ethnographic research within government institutions. Noting the tendency of social scientists to study the state "from above" anthropologists such as Heyman and Smart (1999:15) increasingly advocate research that studies bureaucracies from the inside: "Viewing states from below and within emphasizes the complicated processes of enacting actual laws, policies, justice systems." As Heyman (1995:264) noted in work with American immigration officers, "Bureaucratic work is internally conflictive but appears, in the single-stranded relationship to the exterior, to be definitive ... and rational." Indeed, the policies of the state are enacted amid tension, conflict, and difference, but higher-level bureaucrats and communications employees construct coherent narratives for the public, which tend to provide narrow insight into what actually takes place. Policies and mandates represent the more superficial, outward expressions of the nation-state, perhaps the most visible narratives of state activity and identity. And it is often within the realm of policy and mandate that social scientists conduct their work (Heyman and Smart 1999:15). Written policies, however, represent idealized versions of what *might* be or what *should* happen. In the case of the human smuggling movement in 1999, policy was written retrospectively. Social interactions and messy processes *within* the state, where bureaucrats work through the implementation of policy, are central to its enactment.

Scholars have debated the loss of sovereignty of the nation-state in confronting the forces of free trade and globalization (eg Ohmae 1995;

Sassen 1996). By "studying up," or researching the powerful institutions that regulate human mobility (eg Herbert 2001; Heyman 1995; Hyndman 2000; Nevins 2002), social scientists are poised to enter this dialogue with empirical testimony as to the contemporary powers of the state. In his poststructural approach to state theory, Mitchell (1991:92) remarked that while policies invoke a hierarchy of command, bureaucracies function more along the lines of disciplinary power. Anthropologists and others who approach the state in "everyday" contexts illustrate that the state is not a monolithic actor, but rather a diverse set of institutional subjects (eg Heyman 1995; Nelson 1999). This prompted Diane Nelson (1999), for example, to conceptualize the Guatemalan state as constituted by and constitutive of identity. Her contributions draw heavily upon Foucauldian concepts of power as producing individuals through discourses of nationhood (Foucault 1991, 1995). Nelson and other anthropologists, such as Taussig, are beginning to outline the rough contours of "ethnographies of the state" (eg Gupta 1995; Nelson 1999; Taussig 1997). Their definitions of "the state" are bound up with the ways in which identities are constructed through quotidian practices.

International boundaries occupy visible, powerful locations in the geographical imagination where the nation-state constructs identities (Kearney 1991; Nevins 2002:160). Immigration policies are not ad hoc, but rather strategic positionings of groups of people in relation to the global economy through their identification as particular types of transnational subjects. Identity is central to this process of classification and is constituted through federal immigration policy. Understanding the ways in which the nation-state sees, classifies, and accepts or rejects transnational subjects shows the power of the state to produce identity and thus to materially exclude, as in Nevins' (2002) analysis of the construction of the "illegal alien," which Heyman (1995) identifies as a key context to the organizational world views of Immigration and Naturalization Service (INS) officers. Applying James Scott's (1998) ideas regarding the ways states see and manage from a distance through centralized practices of classification regarding human migration is one way to frame categories of transnational subjects currently circulated in immigration policy.

To see some spaces as belonging to the state and other spaces as nonstate spaces is a false divide. Civil servants work, live, study, and send their children to school and daycare within the communities around them. They rely upon social systems of support and develop expectations in relation to their understanding of what it means to be a citizen and what rights and privileges are entailed therein. I aim, ultimately, to dissolve the distinction between "inside" and "outside" the state through everyday analysis, or a "quotidian interpretation" of the state (Kirby 1997:2). Employees of the state are embedded in social relationships patterned across networks at multiple scales. In other words, the state is shaped by the local and regional communities in which it operates and, in turn, it shapes them. It also shapes and is shaped by powerful transnational imaginaries, through the mediation of transnational movements and relationships. But how and where do we locate the state methodologically? In order to understand the state as a site of identity construction and social reproduction, I pursue feminist geopolitical strategies of embodying and rescaling the state (see Hyndman 2002) through ethnographic research (see Hansen and Stepputat 2001).

After detailing the methodology of the project, I will exemplify a poststructural approach to everyday geographies of the nation-state. This framework entails four elements. First, it includes the roles played by people in enacting the state and, in this case, immigration policy. Second, it places language at the center of struggles over power in which the nation-state attempts to not only make sense of but also impose order on the world of transnational migration at the interface between discourse and materiality. Third, poststructural geographical analysis entails the dissolution of boundaries around governance that become more fluid when viewed through qualitative research; which, in turn, prompts deconstruction of the category of the state. Finally, this approach to the state turns on identity and on the ways in which nationhood is constructed through the location of borders in the transnational geographical imagination.

Methodology

> Disciplinary power ... works not from the outside but from within, not at the level of an entire society but at the level of detail, and not by constraining their actions [those of institutional actors] but by producing them. (Mitchell 1991:93)

As Mitchell suggests, analysis of disciplinary power—in this case, the production of identity through bureaucratic arrangements—must occur at "the level of detail," or, in my estimation, the scale of the everyday. Hansen and Stepputat (2001) advocate localized, ethnographic approaches to the state, centered in the field. Critical ethnography enables an approach to the state as "a set of social practices" (Painter 1995:34) and as a set of diverse institutional actors exercising agency through quotidian bureaucratic arrangements.

I began my research with CIC approximately one year after the first boat arrival. My goal was to gather narratives of the 1999 response to human smuggling in British Columbia (BC) from diverse perspectives through participant observation, semistructured interviews, archival research, and media analysis. For a period of a few months, I participated in the daily exchanges of office life in the regional headquarters of CIC in the BC/Yukon region in downtown Vancouver, without actually doing any immigration-related work. I occupied a desk in the office, reviewed documents, conducted interviews, and "hung out" with employees to the extent that their schedules would allow. This served as a base of operation from which I set up semistructured interviews. Within CIC, I interviewed a diverse set of employees involved in the 1999 response to human smuggling in some capacity, from frontline officers who boarded the boats to officials located higher up in the administration of the department in Ottawa. In interviews with immigration bureaucrats, officers, managers, and high-level officials, I explored the positioning of this movement in relation to other transnational migrations and the decision-making processes surrounding the boat arrivals. Beyond CIC, I interviewed provincial employees and many "others" of the state involved, such as immigration lawyers, nongovernmental organizations (NGOs), and suprastate human-rights monitors. My objectives included understanding the parameters around governance and access to decision-makers. Interview questions addressed the various roles that people played and the challenges to cross-institutional collaboration. Interviews numbered approximately 70.

Documents reviewed included those filed on site at the regional headquarters in BC that pertained to the 1999 response, including instruction manuals, reports, communications strategies, memos, and e-mail exchanges that documented the daily interactions around the response to smuggling. I also reviewed all documents released to the public during the 24 months following the boat arrivals in response to access to information requests. Examining "public" materials alongside "in-house" files enabled me to look at the external and internal articulations of the response. An additional method that painted another layer of context was content analysis of coverage in local and national newspapers.

It is challenging for social scientists to access the state and other powerful institutions ethnographically, and this research, like all field projects, carried with it a host of ethical quandaries. These included the desire to protect those who participated in the study and the privacy of their clients, as well as my own status as a researcher and foreign student in Canada in relation to a powerful organization working in a controversial and dangerous field. The bureaucracy itself is designed to protect employees, clients, and information, and I had to negotiate protective mechanisms throughout the process. This approach is epistemologically and methodologically distinct from the more traditional approaches of political scientists and political geographers to conceptualizations of the state. The research has the potential and also the risk inherent in naming and disrupting the taken-for-granted powers of the state understood and enacted through finer scales of analysis at the level of everyday interactions.

Everyday Geographies of the Response
to Human Smuggling

I now return to and expand on a poststructural approach to everyday geographies of the nation-state, using empirical evidence from the case study of the 1999 response to human smuggling in BC. A people-centered institutional ethnography brings conceptual models inside the state where the messy, conflicted, and collaborative nature of institutional processes leads to deconstruction of the category of "the state." Dissolution of this category, in turn, challenges various theoretical binaries. Primary among these is the division constructed between state and nonstate actors. This poststructural approach to the state entails a shift in scale from the geopolitical to the body (see Hyndman 2002; Mountz 2002; Nelson 1999) and brings to light more nuanced discursive struggles over the language through which transnational migrants are categorized. Many parties have a stake in the labeling of transnational migrations, and power circulates through practices of naming and ordering (cf Sharma 2001). In fact, Hansen and Stepputat (2001:9) argue that the "language of stateness" is the mechanism through which "the state" reproduces itself. Therein lies the powerful interface between the discursive and the material.

The Power to Name

In her documentation of the process through which Canada recruited entrepreneurs from Hong Kong through the business immigration program, Katharyne Mitchell (1993:271) wrote that "The contemporary message of Canadian identity and nationhood is the message of multiculturalism ... [A]ll cultures together will form the essence of what it means to 'be Canadian.'" By the end of the decade, attention to the class of those migrating and the racialization of their relationship to the nation-state had shifted, as had contemporary messages regarding Canada's place in the world of migration. In the context of human smuggling, Canadian identity and nationhood were constructed in opposition to rather than through the promise of immigration. Regarding changes to Canadian immigration legislation in the 1990s, Razack (1999:160) argued that "One of the paramount tasks of border control, and the justification for all new initiatives, became the separation of the legitimate asylum seeker or immigrant from those deemed to be illegitimate." Several months after the boat arrivals, Minister of Citizenship and Immigration Elinor Caplan introduced Bill C-31 as legislation that would preserve the promise of Canada's future through immigration, facilitating desirable, legalized immigrants while protecting the nation against illicit movements.

The discourse surrounding the boat arrivals from China reflected these efforts to categorize according to legitimacy. The magnitude and tenor of the public response positioned the group as particularly egregious. In some ways, however, the smuggled migrants actually represented a typical movement. They comprised but a small percentage of a larger, continuous movement of people smuggled to Canada and the United States on a daily basis via a multitude of methods and routes. Despite the daily arrival of many more smuggled migrants through Canada's airports and across Canadian land borders, scant attention is paid to these movements. There was, however, heightened attention paid by the public, the media, and the state to this relatively small group of arrivals by boat.

In this way, the 1999 arrivals contrasted with the more common narrative of undocumented workers to North America. Often, laborers leave behind families to work in poor conditions for low wages, and the state remains silent, complicit in the inexpensive fulfillment of gaps in the labor market with none of the accompanying rights to social benefits or investments in social reproduction (see Katz 2001b; Rouse 1992). In many ways, undocumented laborers are often overlooked by nonimmigrants and governments alike.

In contrast with the usual "concealments" (see Katz 2001a), however, in response to the boat arrivals from China, a great amount of attention was paid to the identities of the migrants and subsequently, an intense period of identity construction. A media frenzy regarding immigration tends to come at moments of heightened xenophobia, racism, and economic downturns (cf Hage 1998; Nevins 2002). The people who arrived by boat were labeled "migrants" rather than "immigrants," which emphasized that they were not in Canada to stay. Furthermore, they were usually identified as "boat migrants," thus distinguishing them from other people smuggled through Canada. The discourse in the media began with discussion of the migrant body as diseased, racialized, and criminalized. Images circulated of the migrants crowded on boats in close proximity and unsanitary conditions. Initial front-page headlines read "Quarantined" in boldface (*Province* 1999: A1). Eventually, the representations settled into repetitive construction of the binaries—"good" or "bad," "deserving" or "undeserving" immigrants—identified by Razack (1999). In contrast with business immigrants landed for the promise of their economic contributions, the "boat migrants" were constructed as greedy.

Ethnographic research showed that the state also struggled with and held a stake in the discourse surrounding migration. Struggles over language were ongoing in the media and among civil servants from the moment the migrants landed. In an interview in Ottawa, one official explained that there was

> an underlying issue: how to view people like that? We were always hemming and hawing around a politically touchy issue. Even though

they're not refugees, it is possible to see them as people who deserve due process, as people that fled a repressive regime, people who still want to become Canadian. (Interview, CIC, Ottawa, March 2001)

Attention to this discourse illustrates some of the struggles in which the federal government was involved in its negotiations with the public, the media, and other institutions.

Here is a localized example in which language and identity constructions had an immediate impact on access. CIC designated the gym on the military base where the migrants were initially processed for several days as a "port of entry" and their time there as "processing" rather than "detention." As a result, CIC limited early communication between lawyers and migrants. Lawyers contested the designation of the gym as a port of entry, arguing that the refugee claimants *were* in detention and therefore had a right to legal counsel. The BC branch of the Canadian Bar Association made the following remarks:

> The Immigration Bar is deeply concerned with the position of the Department of Citizenship and Immigration Canada that the migrants have no right to counsel for the purposes of their initial interview and Senior Immigration Officer (SIO) interview. The Bar is concerned that migrants do not understand the law, and do not understand that they must initiate their claims before the SIO interviews conclude. (*BarTalk* 1999:1)

Immigration lawyers argued that because the migrants were presumed not to be "genuine" convention refugees, they were granted limited and expedited access to the refugee determination process.

This process of identity construction is consistent with Foucault's (1991) theories of biopower and governmentality, wherein the state manages populations by producing identities discursively through practices of classification and categorization (cf Scott 1998), exercises that entail the material inscription of identities onto the body (see Pratt in collaboration with the Philippine Women's Centre 1998; Pratt 1999). The media thus contributed to the regulation and surveillance of migrant bodies in relation to popular interpretations of immigration policy. The narrative of the illicit entrant affirmed the story of the violation of what was perceived as a nation already too generous with its immigration policies (cf Razack 1997:173). These positionings manifested first in the language and images of representations of the movement. They also, however, contributed to the environment in which migrants experienced the refugee determination process. It is, therefore, important to think about the ways in which governmental policies and procedures unfold: never in a vacuum, but rather recursively, amid social and cultural contexts.

The Deconstruction of Boundaries around "the State"

The state is often misconceived as a unified, homogeneous category (Gupta 1995). But the tension among governmental bodies regarding the response to the boat arrivals suggests that the state comprises a set of institutions operating at different levels across disparate geographies, comprised of individuals working within diverse mandates and frameworks. While CIC held primary responsibility for the response, the department depended on several other institutions to make it happen. As one manager explained, "Smuggling is an immigration problem, but we have no assets, just human resources" (interview, CIC, Victoria, March 2001).

The various institutions that collaborated in the response sometimes became adversarial. Struggles over the treatment of unaccompanied minors who arrived on the boats exemplify such tension. CIC, working within an enforcement framework, sought to treat minors fairly similarly to adults: to move them through the refugee determination process expeditiously and pursue repatriation. However, the province of BC served as the legal custodian of unaccompanied minors[7] and contemplated a range of options regarding their care, accommodation, and legal representation. The Province decided that it was not in the best interest of the children to repatriate them to a family that had sent them abroad, located in a country where they could be endangered upon return. It decided instead to support the minors through claimant and appeal processes as far as they chose to carry their claims (interview, Ministry for Children and Family, Vancouver, August 2001). The provincial and federal governments conflicted over the security of the group homes and institutions where the minors stayed. The minors were susceptible to communication and abduction on the part of the smugglers, who would not receive profits until clients had arrived in their final destination and so persisted toward this objective. In fact, most of the minors followed the claimant process through to completion, were denied refugee status in Canada, and ultimately fled the group homes, usually assisted by smugglers, en route to the US. This result was an affront to enforcement-oriented managers in CIC, but it was viewed more positively by the provincial workers supporting the migrants (interview, Ministry for Children and Family, Vancouver, August 2001). This conflict—one of several between the federal and provincial governments—opened space for alternative viewpoints and debate within "the state" about how to respond to smuggled migrants who themselves comprised a diverse group.

In his exploration of the "thought worlds" of immigration officers, Heyman (1995:271–273) found that immigration officers were influenced by personal histories prior to their entrance to the bureaucracy, and then socialized to a new set of worldviews within the INS.

Noting that "social relationships are produced through the bureaucracy," he (1995:263) argued that immigration officers embody the sovereignty of the state and thus think through their decisions according to the overarching ideas of self and other that manifest at the border. In CIC, as employees explained their day-to-day work in relation to the mandate of the department, the inconsistencies in their objectives illustrate that conflicting perspectives existed not only *among* governmental bodies, but *within* them. Higher up in the bureaucracy, a narrative emerged about transnational organized crime networks facilitating human smuggling and about the protection of sovereignty and the integrity of borders in relation to fighting these nefarious, global forces. Officials discussed detention of smuggled migrants as imperative (interviews, CIC, Ottawa, March 2001). Bureaucrats working in office buildings in Ottawa, however, were far removed from the "frontline work" of those located along borders, in airports, or in inland claim centers. It was easier for these officials to distance themselves from the migrants as individuals and to characterize them instead as a criminal group they worked to deport. The more removed bureaucrats produced cleaner, more simplistic narratives of human smuggling as "bad," enabled by distance, "dehumanization" (Heyman 1995), and simplified narratives of the involvement of transnational organized crime.

Individuals working in distinct locations within the state, however, often work in tension with others in ways that disrupt the cleaner, dominant narratives of the state. Through fieldwork, I moved up and down along the hierarchy of the bureaucracy to interview not only office workers but also those working directly with migrants. Employees lower down in CIC suggested that coherent, publicized narratives were shot through with ironies and inconsistencies. Divergent narratives about the response to the boats related to the locations, roles, and identities of employees within the bureaucracy and to their own histories and social embeddedness in relation to their work. These locations informed the different ways in which they related to smuggled migrants and enacted policy. Those with more personal, proximate involvement produced narratives infused with more emotion, passion, and complexity enabled by intimacy. Some argued that there was never any discussion about why they would suddenly shift policy to wide-scale detention of claimants. Others questioned whether "transnational organized crime" was actually involved. Dissecting these conflicting viewpoints within the state offers the opportunity to recover alternative perspectives not pursued, responses and philosophies beyond those enacted and presented to the public.

According to Heyman (1995:277), the bureaucracy must uphold coherent narratives and implement them despite inconsistencies. The ethnographic strategy of embodiment *includes* narratives "lower down" that not only conflict with public messages but also connect more intimately with both migrants and other institutions. One employee who worked closely with the migrants was herself smuggled to Canada as a child many years ago. She described being overcome with emotion in her initial interactions with the migrants. She characterized her experiences as "very painful," particularly when relating to the women and children from the boats, with whom she empathized. She was especially upset in her interactions with a young woman whom she believed had been raped and wounded during the journey. She reported that many memories had returned as she worked with the migrants. When she tried to talk to a friend about it, her friend reminded her that she was doing her job and to forget about it. To me, however, she described intense emotional experiences connected to her own history with human smuggling (interview, CIC, Vancouver, March 2001).

Likewise, workers in prisons and group homes in BC came to know migrants and were upset by their deportation (interview, BC Corrections Victoria, September 2001). One person mentioned spending many hours on a plane with one of the large groups repatriated to China in the spring of 2000. During the circuitous route back, he came to know the personalities of some of the migrants and to regret that they made the trip in handcuffs, to realize how poorly they were treated once in China and to see the potential gravity of their repatriation. Such employees experienced points of identification, rather than distance and abstraction. Like everyone, they lead lives that are complex, inconsistent, challenging, and interesting. Through emotional processing of their experiences with the migrants, they came to question the simple narratives of the "bad," "illegitimate," and "bogus" claimant. The response to human smuggling in 1999 held great personal impact for civil servants involved, which many contextualized in interviews in relation to other work-related, life-changing events. These experiences opened space for dialogue, in that they foregrounded the subjectivity of those who implemented immigration policy and caused them to reflect on their day-to-day work.

Employees also expressed conflicting perspectives according to their jobs within the department. For example, frontline workers and midlevel bureaucrats frequently expressed frustration with lawyers in legal services whose job it was to provide legal guidance, and with employees in communications whose job it was to communicate events to the public via the media. Lawyers were accused of moving too slowly, taking months to write a legal opinion long after the issue already had to have been resolved on the ground. In contrast, communications people were accused of moving too quickly and communicating too proactively with the media. Despite internal struggles, however, employees sustained a strong culture regarding who was allowed to speak officially for the department. This was the process by which singular, unified narratives of what had happened were articulated to the public. This process signals a place for research that recuperates narratives repressed by the bureaucracy.

Analysis of the boundaries surrounding "the state" also dissolves the artificial separation of state and civil society (Gupta 1995; Mitchell 1991). Even a glimpse at the interactions between institutions renders this distinction blurry. While the federal government held primary responsibility for the response, it relied upon several other institutions —both governmental (eg provincial) and nongovernmental—in order to do so. The United Nations High Commissioner for Refugees, NGOs that supported refugee settlement services, and the Legal Services Society each played roles that were at times collaborative and at others adversarial in relation to the federal government, while simultaneously receiving funding *from* the government.[8] Even when the immigration lawyers or provincial ministries of BC contested federal decisions, such as the decision to detain claimants, they continued to support clients who proceeded through governmental processes. What ensued, therefore, were struggles over language among collaborating institutions. In fieldwork, I explored the venues for dialogue among institutions. Some NGOs and refugee advocates, for example, contested the criminalization of this group by arguing that *all* of their clients had been smuggled during some portion of their journey.

As exemplified by the designation of the military gym where migrants were held as a port of entry, each institution, and every migrant, held a stake in the language of this experience, which in turn influenced access to the nation-state. By seeing the state as an everyday material practice, rather than an abstract concept, and by examining the geography of government procedures, we begin to see the dissolution of the boundaries around governance and the material struggles that manifest in language. Bureaucrats exercise agency in enacting the state amid various social relationships. In so doing, they struggle with the agency of other institutions and with the migrants themselves. The dissolution of the boundaries around the state challenges various binaries between policy and practice, "outside" and "inside," and state and civil society.

Identity, Boundaries, and the Transnational Imaginary

There are moments at which the state, the media, and the public pay more attention to particular border crossings. Nevins (2002) writes about Operation Gatekeeper as one such moment. He and others addressing border crossings between Mexico and the US illustrate the many ironies and inconsistencies with which that border is policed (eg Kearney 1991; Rouse 1992). Since the inception of Canada and the

United States as nation-states, immigrants have been positioned strategically in relation to nation-building in transnational contexts. In Canada, much of the contemporary debate about sovereignty and the integrity of borders relates to insecurity in relation to its more powerful neighbor to the south, especially in light of globalization and free-trade programs of the 1990s. The boat arrivals stirred an intense moment of nation-building. After the public outcry over the attempt to enter illegally and the public discursive construction of the "bogus refugee," we saw an unusual show of force by CIC. As the state "thinks the subject" of the transnational migrant (Lubiano 1996:65), it does so in relation to how it imagines itself in the world.

One high-ranking official in CIC explained the outcry in response to this movement: "It struck a nerve because it was first of all a direct attack on Canadian sovereignty ... because they arrived illegally, not intending to claim refugee status, and because they were clearly not refugees" (interview, CIC, Ottawa, March 2001). This identification of the nation-state in relation to its own public and to the global community is intimately bound up with the policing of international borders (cf Hage 1998; Heyman 1995; Nelson 1999; Nevins 2002; Razack 1999; Sharma 2001). The boat arrivals from China raised important questions regarding Canadians' transnational identification as a humanitarian, refugee status-granting nation of immigrants versus one that is "too soft." The migrants were actually en route to work in the US as undocumented laborers, like the estimated eight million who work for low wages, in poor conditions, without access to social benefits. In fields of transnational migration, this is the classic example of the kind of "vagabond capitalism" or abandonment of social support about which Katz (2001b) has written. The US knows about these populations, but it turns a blind eye because they are central to the US economy, supporting agriculture, industrialism, and the service economy.

The response to this movement was of symbolic importance to the Canadian transnational imaginary: rather than emphasize its more customary popular role as humanitarian (particularly in relation to the US), the federal government instead responded to pressure from national and international publics with an enforcement stance. Popular and legislative discourse regarding immigration shifted towards stronger articulations of legitimate versus illegitimate means of movement. Identifiers of smuggled migrants were wrapped up in this discourse with the constructions of "boat people" and "illegal aliens." The ways in which CIC responded to the smuggling movements—with the largest mass detentions and deportations in recent Canadian history—and engaged in this discourse speak powerfully to the role of the state in relation to transnational movements and the production of trans/national identities. Not surprisingly, Canada played a leading role in drafting the UN Protocols on Human Smuggling and Trafficking (2000) as an enforcer in the global community (interview, Ottawa, March 2001).

Nelson's (1999) conceptualization of the state as constitutive of and constituted by others through identity is central to a political project to intervene in policy. The federal government embarked on an enforcement response to human smuggling that was enabled by discursive practices of identity construction. The identification of the migrants within the transnational landscape of human migration as criminal justified an enforcement response. Those enacting these policies on the ground, however, struggled with their inconsistencies, recognizing that human migration and life histories were more complex than public narratives of policy depicted them. Ethnographic research enables closer examination of points of identification, intimacy, and difference through which the state is constituted. The more personal narratives of the work of government and nongovernment employees disrupt the cleaner national narratives of the Canadian self and other and offer the possibility of reconfiguring those relationships.

Conclusions

While the assumption that wealthy immigrants are good for Canada persists within government circles, a humanitarian acceptance of smuggled migrants remained outside of the realm of possibility. Protestors in the small communities that are resource towns along Vancouver Island where the migrants were off-loaded turned out with signs that said "Canadians first." Feeling social systems crumble around them, they were not willing to have the Canadian government accept poor people from other parts of the world. These were not the wealthy "flexible citizens" sought by governments such as Canada's, those about whom Aihwa Ong has written (1999). In fact, they became migrants whom Canada sought to deter very publicly. The 1999 smuggling movements represented particularly visible border crossings and heightened moments of identity construction for transnational migrants and for the Canadian government and its citizens alike. The arrivals provided an opportunity for the federal government to articulate its objectives to bring the best and the brightest to Canada "through the front door," and simultaneously, to present a global image of "closing the back door" to others.

The state maintains the exclusive right to create and implement laws (Heyman and Smart 1999). This power is reaffirmed through the disembodiment of the state and reified through academic abstractions. Abrams (1988:61) suggested that "[T]he state, conceived of as a substantial entity separate from society, has proved a remarkably elusive object of analysis." Likewise, Mitchell (1991:61) argued that we view the state with "aridity and mystification rather than understanding and warranted knowledge." Failures to locate the state reify its myth-like quality. According to Nevins (2002:160), practices that reify the artificial boundary between state and civil society are depoliticizing, because they assume that the state acts as an autonomous decision-maker in relation to border policing. The "state" may not be knowable as a coherent whole because it does not exist as such. Like other institutions, the state is highly variegated, complex, and entwined in many relationships that are difficult to pry apart. Social scientists are failing to recognize the full political potential of alternative epistemologies of the state. One political task at hand is to explore the inconsistencies in narratives and to seek within them ways to disrupt the most audible material political projects of the state. "And it is here that seizing on the fissures and ruptures, the contradictions in policies, programs, institutions, and discourses of 'the state' allows people to create possibilities for political action and activism" (Gupta 1995:394).

Qualitative research on the day-to-day operation of the nation-state offers a critical approach to counteract the depoliticizing effects of abstractions of "the state," to uncover taken-for-granted assumptions behind public narratives, and to thus dispel the myth of the autonomous state. Embodiment serves as a strategy to locate knowledge and power in a time and a place (see Gupta 1995; Haraway 1988; Rose 1995). Embodiment shows that the state is constituted within and through social relations, not only constitutive of but constituted internally and unevenly through difference. Mitchell (1991:93) argued:

> [J]ust as we must abandon the image of the state as a free-standing agent issuing orders, we need to question the traditional figure of resistance as a subject who stands *outside* the state and refuses its demands. Political subjects and their modes of resistance are formed as much *within* the organizational terrain we call the state, rather than in some wholly exterior social space. (emphasis in the original)

His statement conjures an inherently spatial paradigm at work in most theories of the state, and suggests a place for geographers to conduct qualitative research.

Quotidian geographies of the state challenge what Mitchell calls "the structural effect" of the artificial division between state and civil society. This divide is politically disempowering, because when people believe that the state is all-powerful and mysterious—existing somewhere "out there"—they do not participate in protest (Mitchell 1991:94). *Resistance* to existing narratives need not come exclusively from "the outside" (see Gupta 1995:394). The daily practices and beliefs that inform those who comprise the state can be captured with ethnographic research that demystifies the power of the state and disrupts normalized legal and material relations with alternative narratives from within. Narratives of disruption and difference expose inconsistencies in Canada's self-imaginings. Coherent national narratives fall apart and enable us to conjure new transnational imaginaries of the nation-state in relation to global restructuring and the mediation of transnational migrations. Within the intricate and intimate connections among institutional subjects lies potential for social change.

After I presented this work at the conference of the American Association of Geographers in Los Angeles, Dr. Helga Leitner asked what spaces ethnography opened for political change, wondering if the opinions of individuals could in any way impact upon "the company line" of the department. The response that I hope to have provided in this essay is that *the state does not exist outside of the people who comprise it, their everyday work, and their social embeddedness in local relationships.* While I do not want to go so far as to suggest that individuals alone have great amounts of power within the constraints of the bureaucracy (see Tilly 1999),[9] I do contend that bureaucracy is only as powerful as decision-making processes and participation within the collective. A profound change in an individual decision-maker *is* a profound change within the state. In this way, immigration officers have the potential to be subversive in their day-to-day work, particularly when a critical mass begins to question and challenge policy. While most would not admit to this in a formal, tape-recorded interview, they speak of it openly in their day-to-day work. Ethnographic observation and participation, in its documentation of these frustrations and subversions, can contribute to political breaking points within the state theorized as an institutional arrangement of social practices.

Acknowledgements

Many thanks to Win Curran, Sallie Marston, Katharyne Mitchell, and Cindi Katz for feedback on this essay. I also appreciate helpful reviews from Joe Painter, Alan Smart, and an anonymous reviewer. I am indebted to all of the people who participated in the project and whose time and insight made the research possible. All mistakes are my own.

Endnotes

[1] In 2000, Elinor Caplan, Minister of Citizenship and Immigration Canada, continued to promote but never achieved the objective of attracting 300,000 immigrants—approximately 1% of the Canadian population—annually (cited by Ley and Hiebert 2001:120).
[2] Human smuggling is "the illicit movement of people across international boundaries" (Koser 2001:59). Trafficking entails additional elements of coercion and exploitation and tends to be associated with the movement of women and children into the sex trade. The notion of coercion—people moving and working against their will—is central to the ways in which the United Nations Protocols on Human Trafficking and Smuggling (2000) differentiate between smuggling and trafficking. In practice, however, the distinction is ambiguous, given how little is known about the experiences of those who are smuggled and trafficked over time (see Chin 1999; Kwong 1997).
[3] The migrants are believed to have been destined for the US via Canada. The federal government was able to detain subsequent arrivals on the grounds that they constituted a flight risk and did not possess identity documents.

[4] There have been other high-profile boat arrivals in Canadian history. The most notable arrival in BC was that of the *Komagata Maru*, a vessel that arrived in 1914 carrying over 300 migrants—primarily Punjabi Sikhs—who were subsequently detained on the ship in the Vancouver harbor for two months and then turned back (see Johnston 1979).

[5] An outline of CIC's mission, hanging in the lobby of its regional headquarters (BC/ Yukon), states four mandates: "deriving maximum benefit from the global movement of people ('selection'); protecting refugees at home and abroad ('protection'); defining membership in Canadian society and supporting the settlement, adaptation, and integration of newcomers ('settlement and citizenship'); managing access to Canada ('enforcement')."

[6] In 1985, Evans, Ruschemeyer, and Skocpol published an edited collection, *Bringing the State Back In*. Last year, in *Paradigm Lost* (2002), Aronowitz and Bratsis also lamented the loss of state theory and advocated its return. Feminists, too, have made important interventions (eg Peterson 1992; Watson 1990), with questions such as "Do feminists need a theory of the state?" (Lilburn 2000). Hansen and Stepputat (2001) contribute a helpful review and a series of "ethnographic explorations," and Steinmetz (1999), too, addresses research on the state after "the cultural turn."

[7] Another struggle involving language related to the definition of "a minor," defined at different ages by the provincial and federal governments. This meant that the province considered itself the legal guardian for refugee claimants that CIC held in detention as adults.

[8] Thanks to reviewers for this reminder.

[9] Thanks to reviewers for this reminder.

References

Abrams P (1988) Notes on the difficulty of studying the state. Originally published in 1977. *Journal of Historical Sociology* 1(1)58–89

Aronowitz S and Bratsis P (eds) (2002) *Paradigm Lost: State Theory Reconsidered.* Minneapolis: University of Minnesota Press

BarTalk (1999) The right—and cost—of representation: New tide of migrants raises legal and policy issues. 11(5):1

Calavita K (1992) *Inside the State: The Bracero Program, Immigration, and the INS.* New York: Routledge

Chin K L (1999) *Smuggled Chinese: Clandestine Immigration to the United States.* Philadelphia: Temple University Press

Citizenship and Immigration Canada (CIC) (2000) *Marine Arrivals: Status Update.* 18 February

Ellis M and Wright R (1998) The Balkanization metaphor in the analysis of US immigration. *Annals of the Association of American Geographers* 88(4):686–698

Evans P, Ruschemeyer D and Skocpol T (eds) (1985) *Bringing the State Back In.* Cambridge, UK: Cambridge University Press

Fincher R (2001) Immigration research in the politics of an anxious nation. *Environment and Planning D: Society and Space* 19:25–42

Foucault M (1991) Governmentality. In G Burchell, C Gordon, and P Miller (eds) *The Foucault Effect: Studies in Governmentality* (pp 87–104). Chicago: University of Chicago Press

Foucault M (1995) *Discipline and Punish: The Birth of the Prison.* New York: Vintage

Gramsci A (1994) *Letters from a Prison.* Vols 1 and 2. Edited by F Rosengarten. Translated by R Rosenthal. New York: Columbia University Press

Gupta A (1995) Blurred boundaries: The discourse of corruption, the culture of politics, and the imagined state. *American Ethnologist* 22(2):375–402

Hage G (1998) *White Nation: Fantasies of White Supremacy in a Multicultural Society.* Annandale, NSW: Pluto Press

Hansen T B and Stepputat F (eds) (2001) Introduction: States of imagination. In T B Hansen and F Stepputat (eds) *States of Imagination: Ethnographic Explorations of the Postcolonial State* (pp 1–38). Durham, NC: Duke University Press

Haraway D (1988) Situated knowledges: The science question in feminism and the privilege of partial perspective. *Feminist Studies* 14(3):575–599

Herbert S (2001) "Hard charger" or "station queen"? Policing and the masculinist state. *Gender, Place and Culture* 8(1):55–71

Heyman J (1995) Putting power in the anthropology of bureaucracy: The immigration and naturalization service at the Mexico-United States border. *Current Anthropology* 36(2):261–287

Heyman J and Smart A (1999) States and illegal practices: An overview. In J Heyman (ed) *States and Illegal Practices* (pp 1–24). New York: Berg

Hyndman J (2000) *Managing Displacement: Refugees and the Politics of Humanitarianism.* Minneapolis: University of Minnesota Press

Hyndman J (2001) Towards a feminist geopolitics. *The Canadian Geographer* 45(2): 210–222

Hyndman J (2002) "Mind the Gap: A Conversation between Feminist and Political Geography." Manuscript, Department of Geography, Simon Fraser University

Johnston H (1979) *The Voyage of the Komagata Maru: The Sikh Challenge to Canada's Colour Bar*. Delhi: Oxford University Press

Katz C (2001a) Hiding the target: Social reproduction in the privatized urban environment. In C Minca (ed) *Postmodern Geography* (pp 93–110). Malden, MA: Blackwell

Katz C (2001b) Vagabond capitalism and the necessity of social reproduction. *Antipode* 33(4):709–728

Kearney M (1991) Borders and boundaries of state and self at the end of empire. *Journal of Historical Sociology* 4(1):52–74

Kirby A (1997) Is the state our enemy? *Political Geography* 16(1):1–12

Koser K (2001) The smuggling of asylum seekers into Western Europe: Contradictions, conundrums, and dilemmas. In D Kyle and R Koslowski (eds) *Global Human Smuggling* (pp 58–73). Baltimore: Johns Hopkins University Press

Kwong P (1997) *Forbidden Workers: Illegal Chinese Immigrants and American Labor.* New York: New York Press

Kyle D and Koslowski R (eds) (2001) *Global Human Smuggling*. Baltimore: Johns Hopkins University Press

Ley D (forthcoming) Seeking *homo economicus*: The strange story of Canada's Business Immigration Program. *Annals of the Association of American Geographers* 93(2)

Ley D and Hiebert D (2001) Immigration policy as population policy. *The Canadian Geographer* 45(1):120–125

Lilburn S (2000) Ask not "does feminism need a theory of the state?" but rather, do theorists of the state need feminism? *Australian Feminist Studies* 15(31):107–110

Lubiano W (1996) Like being mugged by a metaphor: Multiculturalism and state narratives. In A F Gordon and C Newfield (eds) *Mapping Multiculturalism* (pp 64–75). Minneapolis: University of Minnesota Press

Mahtani M and Mountz A (2002) *Immigration to British Columbia: Media Representation and Public Opinion.* Research on Immigration and Integration in the Metropolis, Working Paper no 02-15. http://www.riim.metropolis.net/Virtual%20Library/2002/wp02-15.pdf (last accessed 19 February 2003)

Mitchell K (1993) Multiculturalism, or the united colors of capitalism? *Antipode* 25(4): 263–294

Mitchell T (1991) The limits of the state: Beyond statist approaches and their critics. *American Political Science Review* 85(1):77–96

Mountz A (2002) "Embodying the Nation-State: Canada's Response to Human Smuggling." Manuscript, Department of Geography, University of British Columbia

Mountz A, Wright R, Miyares I and Bailey A (2002) Lives in limbo: Temporary pro-tected status and immigrant identities. *Global Networks* 2(4):335–356

Nelson D (1999) *A Finger in the Wound: Body Politics in Quincentennial Guatemala.* Berkeley: University of California Press

Nevins J (2002) *Operation Gatekeeper.* New York: Routledge

New York Times (2002) Canada courts migrant families to revive a declining hinterland. 2 October. http://www.nytimes.com/2002/10/02/international/americas/02CANA.html (last accessed 17 March 2003)

Ohmae K (1995) *The End of the Nation-State: The Rise of Regional Economies.* New York: Free Press

Ong A (1999) *Flexible Citizenship: The Cultural Logics of Transnationality.* Durham, NC: Duke University Press

Painter J (1995) *Politics, Geography, and "Political Geography."* New York: Arnold

Peterson V S (ed) (1992) *Gendered States: Feminist (Re)Visions of International Relations Theory.* Boulder: Lynne Rienner Publishers

Pratt G (1999) From registered nurse to registered nanny: Discursive geographies of Filipina domestic workers in Vancouver, BC. *Economic Geography* 75(3): 215–236

Pratt G in collaboration with the Philippine Women's Centre (1998) Inscribing domestic work on Filipina bodies. In H Nast and S Pile (eds) *Places through the Body* (pp 283–304). London: Routledge

Province (1999) Quarantined. 21 July:A1

Razack S (1999) Making Canada white: Law and the policing of bodies of colour in the 1990s. *Canadian Journal of Law & Society* 14(1):159–184

Rose G (1995) Geography and gender, cartographies and corporealities. *Progress in Human Geography* 19(4):544–548

Rouse R (1992) Making sense of settlement: Class transformation, cultural struggle, and transnationalism among Mexican migrants in the United States. In N Glick-Schiller, L Basch and C Blanc-Szanton (eds) *Towards a Transnational Perspective on Migration: Race, Class, Ethnicity, and Nationalism Reconsidered* (pp 26–47). New York: The New York Academy of Sciences

Sassen S (1996) *Losing Control: Sovereignty in an Age of Globalization.* New York: Columbia University Press

Scott J (1998) *Seeing Like a State: How Certain Schemes to Improve the Human Condition Have Failed.* New Haven, CT: Yale University Press

Sharma N (2001) On being not Canadian: The social organization of "migrant workers" in Canada. *Canadian Review of Sociology and Anthropology* 38(4):415–439

Steinmetz G (1999) Introduction: Culture and the state. In G Steinmetz (ed) *State/ Culture: State-Formation after the Cultural Turn* (pp 1–49). Ithaca, NY: Cornell University Press

Taussig M (1997) *The Magic of the State.* New York and London: Routledge

Tilly C (1999) Epilogue: Now where? In G Steinmetz (ed) *State/Culture: State-Formation after the Cultural Turn* (pp 407–419). Ithaca, NY: Cornell University Press

Tyner J (2000) Migrant labour and the politics of scale: Gendering the Philippine state. *Asia Pacific Viewpoint* 41(2):131–154

United Nations (2000) Protocol to Prevent, Suppress, and Punish Trafficking in Persons, Especially Women and Children, Supplementing the United Nations Convention against Transnational Organized Crime, G A res 55/25, annex II, 55 UN GAOR Supp (no 49) at 60, UN doc A/45/49 (vol 1) (2001). http://www.uncjin.org/Documents/ Conventions/dcatoc/final_documents_2/convention_%20traff_eng.pdf (last accessed 17 March 2003) or http://www1.umn.edu/humanrts/instree/trafficking.html (last accessed 17 March 2003)

Walton-Roberts M (2001) "Embodied Global Flows: Immigration and Transnational
  Networks between British Columbia, Canada, and Punjab, India." PhD dissertation,
  Department of Geography, University of British Columbia
Watson S (ed) (1990) *Playing the State: Australian Feminist Interventions.* North Sydney:
  Allen and Unwin

Index

Printed and bound by CPI Group (UK) Ltd, Croydon, CR0 4YY

09/06/2025

14686100-0001